THE UNITED STATES REFUGEE ADMISSIONS PROGRAM:

REFORMS FOR A NEW ERA OF REFUGEE RESETTLEMENT

D1573353

DAVID A. MARTIN

TO MY PARENTS, LIBBY AND WENDELL MARTIN

*589 75828

Library of Congress Cataloging-in-Publication Data

Martin, David A., 1948-
  The United States Refugee Admissions Program : reforms for a new era
of refugee resettlement / David A. Martin.
      p. cm.
  Includes bibliographical references and index.
  ISBN 0-9742819-1-3
  1. United States Refugee Program. 2. Refugees—Government
policy—United States. 3. United States—Emigration and
immigration—Government policy. I. Migration Policy Institute. II.
Title.
  HV640.4.U54M35 2005
  325'.21—dc22
                              2005043892

Cover Photo: Somali Bantu refugees arrive in the United States.
Photographer: Christophe Calais.

Design: Patricia Hord.Graphik Design, phgd.com

TABLE OF CONTENTS

PREFACE AND ACKNOWLEDGMENTS FOR THE MPI EDITION IX

GLOSSARY OF ACRONYMS XI

INTRODUCTION 1

CHAPTER I. THE CONTEXT 2

A. Obstacles, barriers, and possible reasons against resettlement initiatives 3
1. Pull factors, migration choices, and host country considerations 3
2. Effects on other possible durable solutions 4
3. Other political effects, including equity concerns 5
4. Fraud, distortion, and corruption 5
5. Definitional issues 6
6. Complexity and luck 7
7. Toward a future of case-by-case decisions to resettle finite groups 8

B. Fundamental choices for the US Refugee Program: aims and nature 9
1. Immediate rescue from grave danger versus rescue from a wider range of harms 9
2. The resource competition between assistance and resettlement 13
3. The Presidential Determination: a ceiling or a target? 15
Table I-1. Refugee Admissions and Ceilings, FY 1980 – 2004 17

Annex to Chapter I. Resettlement of the Somali Bantu 19

CHAPTER II. REFORMING THE SYSTEM FOR DECIDING ON RESETTLEMENT INITIATIVES 25

A. The scale of the challenge 25
Table II-1. Refugee Admissions by Priority, FY 1994 – 2003 27
Table II-2. Refugee Admissions for Family-Based Categories, FY 1994 – 2003 27

B. PRM's role 28
1. Overview 28
2. For the future 30

C. The involvement of the rest of the Department of State 31

D. Suggested procedure for deciding on group initiatives 32
1. Refugee Admissions Committee 32
2. Refugee Admissions Committee procedures 33
3. Advantages 34
4. Assuring timely completion of the full Presidential Determination process 34

CHAPTER III. THE PRIORITY SYSTEM FOR ACCESS TO THE ADMISSIONS PROGRAM
AND ARRANGEMENTS FOR URGENT CASES   37

    A. Overview of the priorities   37
        1. The P-1 category: UNHCR and embassy referrals   37
        2. The P-2 category: groups of special humanitarian concern   38
        3. Categories P-3 through P-5 and Visas 93: family-based access 39

    B. Broad restructuring of the priority system?   40
        1. The Frelick proposal   40
        2. Evaluation and recommendation for more modest revision   40

    C. Individual referrals   42
        1. UNHCR referrals   42
        2. US embassy referrals   43
        3. NGO referrals   43

    D. Group access   44

    E. Family-based priorities, including issues of processing bottlenecks and fraud   46
        1. The Visas 93 process for immediate family following to join 47
        2. P-3 processing   48
        3. A universal P-3 category?   51
        4. Functional family relationships   53

    F. Urgent cases   54
        1. General considerations   54
        2. Proposals for a universal in-country designation   55

CHAPTER IV. THE ROLE OF THE DEPARTMENT OF HOMELAND SECURITY   59

    A. The need for a better structure to resolve Department-wide refugee
       and immigration policy   59

    B. Issues affecting individual adjudications   61

    C. Deployment of circuit ride teams and the security of interviewing sites   63

    D. The Refugee Corps   64

CHAPTER V. OPERATIONAL ISSUES AND AN OVERVIEW OF THE RESETTLEMENT PROCESS   67

    A. The basic process   67
        1. Access   67
        Figure V-1. US Refugee Admission Process   68
        2. OPE case preparation   69
        3. Security screening   71
        4. The DHS interview   72
        5. Medical screening, sponsor assurances, and cultural orientation   75
        6. Travel, port-of-entry procedures, and arrival at the destination   76

    B. Overall observations: the need for a resolutely managerial approach   78

C. Specific operational recommendations   81

   1. Overseas Processing Entities   81

   2. Training and preparation of interviewing officers   85

   3. The use of interpreters   88

   4. Requests for reconsideration   89

   5. Security screening   89

   6. The Worldwide Refugee Admissions Processing System   90

   7. Processing at the port-of-entry   92

   8. Adjustment of status   93

CHAPTER VI. THE ROLE OF THE OFFICE OF THE UNITED NATIONS
HIGH COMMISSIONER FOR REFUGEES   97

A. Background   97

   1. The evolution of UNHCR's approach   97

   2. The UNHCR role in the US program   99

B. UNHCR's development of a group referral capacity   100

C. Improving refugee registration   101

CHAPTER VII. STATUTORY AMENDMENTS   106

A. Provide for continued refugee movements at the beginning of the fiscal year,
even if the Presidential Determination is delayed   106

B. Allow congressional consultation by both Cabinet secretaries and deputy secretaries   107

C. Repeal the ceiling on asylee adjustments   107

D. Reconsider the ceiling on refugee and asylee status grants based on
coercive population control measures   109

E. Consider admitting overseas refugees as lawful permanent residents   110

F. Allow the President to designate specific classes of persons to be admitted as
Section 207 refugees without individually applying the Convention refugee definition   111

Annex to Chapter VII. Statutory Amendment Governing Refugee Admissions
Under INA § 207   115

CONSOLIDATED RECOMMENDATIONS   119

AFTERWORD   126

INDEX   130

Preface and Acknowledgments for the MPI Edition

It was a bit daunting to be asked, as I was by the Department of State in early 2003, to take on a major project that might lead to wide-ranging reforms to America's refugee admissions system. Refugee resettlement is a vast and intricate subject, an insight of which I was constantly reminded in the course of the interviews and research for this book. Many areas I thought I understood fairly well, based on many years of writing and government service in this field,* proved to have additional layers of complexity or mystery. Fortunately, the people I interviewed were unfailingly helpful and patient in explaining the critical details I needed to understand. I have tried to present faithfully what I learned, but I remain aware of the gap between the panoramic view I attempted to capture and the detailed expertise held by those who were my guides into specific elements of the process.

By design, this study focuses on refugee *admissions* — that is, the early stages of the resettlement process, up to the point when refugees arrive at their destination community. That arrival, however, by no means marks the end of resettlement. A great deal of work remains, for sponsoring organizations, government officials, and above all for the refugees themselves, to assure that each family and individual settles successfully into life in the United States. Many of the people with whom I spoke in the course of my research are also deeply involved in that complex, potentially rewarding, but always challenging integration process. My assignment was sufficiently formidable, however, without trying to cover that stage of resettlement.

My chief recommendations for reform are printed in bold type throughout the chapters and also gathered in a single consolidated listing at the end of this volume. Some reflect strong convictions I reached in the course of analyzing particular problems, but many others embody far closer judgment calls, and a reader might well conclude that a differently structured reform would be wiser. I have tried my best to describe the problems and the issues fully, as well as the competing ideas I heard for how to address them, so that readers — including those with ultimate decision making authority over parts of these processes — would have the material at hand to make their own judgments.

This book is based heavily on over 100 interviews of government and international organization officials, nongovernmental organization representatives, scholars, and occasionally refugees themselves. Most of those interviews took place in the Washington, DC, area, but the project also carried me to New York, Geneva, Rome, Accra, Abidjan, and Cairo. I supplemented the in-person interviews with phone conversations where warranted, and a host of persons, both in government and in the NGO world, took time to write out detailed comments and suggestions.

I decided in the early stages of the project to conduct interviews on a not-for-attribution basis. The last few years have been extraordinarily difficult times for the US refugee admissions program, and the difficulties have stirred passions and sometimes caused tempers to flare. Nonetheless, the resettlement system

---

* I served as Special Assistant to the Assistant Secretary for Human Rights and Humanitarian Affairs, Department of State, from 1978 to 1980. During that period the Refugee Act of 1980 was drafted, debated, and enacted, and during much of that time the refugee admissions program was part of the bureau to which I was attached. From 1995 to 1998, I returned to government as General Counsel of the Immigration and Naturalization Service, a job that often entailed involvement in refugee and asylum issues.

requires the various players, governmental and nongovernmental, to continue to work together as part of an ongoing process. I wanted to receive my interlocutors' candid views on the operation of the system and their suggestions for changes, but I encountered reluctance if they felt that their words might be publicly attributed to them. Hence the not-for-attribution approach. That method also carries certain well-known drawbacks, to be sure. It could allow for rumor or unfounded suspicions to be voiced, and it may hamper later efforts to verify or disprove what I report here. Nonetheless, I tried not to include information or allegations unless corroborated in some fashion. (A thick stack of binders and files contains the interview notes and records upon which my account here is based.) In any event, it was apparent that nearly everyone approached the interview with the attitude that they would strive to convey as complete and accurate an account as they could, even when they had strong views on the subject or the actions of other players. I came away with a wide array of angles of vision on common incidents and problems. A great many people care deeply about the health of the US refugee admissions program, and they were extraordinarily generous with their time, in order to make sure that I would be fully informed.

That interview method precludes recording detailed acknowledgments of the assistance I received, but I hope that those with whom I talked will see something of their teaching here and will know of my gratitude for their assistance. I do want to say a special word of thanks, without naming specific names, to the staff of the two key US government units whose practices are centrally examined here: the Bureau of Population, Refugees, and Migration (PRM) in the Department of State, and the Bureau of Citizenship and Immigration Services (USCIS), in the Department of Homeland Security. They were extraordinarily generous with their time during initial and often repeated interviews, and in carefully going over drafts that eventually resulted in this book. This work has also benefited greatly from the feedback I received at public meetings on earlier drafts, held in winter and spring 2004. Pam Messina at the University of Virginia School of Law provided painstaking assistance in the preparation of the final report manuscript. And for thoughtful and diligent research assistance, I want to express warm thanks to Elizabeth Reilly-Hodes, Tina Tran, and Thomas Wintner.

This project resulted in a completed report that was presented to the Department of State in late August 2004. Not long thereafter I had the good fortune to be invited to join the Migration Policy Institute as a Nonresident Fellow. Discussions with the Institute's leadership suggested that it might be useful to turn the report into a book for publication under MPI's auspices, so that it would be available in a more accessible hard-copy form and perhaps thereby stimulate wider attention and debate — and maybe also speed action on possible reforms. I am grateful to the Department of State for its permission to publish the volume through MPI. The report appears here essentially as it was presented to the Department of State, although I have taken the opportunity to smooth out infelicitous phrases, with the assistance of a skilled copyedit by Amelia Brown. I have also added a new Afterword that brings the picture of the refugee admissions program up to date. I am deeply grateful for the broad support MPI has provided, and particularly for the diligent work of Jonathan Pattee to bring this publication to fruition.

David A. Martin
Warner-Booker Distinguished Professor of International Law
Charlottesville, Virginia
March 2005

GLOSSARY OF ACRONYMS

ADAG – Associate Deputy Attorney General

AG – Attorney General

AOR – affidavit of relationship (a document used to start the process that may lead to refugee admission under family-based access priorities)

BID – best interests determination (a determination by a child welfare professional, generally required before major decisions are made regarding unaccompanied minors)

BTS – Directorate of Border and Transportation Security in the Department of Homeland Security

CBP – Bureau of Customs and Border Protection, a component of BTS

CIA – Central Intelligence Agency

CIS – See USCIS.

CLASS – Consular Lookout and Support System

DAG – Deputy Attorney General

DHS – Department of Homeland Security

DRL – Bureau of Democracy, Human Rights, and Labor in the Department of State

EAD – employment authorization document

EOIR – Executive Office for Immigration Review in the Department of Justice

FAM – Foreign Affairs Manual

FBI – Federal Bureau of Investigation

FY – fiscal year

HIAS – Hebrew Immigrant Aid Society

IOM – International Organization for Migration

ICE – Bureau of Immigration and Customs Enforcement, a component of BTS

ICMC – International Catholic Migration Commission

INA – Immigration and Nationality Act of 1952, as amended

INS – Immigration and Naturalization Service

IRC – International Rescue Committee

JVA – joint voluntary agency

LPR – lawful permanent resident

MRA – Migration and Refugee Assistance (the principal funding account for State Department programs aiding refugees

NSC – National Security Council

NGO – nongovernmental organization

OPE – overseas processing entity

ORR – Office of Refugee Resettlement in the Department of Health and Human Services

P-1, P-2, etc. – designations for the priority categories that structure access to the US Refugee Program, explained in detail in Chapter III

PD – Presidential Determination (the document issued annually by the President to set the total number and allocation of refugee admissions for the coming fiscal year)

PRM – Bureau of Population, Refugees, and Migration in the Department of State

RAVU – Refugee Access Verification Unit of USCIS

RCUSA – Refugee Council USA (umbrella organization of resettlement-focused voluntary agencies)

Refcoord – refugee coordinator (a State Department officer in selected posts abroad)

RFR – request for reconsideration

RPC – refugee Processing Center (a key facility in the refugee admissions system, located in Arlington, Virginia)

RRF – resettlement registration form (a UNHCR document)

RSD – refugee status determination (the term is usually applied to this process as carried out by the UNHCR)

RSO – regional security officer (chief security officer for an embassy)

SAO – security advisory opinion

TPS – temporary protected status

UNHCR – United Nations High Commissioner for Refugees

USCIS – Bureau of Citizenship and Immigration Services, part of the DHS (also sometimes referred to simply as CIS)

USRP – United States Refugee Program

Visas 92 and 93 – the systems that are used for the admission of immediate family members who are following to join persons granted durable status in the United States based on their fear of persecution in the country of origin. The Visas 92 system is used for family members of persons granted asylum under INA § 208, and Visas 93 for family members of persons admitted as part of the overseas refugee resettlement program under INA § 207.

Volag – voluntary agency

WRAPS – Worldwide Refugee Admissions Processing System (key database used in the refugee admissions system, managed by the RPC)

Introduction

The United States Refugee Admissions Program: Reforms for a New Era of Refugee Resettlement

The United States Refugee Program (USRP) is at a crossroads, and many people would say it is in crisis. The most obvious symptoms are a steep fall-off in refugee admissions for fiscal years (FY) 2002 and 2003 to below 29,000 annually. (For a comparison, actual refugee admissions for the previous five years averaged almost 76,000.) Because FY 2002 began twenty days after the September 11 terrorist attacks, observers often attribute the program's travails to the enhanced security measures introduced in response. Those measures played a role, but they are by no means the only source.

In fact, FY 2002 brought the United States to the end of several familiar elements of past refugee programs, placing us into a significantly new context for US refugee resettlement — a difficult transition whose dimensions were obscured by the September 11 responses. Largely gone are the massive, steady, and more predictably manageable programs that had dominated US admissions since the passage of the Refugee Act of 1980 — the Indochinese and Soviet programs, followed for a few years by programs for those fleeing the former Yugoslavia. We are in a distinctively new era for refugee resettlement, and we need to recognize the true dimensions of the change. The new era brings both disadvantages and important new opportunities for the program to reflect on its core objectives and to respond to a wider range of genuine refugee needs.

For the future, refugee admissions will be characterized by the combination of many smaller-scale resettlement programs, mostly originating in difficult locations that will shift from year to year, each presenting significant and distinct policy challenges. The challenges consist not only of processing and logistics, though these are substantial, especially in an era of heightened security concerns. They consist also, and more importantly, of the complicated steps required to achieve agreement among the relevant US government — and often international — players on the groups and individuals that should be the beneficiaries of resettlement. A sensible system that does not make it too hard to say yes to new priority categories for resettlement is absolutely essential to our post–Cold War refugee admissions program. Without the capacity to approve new resettlement initiatives nimbly, even expansive gains in operations, including in the security screening system, will not achieve significantly improved admissions. Without that capacity, we will also be unable to capitalize on the genuine humanitarian opportunities that this new era presents.

The refugee resettlement system must evolve in response to this distinctly new climate, in both outlook and operations. Several useful changes are in the works, but others are missing or underdeveloped. This report, commissioned by the US government, represents an effort to describe the program, identify the problems and challenges, and provide concrete suggestions for improvements, both short-term and long-term. It is based on extensive interviewing and research carried out over ten months in 2003 and 2004.

CHAPTER I

THE CONTEXT

ritique of the past two years' admissions performance often takes this form: "There are fourteen million refugees in the world. Why can't they find 70,000 to admit?"[1] To many it seems an obvious question, and its unspoken premise suggests a lack of will, lack of effort, or outright resistance to a vigorous resettlement program on the part of those running the system. The question is well worth asking, but the underlying premise is not fair to the dedicated individuals who work in the various offices responsible for pieces of the admissions system or to the real dilemmas that must be faced honestly in making decisions to resettle. There are often good reasons not to resettle particular populations, or at least to defer any resettlement until other possible responses to the situation have been fully explored and allowed to develop. Moreover, even when a preliminary decision to resettle a particular group is made, actual movements may be delayed for lengthy periods because of difficulties in securing the cooperation of the host country or other key international actors, or as a result of unforeseen political complications or simple bad luck. Many of these factors — combined with the historical reality that we now lack a large and steady anchor resettlement program from a particular region that can be counted on to bring tens of thousands as part of an established pipeline — help to account for the low admissions totals in FY 2002 and 2003.

Section A of this chapter explores these genuine and legitimate barriers and obstacles to resettlement, as well as factors that might properly counsel against a resettlement initiative in specific circumstances. Critics of the USRP's recent performance often underestimate or obscure these challenges, while government officials take exception to critiques that do not do justice to the constraints under which they labor. In fact, refugee migrations and refugee resettlement represent highly complex phenomena. Refugee admissions cannot be based solely on any single-factored analysis. Instead, resettlement decisions must take careful account of the inherent dynamics of refugee situations, which vary greatly from place to place. A candid and rigorous look at those challenges is not antithetical to the vital humanitarian aims of refugee resettlement; in fact, it is necessary in order for the program to serve those aims more effectively.

Nonetheless, to acknowledge these points — to be more judicious in giving them their due weight — does not require surrendering to them. Reasons not to resettle a particular population may be legitimate, but they are rarely decisive. A major flaw in the current system is the lack of an institutional framework that consistently brings to bear the good reasons in favor of resettlement, at least for specific and carefully chosen groups, so that balanced and sensible choices can be reached to produce a refugee program on the scale made possible by the President at the beginning of the fiscal year. Section B begins an examination of the reasons for this flaw, dissecting an ambivalence about the aims of the system and about the outlook that should govern. It recommends an end to this ambivalence and a firm acceptance of objectives that go beyond resettling those in immediately life-threatening circumstances. The section also proposes shifting to treat the annual refugee number set by the President as an admissions goal and not a mere ceiling. If such a shift is accepted, then determining how to reshape other operational elements of the system becomes easier — questions that are taken up in detail in later chapters.

A. Obstacles, Barriers, and Possible Reasons Against Resettlement Initiatives

I. Pull Factors, Migration Choices, and Host Country Considerations

Decisions to resettle have political impact, arousing political support and political resistance, domestically and internationally, that must be worked through before deciding whether, and if so exactly whom, to resettle. A key feature is this: The refugee populations that make up the generally used estimate of twelve to fourteen million refugees worldwide are not a static pool that can simply be dipped into to ladle out however many people the United States or other resettlement countries might want to admit.[2] The act of resettling, even the act of openly discussing a major resettlement program, affects both future migration and the attitudes and actions of existing camp populations. It can affect the politics in the country of origin as well as the country of asylum, and it can have unintended consequences in discouraging other — and sometimes superior — durable solutions. Effective resettlement must take into account each of these elements, realistically and tough-mindedly.

Refugees are not a breed apart. Nearly all have had prior settled lives, often thriving existences, as farmers, merchants, herders, teachers, businesspeople, students, government officials. They are not just the passive objects of domestic or international policy, the helpless or inert victims often portrayed in the media. They are subjects, persons with objectives and life-plans and the capacity to take action to better their own lot if given a reasonable chance. Most never expected to find themselves tagged with the label of refugee, and most find the restrictions and boredom that are characteristic even of a well-run refugee camp stifling and diminishing.

Although we often speak of refugees as having been driven from their homes, in fact the exit decision is rarely so stark. Short of truly desperate emergency evacuations, refugees exercise choice over whether and when to leave and, to some extent, where to go. Moreover, the escalation of dangers is often gradual. Conditions deteriorate in the home country, economically, politically, militarily, or as a combination. At some point the conditions — threats, persecution visited on associates, ethnic conflict, the depredations and dangers of a civil war — reach a point that an individual, a family, a clan, or a village decides to pick up and leave. They may head for another part of their own country, becoming internally displaced persons, or they may cross an international border, definitionally a key element in their being counted as refugees. But in most such situations, even when the dangers are great or the persecution widespread, others choose to remain behind — based on courage, optimism, foolhardiness, misinformation, patriotism, inertia, or simple devotion to their own home, farm, or village.

Where refugees go and when they leave their country of origin are influenced by their understanding of what awaits them in the destination, measured against the dangers if they remain at home. This dynamic is the source of one of the major complications in resettlement decisions. Dangers in the home country are always matters of degree. Many choose to stay in familiar territory and cope with risks, even severe risks — particularly if life across the border appears to offer little prospect for a meaningful existence for oneself and one's children. But if that cross-border picture changes because the chance for resettlement out of the camps to a prosperous and stable country is introduced, the dynamic is altered. If the resettlement offer is perceived as open-ended, then the potential refugee's calculus for departure can be significantly influenced. Resettlement offers therefore can create a magnet effect — what the Office of the United Nations High Commissioner for Refugees (UNHCR) often calls a "pull factor." Carelessly managed resettlement, even on a large scale, may actually wind up increasing the size of camp populations in the first-asylum country, if out-migration fails to keep pace with new arrivals drawn largely by chances for resettlement. To say this is not to disparage the real dangers that propel refugee movements. It is simply to recognize that human beings often choose to put up with dangers. Refugee flight is rarely a clear-cut decision, and refugees consider more than just the condition of their home territory when deciding to leave.

Host countries are certainly aware of these effects. They, or at least certain key factions within the host government, such as the military, may resist the beginnings of a US resettlement program from their country, precisely because of fears about the potential for new migration — migration that otherwise would be deterred by knowledge of the conditions of camp life. (Host countries sometimes keep camp conditions stark in order to discourage additional movements.) US ambassadors also may be acutely sensitive to such concerns or factions within the host government, and they may weigh in with this viewpoint forcefully early in the internal US government process for considering new resettlement initiatives.

In the large refugee programs of the past, for reasons specific to each, the magnet effect was of more limited concern, at least during crucial stages. In Indochina, the United States felt a sufficient historical responsibility for the persons fleeing Vietnam that early moves (from 1975 through the mid-1980s) were essentially premised on the idea that this country and its international partners would find room for all who escaped.[3] When the numbers leaving Vietnam moved upward in the late 1980s after an earlier decline, however, the international community became more openly concerned about pull factors. In response, the Comprehensive Plan of Action, adopted in 1989, introduced a screening process, coupled with potential returns, that was meant to reduce further outflows.[4] With the Soviet program, a similar Cold War dynamic undergirded a broad welcome for virtually all who could manage to leave.[5] Significantly, in that context, any magnet effect was counterbalanced by the continuing presence of Soviet exit controls, which in fact generally kept outmigration to levels that the United States and other transit or resettlement countries considered manageable. When the Soviet Union disbanded, some observers predicted huge new outflows, especially to Europe. Had they occurred, resettlement programs would probably have had to adjust in response. But flows on that scale did not materialize, and the continuing US resettlement program from the former Soviet Union experienced a significant decline during the succeeding decade, despite specially generous eligibility standards introduced by the Lautenberg Amendment in 1989.[6]

As that experience indicates, predictions about pull factors are not an exact science. But any responsible system must factor the risk of a magnet effect into resettlement decisions — an effect that may be more easily triggered today, given the development of instantaneous global communications. Moreover, it can certainly be expected that host governments, as well as US ambassadors and the State Department's regional bureaus, among others,

will upon occasion press this consideration during debates over new resettlement initiatives. Obviously, in the absence of host government support or at least acquiescence, resettlement processing cannot take place. This element of resettlement decision making is sometimes downplayed or overlooked by critics, believing that US pressure or inducements can always overcome such resistance. That view is an exaggeration. US officials wishing to launch a resettlement initiative often find host governments quite entrenched on such issues, particularly if the latter believe that resettlement will trigger an increased inflow or that the international community's support will wane after an initial enthusiasm, leaving them with sole responsibility for an expanded population.

Nonetheless, several deliberate tools can be used to minimize the magnet effect. Prominently mentioned during project interviews was a strategy of focusing resettlement initiatives on well-defined groups whose boundaries are clearly marked — so that persons contemplating new cross-border migration understand that they simply will not qualify. These observers also counseled withholding publicity about such a plan, most of the time, until the basic selection or access groundwork is nearly complete. The wave of the resettlement future is probably what some persons interviewed for this project called "finite groups."

2. Effects on Other Possible Durable Solutions

Resettlement also has an impact on the decisions of existing camp populations. Voluntary repatriation is usually considered the most desirable of the three main durable solutions for refugee crises (the others being resettlement or local integration in the first-asylum country). Over the past fifteen years, international action has helped broker the settlement of many long-standing civil wars, permitting wide-scale returns. Other international initiatives during this period, including the increasing use of humanitarian military intervention, have helped to remove abusive regimes from power, allowing the regime's past targets to repatriate in relative safety.[7] Successful repatriation has reached a surprising and gratifying level that few might have expected in 1990, and resettlement should not serve to discourage or hamper such outcomes.

Repatriation often requires careful negotiations involving the host country, the source country, and various international actors, importantly including the UNHCR, and it must take account of reactions by the refugees and their leaders.[8] Initiatives to this end may be skewed or complicated if a resettlement country introduces an offer of resettlement for camp populations at an inopportune moment.[9] Similarly, negotiations to achieve agreement on local integration could be disrupted if resettlement elsewhere is suddenly on offer. UNHCR has on several occasions counseled against resettlement for given populations that otherwise might seem eligible for US resettlement, precisely because the Office believes that negotiations might soon open the way for voluntary repatriation — or indeed for local integration. Of course, such predictions are themselves always open to debate, and they can sometimes be employed simply to avoid taking a fresh look at a wider range of possible solutions. But they cannot be simply dismissed. Moreover, UNHCR opposition to resettlement can prove a substantial obstacle to the launching and administration of a successful initiative, because of the crucial role UNHCR often plays in managing refugee camps.

3. OTHER POLITICAL EFFECTS, INCLUDING EQUITY CONCERNS

Some refugee situations do not lend themselves to resettlement for other reasons. Possibly the largest single group among the conventional total of twelve to fourteen million refugees worldwide consists of an estimated three million Palestinians.[10] The politics of both the host countries and the United States have precluded any significant US resettlement program for Palestinians.

Other populations, though lacking the same political obstacles, may present other difficulties. For example, the scale may simply be so large that resettlement could never conceivably produce a durable solution for more than a tiny proportion of the population. This was the judgment for many decades regarding Afghans displaced to nearby countries, whose ranks once numbered as many as six million refugees.[11] Viable resettlement must then be based on a transparent selection principle that is logistically manageable and avoids creating tensions in the relations among various subgroups that will remain in the camp population (or at least minimizes such tensions). Family or other close ties to the United States could provide a basis for selection, as could length of stay in the camps. Still, determining those features is often difficult, partic-

ularly if the chaos of flight or the disorder of camp governance has prevented the maintenance of reasonable civil records (births, deaths and marriages), or in the absence of a reliable registration system that can be used to demonstrate the length of a refugee's stay. And if the selection grounds are not clear or easily determined, the risk of a pull factor rises.

Some such selection criteria can be challenged on equity grounds: is it really fair to resettle, say, the few who have made their way to a more easily accessible processing site, while ignoring others who face more severe dangers in other locations? On the other hand, the equity concern has sometimes been significantly overplayed in debates over US resettlement. Taken to its extreme, it would bar virtually any resettlement unless all who are similarly (or more severely) threatened can be included — a virtually impossible standard to meet. The inability to respond to all need of a certain kind or magnitude is not a valid argument against responding to any part of the need. The humanitarian premises of the admissions program call for response when possible, even when it is messy and incomplete, and even when accompanied by genuine anxiety over the inability to offer a solution to others.

4. FRAUD, DISTORTION, AND CORRUPTION

In any selective system, fraud is an inescapable problem. After all, resettlement usually represents major gains in life prospects, often well beyond even what the nondisplaced local population living near the refugees could ever reasonably expect. Hence the temptation is great. Out of desperation or manipulation, or based on the coaching of an entrepreneur collecting a fee for such advice, applicants for resettlement may tailor their stories to fit what they understand to be the requirements of the program (often called the "camp story" problem) — as a great many persons interviewed for this study took pains to emphasize.[12] Importantly, these warnings about the likelihood of fraud in connection with a resettlement program were heard at least as much and as vehemently from humanitarian workers as they were from persons with enforcement roles.

It is probably true that this problem has worsened in recent years. With the expanded reach of criminal enterprises, including human traffickers, and with improved global communications,[13] anecdotal evidence suggests that organized fraud crops up earlier and in more sophisticated forms in refugee situations. For this reason, several persons interviewed for this project emphasized the need for what some called a "stealth" approach to resettlement. That is, preliminary work that will fix or record key individual characteristics or histories — such as detailed questioning as part of camp registration or a UNHCR population verification exercise — should be completed to the greatest possible extent well before any public mention of a possible resettlement initiative. At such an early time, the interviewer is far more likely to obtain a full and candid picture of the person's true situation, undistorted by his or her guesses about what will maximize chances for resettlement (or by the coaching of a third party). Such secrecy is difficult to achieve, however, because complex programs necessarily require the early and sustained involvement of a great many players from governmental, international, and nongovernmental ranks.

Another, related form of distortion is also possible, particularly if the priorities for resettlement are not well-conceived. For example, I heard concerns expressed that some of UNHCR's traditional categories for resettlement referrals, especially the category for "women at risk," can become self-fulfilling. When it becomes known that resettlement is possible on this ground, families may separate to enable the woman to win a referral for herself and the children — and perhaps be able to bring the husband later. Further, some women successfully heading households in a refugee settlement may begin to portray their situations in a sharply different light, or even expose themselves to greater dangers, so as to come within the category. This potential distortion deserves closer attention, and it may well be that more carefully described or context-specific categories could achieve much of the objective without inducing such manipulation.

The temptations in this field have also sometimes resulted in damaging corruption or manipulation on the part of certain UNHCR officials or others in a responsible role, who find they can extract large bribes or other personal favors for moving certain cases to the head of the resettlement line. On occasion, as happened in Nairobi in 2000, resettlement was suspended until UNHCR fully dealt with the issue. It is important to note that UNHCR has taken serious steps in response and is working to implement genuine checks and balances to counter corrup-

tion in new management and registration systems.[14] Some programs, particularly family-based resettlement programs in West Africa, have been marred by a high level of fraudulent claims. But US government initiatives over the last two years, many developed in close coordination with refugee nongovernmental organizations (NGOs), have provided important new tools to detect and deter fraud. (See Chapter III.) Continued vigilance is necessary, but measures are available to address these problems, and the agencies involved are capable of refining their techniques as needed. The system must remain closely attentive to fraud and corruption at each stage, but these risks should be addressed directly, rather than used as a basis for diminishing US response.

5. DEFINITIONAL ISSUES

A further factor complicates efforts to agree on which refugees to resettle out of a conventionally counted world total of twelve to fourteen million. The popular conception of refugee differs from the legal definition governing US refugee admissions. That legal definition, based on the 1951 United Nations (UN) Convention relating to the Status of Refugees,[15] defines a refugee as a person who is outside his or her country of origin owing to a "well-founded fear of persecution on account of race, religion, nationality, membership in a particular social group, or political opinion." When applied with precision (as it is in the US asylum program, which is administered solely in US territory), the definition requires a rather specific showing that the person, or a group with which he or she is identified, is likely to be targeted for persecution on the basis of one of the five grounds. Civil war and domestic disturbances, without more, do not provide a basis for meeting the Convention refugee definition. Those who flee even intense fighting are not covered, unless the combatants had one of the stated reasons for targeting the individual or group that has fled. Even though the definition is usually applied with a somewhat more generous approach in the overseas refugee program than for purposes of asylum, overseas officers still must find a sound basis in the information provided during the interview, or in other circumstances affecting the applicant, for making the legally required findings.

Some persons readily labeled refugees by the press and public cannot make this showing. That is, the popular conception of a refugee is more expansive than the legal definition. Quite understandably, the popular view tends to include anyone who has crossed a border because of real dangers in the home country, whatever their precise nature. Those who have fled civil war are routinely called refugees, and flight from a country where persecution goes on, without any close attention to whether the individual can show good reason why he or she is likely to be targeted (much less whether the harm would be based on one of the five Convention grounds), can also result in popular application of the label. Moreover, in many circumstances, broader legal definitions than the one enshrined in US law are employed. For example, the Organization of African Unity's treaty on refugees embraces both the UN Convention refugee definition and also those who have been compelled to leave their homes and cross a border "owing to external aggression, occupation, foreign domination or events seriously disturbing public order."[16] UNHCR uses this latter definition as the basis for much of its work in Africa. It is also authorized, in some settings, to use group-wide "prima facie determinations" of refugee status as the basis for its involvement, particularly to provide assistance to displaced individuals. And for certain purposes, other UN legal instruments also bring populations that do not meet the Convention refugee definition within the UNHCR's mandate.[17] In each case, there are good reasons, founded in an overall assessment of genuine dangers, for treating the group as refugees, particularly for purposes of generating broad and urgent international action to feed and shelter the displaced and to provide them elementary protection. The usual estimates of global refugee populations employ the broader definitions, at least for some regions.

The law governing US admissions provisions does not incorporate these wider conceptions, even when they have been the basis for international assistance in which the United States generously participates. (Chapter VII argues for a statutory amendment that would expand eligibility for US refugee admissions in a carefully structured manner.) Criticism of US admissions performance sometimes overlooks these constraints. Planners cannot uncritically use these global totals in choosing groups to process for US resettlement, but instead must be sensitive to the legal constraints that ultimately govern decisions by the interviewing officers deployed by the Department of Homeland Security (DHS).

6. COMPLEXITY AND LUCK

Even when a decision is made to resettle a particular group, the actual movement to the United States may be delayed by months or years, owing to operational factors that are not wholly under the control of US government officers. The refugee resettlement machinery is highly complex, and dozens of pieces must line up successfully before resettlement takes place. (Chapter V, Section A, describes this machinery in greater detail.) If one piece is knocked out, a host of other good work to promote resettlement may produce no concrete results — and may then go totally unnoticed by critics. At the very least, time will be lost while that one piece is brought back into alignment. For example, just when the Department of State's Bureau of Population, Refugees, and Migration (PRM) expected to move significant numbers of approved refugees from Nairobi toward the end of FY 2003, the Kenyan government suddenly and unexpectedly announced that all departures would require approved exit permits, which virtually none of the persons in Nairobi awaiting travel to the United States possessed. (Further negotiations succeeded in overcoming much of the problem, but movements were impaired for a brief time.) On other occasions, populations that had undergone most of the preinterview processing could not receive final Immigration and Naturalization Service (INS) or DHS review because sudden deterioration in the security situation at the interview site resulted in canceling or postponing a circuit ride.

Often the program cannot simply pick up where it left off once the immediate problem is overcome. Delay often requires redoing certain laborious steps in the process, because fingerprints and other security clearances, for example, as well as medical clearances, are valid only for a limited period — usually for six or twelve months. The various delays and complications that arose with new procedures adopted in late 2001 have frequently necessitated new clearances of this sort before actual movements could resume. That the resettlement pipeline has functioned relatively smoothly over most of the life of the USRP is a testament to the government officials and NGOs, along with UNHCR and International Organization for Migration (IOM) personnel, who play the key roles and are often quite resourceful in coping with sudden complications. But the effects of the program's unavoidable complexity, which has compounded since September 11, 2001, are sometimes overlooked by critics of recent performance.

The resettlement of the Somali Bantu provides an example of the possible difficulties, as well as the role that bad luck can play. Here the problem was not any difficulty in reaching US government agreement on designating the group for priority resettlement, because some 11,000 Somali Bantu were approved as a P-2 priority group in late 1999. They were not expected to move immediately, because time was clearly needed for UNHCR to undertake a challenging verification exercise to assure the integrity of the lists that would be used for access to US interviews. As it happened, it took until December 2001 to complete that exercise. In the meantime, PRM decided it had to move the Somali Bantu to another camp in Kenya, because processing in the original camp was too dangerous. That expensive move, a bus trip of 900 miles, was completed in the summer of 2002. It was then expected, however, that the Somali Bantu would provide a substantial portion of the resettlement caseload at least by FY 2003, as the system worked to regain its balance in the aftermath of September 11, 2001. Owing to a striking series of complications and even natural disasters, however, interviews had to be postponed on several occasions, and movement to the United States in that period was limited to about 800 persons. (These difficulties are described in more detail in the annex to this chapter.) Most of that population is expected to resettle to the United States in FY 2004, although ongoing security concerns in Kenya wound up delaying the initial dispatch of DHS officers to the processing camp for interviewing. Overall admissions performance could have been 20-30 percent higher in FY 2003 if the Somali Bantu program had not encountered these difficulties.

Fortunately, few programs have been as relentlessly beset by misfortune and delay as the Somali Bantu effort, but that history and the pitfalls it exemplifies need to be kept in mind in judging admissions performance. It also signals that the USRP needs to manage the refugee pipeline in a way that can accommodate such complications and delays without losing all momentum for a robust admissions level.

7. TOWARD A FUTURE OF CASE-BY-CASE DECISIONS TO RESETTLE FINITE GROUPS

For all these reasons, one cannot simply throw a dart at a map, even in a region marked by large refugee flows and genuine privation, and begin resettling refugees. Nor should the US program be based on fixed criteria that trigger resettlement

when a single factor is satisfied (such as populations who have spent more than X years in a camp, or women and children at risk of specified harm).[18] The factors that must be considered are inevitably complex and interconnected. Because of host-country or UNHCR resistance, desires not to torpedo chances for repatriation, difficulties of equitable and manageable selection through processes that assure integrity, definitional disconnects, and particularly concern not to induce unmanageable further migration, choices to resettle specific groups or categories must be done carefully and case-by-case.

This is a crucial feature of the modern refugee resettlement era. We are extremely unlikely in this new century to find the United States or any other country willing to make an open-ended commitment to resettlement of virtually all who escape a designated nation — the type of commitment that prevailed for refugees from the Soviet Union and, for the first decade of the program, for Vietnamese refugee resettlement. Absent that sort of political decision, resettlement initiatives will be marked by the need to draw clear lines around the group to be admitted, so as to minimize fraud and to discourage future migration of others who might hope to be included in the resettlement. The quest will be for *finite groups*, and resettlement will work best if much solid work on identification and line-drawing can be completed before resettlement plans become known in the refugee camp or settlement.

A further caveat is in order. For almost any refugee situation, serious reasons can be presented as to why resettlement should not be pursued, or at least why it should not be pursued at the current time. Postponement might allow other solutions to the displacement to develop. If each refugee situation is viewed only in isolation, those reasons can be made to appear far more concrete and solid than the arguments in favor of resettlement. In almost any such circumstance, voices will be heard stating that the less risky course for American policy is to deny or defer any resettlement initiative.

But to note these real and important complexities is not to suggest acceptance of the current performance. All these factors may deserve attention, but they are simply cautionary considerations, not absolute trumps that should defeat the initiation of significant refugee resettlement from given regions. In an era that will require multiple decisions each year on resettling specific groups, the challenge is to reform the US decision-making system, as well as certain operational practices, so that we can take better account of the positive arguments in favor of resettlement and fully deploy available measures that minimize the obstacles.

The next section considers certain foundational questions that must be addressed in order to strengthen such a system. Later chapters turn to more specific operational recommendations.

B. Fundamental choices for the US Refugee Program: aims and nature

The US Refugee Program has suffered from a lack of clarity regarding its principal aims and fundamental character. Many players in specific debates over new resettlement initiatives hold subtly different conceptions of the primary objectives, so that what looks like a debate on whether to resettle a specific group is really an unspoken dispute over underlying objectives. Getting that deeper debate out in the open would help unclog deadlocks in deciding on specific groups. Clear direction on these points from the President or the Secretary of State would also structure and simplify future decision making. And such clarity would also be quite helpful in making specific decisions on how to improve the details of operations.

The different views can be placed in two separate camps, marked by these interrelated polarities:

■ resettlement focused on immediate rescue from grave dangers versus resettlement that accounts for a wider range of genuine harms

■ resource priority for assistance versus resource priority for resettlement

■ the refugee admissions number in the annual Presidential Determination as a ceiling versus that same number as a target.

To paint it this way is to oversimplify, of course. No one wants refugee resources to go only to assistance in first-asylum countries or only to resettlement. No one in the second camp wants to eliminate the capacity to use the program to rescue people who would be gravely threatened, harmed, or killed without swift resettlement initiatives. Under any system, the first claim on admission spaces should always be for such rescue, where possible; further, the

system should prioritize the use of admissions, wherever a resettlement initiative is otherwise feasible, based on the degree of risk or suffering that the particular population faces. Moreover, good and respectable arguments support both approaches, so that the choice between them (or among various shadings) is not any easy one. Nonetheless, considering the different views in this simplified fashion can help illuminate some fundamental choices that those guiding the program need to make.

1. Immediate rescue from grave danger versus rescue from a wider range of harms

The contending positions. One view sees US resettlement spaces as a scarce resource to be used only when needed in order to rescue persons whose lives would otherwise be in grave and immediate danger. The beginnings of the Indochina resettlement program in the late 1970s have often been seen as an example of this approach. As the numbers exiting Vietnam surged in 1978, some first-asylum countries in the region physically pushed refugees back across their land borders or repelled vessels overcrowded with desperate families, sending them back out to likely death at sea. Only when the world community in 1979 pledged essentially to resettle elsewhere all who were permitted first asylum did those countries relent.[19] They agreed to permit landings and ongoing care and maintenance in camps on their territories, where the processing for resettlement then geared up in earnest. Macedonia's treatment of those fleeing Kosovo in early 1999, holding them in deeply hazardous conditions in fields near the border, also prompted a similar rescue initiative.[20] When many other countries offered to take at least some of the population sheltered there for either permanent or temporary haven, Macedonia changed its approach and began to allow the care and maintenance of new arrivals in more secure facilities.

This rescue-based view also countenances launching resettlement when persons who had found a tolerable welcome across the border suddenly become highly vulnerable in the first-asylum country. The conception of the recent resettlement program for selected Liberians from Cote d'Ivoire provides an example. Until recently, the Ivorian government and populace had generally accepted Liberians displaced by Liberia's long-running and brutal civil war. A great many were able to find a fairly stable existence in the western part of the host nation or in the capital, Abidjan. But when civil war erupted in Cote d'Ivoire itself in September 2002, the populace blamed much of the problem on foreigners. Tolerance changed to vituperation. Liberians sometimes became the targets for community violence, and many were forced to relocate to a handful of camps where their protection and subsistence remained tenuous.[21] Based on a group referral of "vulnerable Liberians" by UNHCR in early 2003, the United States speedily initiated a resettlement program focused on approximately 8,000 Liberians from specific camps and urban centers.

A resettlement program built on the narrow rescue principle is inherently volatile. Acute vulnerability waxes and wanes, and resettlement volume could be expected to rise and fall in response. Small populations chosen under this approach can perhaps be wholly rescued with a few months of processing and transportation, and new resettlement initiatives will not necessarily fill the gap, unless of course a new life-threatening crisis materializes elsewhere. Larger populations raise other issues. If the launching of a resettlement program succeeds in securing acceptance of first asylum in countries close to the source country, or in diminishing popular backlash among the host population, then the immediate vulnerability is reduced. Over time, the interim arrangements, including international aid for the care and maintenance of refugees in the first asylum country, may ease the host country's resistance to longer-term stays in camps or even to local integration for a portion of the refugee population. If so, vulnerability has diminished and resettlement may be curtailed or stopped, or at least arguments for reducing or ending the resettlement program will be pressed with greater vigor. That is, it is always open to argument just how serious the current vulnerability may be. On the other hand, the first asylum countries may believe that they have an ongoing deal, and may object to even modest efforts to trim resettlement flows — perhaps to the point of threatening to renew rejections at the frontier. Something of that latter dynamic persisted through the 1980s with the Indochinese program, and resettlement did not significantly diminish even after pushbacks had been curtailed.

The Indochinese program demonstrates that rescue-based approaches can result in a steady stream of resettlement, extending over many years. But such circumstances are likely to be rare, and for such a program to continue taking in large numbers for a

lengthy period will probably require support that derives from other sources. The Indochinese program of course had such wellsprings of support — based on this country's lengthy involvement in Vietnam and links to many of the people who were potential victims, as well as the program's congruence with Cold War objectives. But even so, a current of resistance to Indochinese resettlement was evident in the later years of that program, arguing that the program had outlived its original rationale and had transmuted into a tacit immigration program.

The primary alternative approach is to see resettlement, in addition, as a durable solution that should be used to respond to a wider range of dangers. This approach does not deny that resettlement is a scarce resource, but it sees a broader spectrum of circumstances as justifying concerted action to resettle, even if the persons involved are not in immediate life-threatening danger.[22] Proponents of this view argue that the United States should actively consider resettlement, for example, for populations that have spent many years of stay in a refugee camp, particularly if the conditions are severe and provide little productive activity for the refugees, limited educational opportunities for their children, or other features that betoken a lingering and profound waste of human potential.[23] Not all such circumstances will necessarily be good candidates for US resettlement, of course. Such initiatives should not thwart voluntary repatriation, if it is reasonably imminent. They should be designed to augment, not to overcome, the possibilities for improved camp life and even local integration. And they should generally be launched only where other circumstances, such as a good camp registration system, can help minimize any magnet effect and provide safeguards against fraud.

This view shares with the narrow rescue outlook an understanding that the USRP must be reserved for uses that alleviate serious human suffering, but it finds that criterion satisfied even if conditions are not immediately life-threatening. In particular, when camp life is little better than human warehousing, and where it has persisted in this mode for several years, resettlement must enter the picture as a potential durable solution. In interviews for this project, proponents of this view often recalled their own experiences visiting bleak refugee camps years after the initial flight and coming face-to-face with the profound wastage of human lives represented by such an enforced existence, particularly for the children forced to grow up under such conditions. They argued that this approach is simply a different species of rescue — saving people from a prolonged strangling of their life chances and not just from fast-working dangers. Bill Frelick describes the need in these terms:

> Millions of refugees worldwide have been relegated to a limbo existence, warehoused in camps or settlements with no prospects for voluntary repatriation or local integration. Children born and raised within the confines of camps often never see normal life outside the fences. These populations often become dependent and despondent, with predictably negative social consequences.[24]

A program founded on the second outlook can more readily be designed for stability of flow and predictability over time. Although this approach would by no means preclude the use of resettlement spaces for the situations targeted by the first view — indeed, they should claim first priority — it permits greater balance and advance planning for that (normally) substantial part of the program that would not be based on the narrowest version of rescue. Moreover, this wider perspective better allows for an approach that is coming to be known as the strategic use of resettlement.[25] That is, the world community should think about using resettlement offers to help encourage receiving states to maintain first asylum,[26] to break up negotiation stalemates that keep refugees stuck in stark camps, and especially to use resettlement as one component in a comprehensive solution. Such solutions work to end refugee exile through a combination of voluntary repatriation with resettlement for those subpopulations for whom repatriation remains too dangerous despite a general settlement.

No official, to my knowledge, has definitively declared that resettlement should be limited to immediate rescue and acute vulnerability. But my interviews for this project did suggest that there were times when key decisions, for example to turn down or at least postpone the designation of additional groups for priority access to the USRP, were ultimately swayed by arguments seemingly based on the narrower rescue principle. Quietly, at crunch time, the fact that the potential beneficiaries are not in immediately life-threatening situations can

prove decisive in rejecting the initiative. At the least, opposition to a new initiative put forward by other bureaus or agencies involved in refugee resettlement may gain force from the claim that resettlement is not needed for the immediate saving of lives.

The narrow rescue perspective offered as an antidote to interest group politics. Several interviews for this project produced this observation: The narrower rescue-focused perspective has been embraced as a reaction against distortion of the admission program's true objectives. Unless the program is limited to lifesaving initiatives, it will be diverted too easily into serving other foreign policy goals, or it will be captured by interest-group politics and will devote too many spaces to refugees whose main claim to priority is simply a strong constituency in the United States — thereby straying from the program's true humanitarian purposes.

Some who voiced this complaint pointed to the Indochina resettlement program, which in their view continued far longer than it should have — moving from a legitimate rescue effort in the late 1970s to a de facto immigration program. Many UNHCR officers apparently share this outlook; the Indochina experience has contributed to a negative attitude within UNHCR toward giving prominence to resettlement as a durable solution — an attitude the organization is now working to reverse.[27]

The example most frequently mentioned in connection with this type of complaint was the Lautenberg Amendment.[28] Originally passed in 1989, the amendment responded to a sudden change of policy by the executive branch in 1988 that called for strict application of the refugee definition in all overseas refugee processing. As a result of this 1988 change, many applicants in the Soviet program and, to a lesser extent, in Indochina found their cases unexpectedly rejected. Some from the Soviet Union were already in transit centers in western Europe, without obvious options. Both they and the transit countries had expected that virtually all such applicants would be moved onward speedily as part of the US resettlement program. After debating several possible legislative remedies, Congress enacted a provision that authorized the approval of refugee applications from specific categories of applicants in the Soviet Union, Eastern Europe, and Indochina based on a markedly less demanding showing of risk. The Lautenberg Amendment was adopted as a temporary measure, destined to sunset after one year, but it was then extended for an additional two years and has been routinely extended ever since, with some modifications — even though the Soviet Union has since disappeared from the map.

Some of the current critics accept that respectable arguments supported the original enactment and perhaps even the continuation, during the uncertain period that immediately followed the breakup of the USSR, of some of the special categories, many of which focus on Jews, Evangelical Christians, and other religious minorities. But they question the continuing need for such a special provision under current conditions, believing that normal refugee standards allow ample scope for resettlement of those truly endangered. Many people interviewed for the project voiced skepticism about these differential standards under current conditions, yet none expected Congress to allow the amendment to expire. They view Lautenberg as a chief example of resettlement priorities that become unjustifiably entrenched owing to congressional inertia and domestic politics.[29]

Others have expanded on the critique of interest group actions. In their view, the voluntary agencies that have long participated in US refugee initiatives, both overseas and domestically, have to a significant degree captured the process and turned it to serve their own narrower interests. Sometimes these critics mean simply that the USRP often favors admission of groups that are tied by ethnicity, religion, or other features to a particular US voluntary agency (volag). But a stronger version of this critique alleges that a different type of self-interest governs — the desire to maintain the flow of federal funds to the volags themselves and their top officers. The campaign to return resettlement numbers to their historic levels is sometimes portrayed as a mere self-interested effort to hold on to volag contracts with the government and to keep volag offices fully staffed.[30]

NGO representatives reject the charge of narrow financial self-interest as the basis for their actions or for their recommendations on groups that should have priority access to the USRP. But some interviewed for this project defended placing at least some priority on choosing groups that have a support base already present in this country. In selecting among millions of genuinely good candidates for resettlement, they maintain, taking those with a

support community already in place maximizes successful resettlement outcomes as well as long-term support for the US Refugee Program. They emphasized, however, that such a rationale should not be the sole criterion for setting resettlement priorities, and they pointed to many counterexamples, like the Somali Bantu, to show that the NGOs do not limit their support solely to persons or groups closely identified with a volag's prior missions.

The strongest versions of the interest group capture claim are unfair. Although there have been instances of financial or management abuses, the NGOs active in this field have historically been energized not by federal contracts but by their officers' and volunteers' real-world experiences with refugees — both in camps abroad and in the process of resettlement in this country. Traditionally, these organizations have brought to bear their own resources — often in significant proportions — and most got into the refugee assistance and resettlement business decades before the current structure of federal contracts and grants was in place. Many draw upon a faith-based tradition of assistance to the needy, and the secular organizations as well can generally point to a long history of humanitarian action wholly divorced from federal largesse. This reflects a proud American tradition.

It is highly important that this tradition not wither, however, and some persons interviewed raised strong concerns along these lines. Volags today vary significantly in the extent to which they raise funds privately to augment their services supporting refugee resettlement, and in the percentage of funding they apply to direct assistance rather than administrative costs.[31] Those that now bring little to the task besides what they receive in government funding (through reception and placement grants from the State Department or other forms of assistance funded by the Office of Refugee Resettlement in the Department of Health and Human Services) are not living up to the public-private partnership standards that should prevail. These public grants are not sufficient by themselves to make for a successful transition for arriving refugees, because the system assumes that the public funding will be augmented by private resources, either financial or in-kind. Volags need to be vigilant to assure that all their local affiliates are providing fully adequate services for the refugees entrusted to their care.

As to the gentler version of the interest group claim, one cannot expect that persons deeply involved with refugee assistance and resettlement would be agnostic on resettlement priorities or that they would shy away from supporting refugee groups to which they have ties. Our democratic system makes such advocacy legitimate, even on the part of persons or entities affiliated with organizations that have contractual ties with a government program. Those with decision-making responsibility may properly consider such background factors (and the possible role of self-interest underlying particular proposals for resettlement initiatives), but they should not be surprised that NGOs will press their proposals doggedly and criticize government decisions with which they disagree.

Of wider effect may be a related feature that requires attention. Interviews for this project turned up a surprisingly widespread feeling, including among congressional circles, that the refugee program has gotten away from resettling "real refugees" — a development many attribute to exaggerated interest group influence. Although this theme has been somewhat submerged in public statements in recent years,[32] the risk exists that it will find more prominence as the program regains its momentum and reaches higher admission levels. Given that the new era may require a dozen or more decisions each year on new resettlement initiatives, more occasions may arise for critics to charge improper influence. Some recent legislative proposals, meant to give NGOs wider authority to help set admissions priorities through "refugee response teams" perhaps composed exclusively of NGO personnel, are freighted with long-term peril of this sort.[33] Such proposals might succeed in getting admission numbers up, but at the likely cost of feeding a backlash against what critics will see as interest group distortion. This is a subtle point, and the devil is in the details of the NGO role. It is of course appropriate and desirable for the government to use the expertise of NGOs more systematically in casting a wide informational net and developing the best possible data for identifying manageable and appropriate resettlement initiatives. (This measured approach has been taken in PRM's recent initiatives to include NGO representatives in "targeted response teams" that undertake quiet field investigations of possible resettlement initiatives.) But any legislation on these subjects should make it clear that the ultimate decisions, both to initiate a detailed look at a population and ultimately to decide to target it for resettlement, remain in the hands of government officials.[34]

The concern about possible distortions of refugee policy is legitimate. But we do not require a tightly restrictive rescue principle to avoid them. A better designed decisional structure — one that proves it really can produce regular decisions on resettlement initiatives after a rigorous examination of need, broadly understood, as well as of constraining factors — can accomplish this objective. Chapter II recommends such a structure.

2. THE RESOURCE COMPETITION BETWEEN ASSISTANCE AND RESETTLEMENT

The pull of the narrow rescue outlook draws additional force from another element sketched in the introduction to this section. To a certain real extent, resources for resettlement are in competition with resources for assistance, and it is a fact that funds spent on assistance will go further and immediately aid many more people. Resettling a single refugee costs many thousands of dollars. That same sum of money, applied in the first asylum country, could feed and shelter many dozens of persons in a refugee camp for a year. Many persons in the refugee field, both government officials and NGO workers, are drawn to this "more bang for the buck" argument in giving a strong priority to assistance over resettlement. Of course resettlement must be preferred, they would acknowledge, if the alternative is refoulement or death, or if conditions in the camp are excessively dangerous for a vulnerable individual or group. But short of such a threat, protracted refugee situations should evoke an assistance response, not resettlement. (Another way to describe this view, using UNHCR terminology, is that it emphasizes resettlement as a tool of protection, rather than as a durable solution in its own right.)

If the competition for resources is viewed as a zero-sum game, where money given to one function inevitably diminishes the resources available for the other, the assistance side has a strong case. But that is probably an inaccurate way to view the issue. In the long run, resettlement almost surely enhances the support and resources available for all parts of US refugee activity. The USRP has brought 2.5 million refugees to a new life in the United States since 1975. They have settled in all fifty states, and a great many communities have developed vibrant support networks to welcome the new arrivals. The participants in those networks often find themselves drawn increasingly into wider efforts to support refugees, including many participants who previously had no real acquaintance with or interest in international human rights or refugee issues. In interviews for this project, some recounted what a profound impact their first experiences in private resettlement work had had on them and their fellow volunteers. Even US citizens not directly involved in such networks wind up gaining personal acquaintance with fellow community members who — they eventually learn — came to the United States as refugees. This personal contact, this immediate sharing of the stories of flight and survival and gratitude at the opportunities that US resettlement provided, has created warm local support for refugees in a wide range of communities. Such support readily translates into personal donations and political initiatives for refugee assistance activities of all kinds, both in the United States and abroad. Of more focused significance, members of Congress often invoke their own personal experiences with refugees in their home-state communities as a way of explaining, justifying, or trumpeting their own support for refugee funding and refugee initiatives — funding that also includes ample support for assistance to refugees and displaced persons outside the United States.

A study of resettlement in Europe and the United States, undertaken jointly by the European Council on Refugees and Exiles and the US Committee for Refugees, commented on these spin-off benefits:

> Finally, there are political and educational benefits to resettling refugees, as shown by the outpouring of public generosity in Europe and the United States toward Kosovar refugees evacuated from Kosovo and Macedonia during the Kosovo crisis in the spring of 1999. The resettlement of these refugees . . . helped to educate the public about the plight of refugees and generated considerable public support, not just for refugee resettlement but for other humanitarian programmes as well.[35]

Nonetheless, in the short run the competition for resources can remain quite real and immediate — and proposals for specific resettlement initiatives have usually come up for consideration individually, demanding short-run decisions. The annual budget-

ing arrangements for the refugee function compound the pressures. They leave it to the State Department, in the main, to divide up refugee funding (the Migration and Refugee Assistance (MRA) account) between resettlement and assistance annually and to adjust the totals during the year through the standard reprogramming procedures. If a group admission proposal comes up at a time when assistance budgets are stretched, or when new flows have prompted UNCHR appeals for additional assistance funding, incentives will obviously exist to preserve the resources for assistance, in order to benefit the greater number of people. This tension is likely to grow more acute if budget pressures over coming years reduce the MRA account. In any event, the dilemmas are real and must not be underestimated.

RECOMMENDATION I-1: The US Refugee Program should be explicitly based on a broad perspective about the use of resettlement. The President, the Secretary of State, the Secretary of Homeland Security, the Assistant Secretary for PRM, and the Director of the Bureau of Citizenship and Immigration Services (USCIS) should make it abundantly clear that the USRP is not limited to rescue from grave life-threatening dangers, but will work actively to rescue displaced individuals and groups who face a wider range of harms, including the wastage of human potential that can result from protracted stay in a refugee camp. These latter needs are real and compelling, and there are large populations meeting these wider criteria. Therefore, the program can still be prudent and selective in choosing among them, with full attention to countervailing factors such as possible magnet effects, other political impacts, and near-term prospects for voluntary repatriation. This approach should be accompanied by a determination to sustain fully viable budgets for refugee assistance, minimizing as much as possible any direct financial competition between assistance and resettlement.

On the other hand, if the Administration and the State Department are unprepared to make a firm declaration of this sort, including adequate funding for both admissions and assistance, they should then be fully candid and consistent about the likely outcomes in the current era, which lacks large-scale programs like those formerly in place for Indochina and the Soviet Union. That is, without new initiatives premised on this broader perspec-

tive, admission totals will almost surely remain low and admissions will fluctuate widely, whatever other operational improvements are introduced for processing those given access to the program. Without top-level candor on these points, officials responsible for the system are placed in an extremely difficult and unfair position. They will be judged by most outside observers against a high admissions total placed in the annual Presidential Determination, but not given the more specific policy directives and resources that are indispensable to meet that benchmark.

3. THE PRESIDENTIAL DETERMINATION: A CEILING OR A TARGET?

The contending perspectives. The approach based on immediate rescue from grave dangers coexists comfortably with the view that the number of refugee admissions set annually by the President is simply a ceiling and not a policy goal. That number is established following the submission of a report to Congress that sets forth a proposed level and allocation of admissions, along with a range of additional information required by statute.[36] Following Cabinet-level consultation with the House and Senate Judiciary Committees, usually carried out by the Secretary of State, the President issues a final Presidential Determination (PD) that sets admission levels and broad regional allocations of the numbers that will govern for the coming fiscal year. The law includes an additional provision for increasing the numbers midyear through a new PD based on "an unforeseen emergency refugee situation," but such an increase has occurred only three times since the adoption of the Refugee Act in 1980.[37]

Over the years PRM officers have often repeated, in response to criticism of admissions totals that fall below PD levels, that those numbers are ceilings, not policy goals. In this conception, if conditions unfold such that we do not need to use the full PD number — or even a significant fraction of it — this outcome does not contravene the President's decision; perhaps it should even be seen as a triumph for overall refugee policy. Critics counter that millions of refugees remain in conditions of stifled development and more subtle dangers, even if not in immediate life-threatening jeopardy, and that it is a shame to let the precious resource of presidentially determined admission slots simply lapse.

Why the Refugee Act does not settle this issue. It is correct that the ceiling-not-a-goal view predominated at the time of the adoption of the Refugee Act of 1980[38] and also provided an appropriate way to understand the PD number in the early years of operation under the Act. Hence the government officers who press this understanding have solid historical support for their position, and NGO critics should be more willing to acknowledge that the burden of proof falls on those who would take a different tack. But it is a burden of proof that can be carried, at least as a matter of current policy that could make for improved operation of the system. The early predominance of the ceiling-not-a-goal view was largely a product of the particular times and of carryover attitudes deriving from the statutory structure that immediately preceded the Refugee Act. Moreover, the legislation by no means mandates that the President's determination serve only as a ceiling. In deciding how to treat the PD number today, we should take into account the significant evolution of our refugee admissions system since 1980, as well as the functional implications of each of the competing visions of its role.

Before adoption of the Refugee Act, US law had provided for a statutorily fixed ceiling of 17,800 "conditional entrants" annually.[39] Until 1975, when Saigon fell and the South Vietnamese government collapsed, most of these numbers had been used for a modest and steady stream of East Bloc refugees who made it to western Europe and were processed by voluntary agencies that had been in that business for decades. On those occasions when greater needs arose, including 1975, they had been met through use of the Attorney General's parole power, but there was widespread dissatisfaction with that mechanism, particularly in Congress (which viewed large paroles as an inroad on congressional prerogatives) and also often on the part of Attorneys General.[40] The effort to pass a new Refugee Act was motivated by several important desires: to provide an alternative to parole for larger numbers of refugees by raising the numerical ceiling, to expand the definition of eligible refugees (previously only those from Communist countries and the Middle East could qualify), and to make sure that those brought as refugees could eventually secure full permanent residence status without the need for discrete special legislation.[41]

It is essential to keep in mind, however, that the Refugee Act was considered and adopted in the midst of a rapidly changing resettlement program, and the views of many legislators and executive branch officials evolved considerably during that time, as events forced rethinking of the types of refugee needs that were likely to be encountered. Early versions of the legislation were drafted in 1977 and early 1978, well after the sudden Vietnamese exodus of 1975 had ended, but before people foresaw any major new wave of boat departures. Resettlement totals in 1977 were low, and the major impetus for new legislation at that moment was lingering dissatisfaction with the limited arrangements that had been available to deal with the 1975 crisis. Early versions proposed to increase the annual ceilings to 40,000 or 50,000 — a significant increase and a number thought sufficient for foreseeable flows short of desperate emergencies like that of 1975, which was deemed unlikely of repetition.[42] By the time serious consideration of the bills began in the new Congress that convened in 1979, however, an enormous new wave of "boat people" had commenced, and refugee arrivals in the first-asylum countries of Southeast Asia (by both land and sea) exceeded 60,000 per month in May and June of that year.[43] Major outflows seemed likely to persist for years. By the time of enactment, President Carter had already pledged up to 14,000 US refugee admissions *per month*, as a response to the severe crisis in Southeast Asia. The US government, along with its NGO partners, was busily deploying resources and developing innovative processing techniques (considerably different from the traditional machinery used by the United States for refugees processed in Europe) to deal with this vastly changed refugee scene.

As American pledges expanded, they obviously outran the firm 50,000 ceiling that had been confidently placed in the administration's internal draft bills in 1978 and early 1979. Not only was that particular ceiling inadequate, but key players for the executive branch came to realize that any fixed ceiling was always vulnerable to being overtaken by events. Before the legislation was actually introduced in spring 1979, the administration redrafted the earlier versions to introduce a new and flexible procedure, which remained in the bills as initially passed by the House and Senate. That draft legislation set the annual admission level at 50,000, but allowed the President to raise it at the beginning of each fiscal year, after consultation with Congress. The provision ultimately enacted as INA § 207(a)[44] reflects a slight but important variation, introduced

as a result of negotiations while the bill was before the conference committee. The final version deleted the 50,000 benchmark or default level after the first three years, leaving it entirely up to the Presidential Determination to set the admissions level every year, following the prescribed consultation.[45]

Discussion of this new mechanism at that time generally used the terminology of ceilings, but not out of any deeply considered rejection of the idea that the numbers might also serve as goals or operational targets. That question never came up, as such. Instead, the terminology persisted because administrative practice under the earlier fixed-level laws had always spoken in those terms. Moreover, the participants realized that the extraordinarily high admissions levels of 1980 (which eventually brought over 207,000 refugees to the United States that fiscal year) were not sustainable. Major diplomatic efforts were under way to reduce the emergency pressures and find ways to bring the Indochinese flow within a more manageable framework. In that climate, it was quite appropriate to speak of the new levels as ceilings and to make it clear that the managers of the system were expected to bring admissions numbers below the high maximums the President was setting, whenever conditions enabled such a result. At that specific time, the PD number truly was a ceiling, not a goal.

Over the succeeding decades, the nature of the refugee admissions program has evolved considerably. The new processing techniques hastily cobbled together in the late 1970s, involving heavy reliance on NGOs to handle much of the paperwork and prepare cases for INS review (the joint voluntary agency (JVA) system), became more routine and sophisticated, and they were extended to other refugee situations as well. Additional refugee populations were resettled, in modest proportions, from Latin America, the Middle East, and Africa. Refugee resettlement became more institutionalized. Planning mechanisms developed, officers began to speak of a resettlement pipeline, and NGOs added staff and developed an enduring network of field offices throughout the United States to help manage the reception and integration of arriving refugees. This evolution represents a major triumph of the USRP — creating and sustaining such a system at reasonable cost levels, importantly involving a major public-private partnership. But with machinery on this scale, it is difficult to make sud-

TABLE 1-1

REFUGEE ADMISSIONS AND CEILINGS, FY 1980 - 2004

FY	Admissions	Original Ceiling	Revised Ceiling	Admissions as % of ceiling*
1980	207,116	231,700		89
1981	159,252	217,000		73
1982	98,096	140,000		70
1983	61,218	90,000		68
1984	70,393	72,000		98
1985	67,704	70,000		97
1986	62,146	67,000		93
1987	64,528	70,000		92
1988	76,483	72,500	87,500	87
1989	107,070	94,000	116,500	92
1990	122,066	125,000		98
1991	113,389	131,000		87
1992	132,531	142,000		93
1993	119,448	132,000		90
1994	112,981	121,000		93
1995	99,974	112,000		89
1996	76,403	90,000		85
1997	70,488	78,000		90
1998	77,080	83,000		93
1999	85,525	78,000	91,000	94
2000	73,147	90,000		81
2001	69,304	80,000		87
2002	27,110	70,000		39
2003	28,422	70,000		41
2004**	52,500	70,000		75
Total***	2,234,374		2,646,700	84

* Revised ceiling is used, where applicable.
** 2004 admissions projected.
*** Ceiling total includes final ceilings for each year, after revision where applicable.
Source: Bureau of Population, Refugees, and Migration, June 2004.

den changes, of level or location. Solid planning and clear benchmarks of performance can be of considerable use.

Perhaps most importantly, even after the Indochinese and Soviet refugee streams declined, succeeding Presidents and Congresses kept the admissions numbers (and accompanying budgetary support) at levels that could not have been envisioned in 1980 for noncrisis periods. Refugee admissions declined from over 207,000 in 1980 to below 62,000 in 1983, but then stabilized somewhat above the latter level through much of the 1980s, rising once more over 100,000 from 1989 through 1994. See Table I-1. As these statistics would suggest, refugee admissions have drawn strong support from a coalition that cuts across party lines and across the divisions that mark out competing camps on other issues. The annual numbers have evolved into an increasingly well-established humanitarian resource to be employed in service of the nation's historic humanitarian objectives. This evolution has come about in significant part because of what this nation has learned about the human value of refugee admissions. Countervailing currents exist, to be sure, and skepticism lingers over some elements of the refugee program that deserves to be taken seriously. But the reality of this highly successful program suggests the value of a steady and reasonably high-capacity resettlement program, even after the decline of what had been its historic mainstay components.

Evaluation. If the admissions program becomes based on the broader perspective of refugee resettlement needs, as is strongly recommended here, then the US Refugee Program should treat the PD number as a goal and not an optional ceiling. Once the focus is expanded beyond immediate rescue, a great many refugee situations come into view as good candidates for possible resettlement, with real humanitarian gains to be realized by offering thousands of men, women, and children who lack any reasonable prospect of voluntary repatriation, the chance to escape from human warehousing. When such a valuable humanitarian resource, determined by the President and supported by Congress, is available, refugees should not be left either in immediately dangerous situations or in multiyear idleness and privation in a refugee camp.[46] Seen as a goal or target (with appropriate tolerances given the volatility of refugee situations), the PD number then provides a useful baseline for accountability addressing both pipeline development and operational management. This outlook would help all relevant players gauge their own performance and plan proactive efforts accordingly.

Such an approach would carry an additional structural advantage. As noted, it is often easy to marshal arguments against new resettlement initiatives. There truly are risks and imponderables with virtually any such effort, which are quite properly taken into account before making an access decision. These include chances of triggering a new pull factor, the risk of disrupting other promising political developments, or logistical and security challenges involved in processing the particular group. But it has often proven difficult in governmental (and international) deliberations to assure systematic consideration of steps that can minimize those risks or of the reasons why it may be time to nudge the political calculations in a different direction. At a

time when many new group-access decisions will be required each year, the system sorely needs ongoing incentives that can counter the structural bias toward letting the negative case win the day. Treating the PD number as a target helps provide such a counterbalance. The central question in the current era of refugee resettlement must be which resettlement initiatives present the fewest drawbacks or disadvantages — not which have none, for that will almost never be the case.

One further caveat is in order. For the PD number to serve this accountability role effectively, it must be set at a realistic — even if designedly challenging — level. Large programs like this cannot easily make sudden changes. The refugee program has had to cope with many difficult operational alterations in the wake of the September 11 attacks, and it has taken a couple of years for the component parts to adjust to the new requirements. Many of these pieces are just now beginning to settle into ordinary and predictable operation, a development that holds real promise for FY 2004 and beyond. But the system has not yet been sufficiently retooled to deal with the second challenge, that of having to identify a host of new group resettlement initiatives each year. Resources are only now beginning to be dedicated to that function on the scale needed — partly because until recently so much time and energy had to be devoted to the more pressing operational tangles. Throughout this time, the annual PD number has been set at 70,000 — with the best of goodwill, perhaps, but without sufficient realism about the system's limitations, the scope of the post–September 11 adjustments, and the time frame needed to accomplish them. It is important — and achievable — for the system in FY 2004 to reach an actual admissions level above 50,000, and such an outcome would provide welcome momentum for continuing a strong upward trend for succeeding years. But a full transition to a workable goal-not-a-ceiling approach is not feasible until FY 2005.

RECOMMENDATION I-2: The number of admissions set in the annual Presidential Determination should be treated as a goal, not a ceiling. It should therefore provide a firm benchmark (following a reasonable transition process) for accountability of the offices that have a role in access decisions and management of the system, including not only PRM and USCIS but also the regional bureaus of the Department of State and

the enforcement bureaus of the Department of Homeland Security. Because of the potential volatility of refugee flows, and the program's vulnerability to unforeseen problems, the benchmark should apply with reasonable tolerances, which can probably diminish once a system built on this new approach has matured. To perform this function, the PD admissions number must be set at reasonable, though challenging, levels congruent with the resources being made available through the budget process.

Access decisions should still pay attention to countervailing factors, both logistical and political, that might appropriately weigh against a resettlement initiative. Such decisions must still be done case-by-case, with full attention to the context. But treating the PD as a firm goal by which performance will be measured will help counter a long-standing tendency to give undue weight to the disadvantages of a proposed initiative.

Annex to Chapter 1

Resettlement of the Somali Bantu: A Case Study of Processing Complexity and Unforeseen Delays

The Somali Bantu are the descendants of southern Africans who were brought to East Africa some 200 years ago, largely as slaves. Although many eventually integrated to some extent with Somali society, a portion remained in destitution, held to menial labor and subjected to extensive discrimination. When the Somalian civil war broke out, many fled to Kenya, along with tens of thousands of other Somalis. The Somali Bantu remained the victims of discrimination, violence, and abuse, including rape, in the camps where they lived in northeastern Kenya near the town of Dadaab. Moreover, it was judged that they had no real prospects of a safe return to Somalia, even if more peaceful conditions could be established there for most of the population. The US decision in 1999 to designate the Bantu was based on an earlier UNHCR list, and it contemplated that the UNHCR would undertake a careful verification of that list before other resettlement processing began. Verification plans took some time, particularly in the face of desperate efforts by other Somalis in the Dadaab camp to claim Bantu status or family connections. The additional planning and preparation time proved worthwhile, however,

because a thorough verification was finally carried out in December 2001.[47]

In the meantime, UNHCR and USRP partners discussed other operational elements of the plan. Dadaab, a collection of camps in a part of Kenya marked by banditry, housed some 130,000 people, mostly non-Bantu Somalis. Although some initial processing had been done there, Dadaab was judged unsafe for the later stages, both because of resentment against the now-favored beneficiaries of resettlement and because of broader security risks to US government and NGO personnel there. PRM therefore decided to move the 11,000 Bantu to Kakuma camp in northwestern Kenya — a journey of 900 miles by bus convoy. Construction of new facilities in Kakuma cost over a million dollars and consumed many months (creating facilities that would remain useful for other activities in Kakuma even after the Bantu departed), and the move finally took place over the summer months of 2002.[48] The first group of DHS officers was supposed to go to Kakuma in July, but that circuit ride was called off after the security situation suddenly deteriorated there, sparked to some extent by rumors and misunderstanding of the resettlement plans. NGO processing staff were evacuated, but returned not long after to prepare cases for a circuit ride that eventually took place in October 2002. The October processing was hampered by a dispute over the quality and possible corruption of interpreters, which was eventually resolved with a decision to use IOM-provided interpreters brought in from Nairobi. Several hundred cases were approved during that time, but postapproval processing was delayed, and almost none of these cases were able to travel to the United States over the following year. This lag necessitated a new round of security and medical clearances, because such clearances are good only for a limited period. In the meantime, the DHS called off planned circuit rides in the winter and spring of 2003, owing to new security incidents and concerns. On several occasions, these problems cropped up just as a new DHS team was about to be dispatched from the United States. Even if those problems were resolved within a few weeks, the originally planned temporary-duty DHS team usually could not be put back together, because its membership was drawn from other units of the DHS that could not keep those officers indefinitely available for refugee processing work. Hence it might take many more weeks or months to reassemble an interviewing team.

To respond to these heightened security problems at Kakuma, PRM eventually arranged with IOM and other partners to construct new fences and watchtowers. But natural disaster then piled on top of the usual security problems to cause further delay. In May 2003 unusually heavy rains brought flooding to Kakuma and forced the suspension of that work and of NGO processing. In July 2003 the embassy's regional security officer finally approved the bolstered facilities at Kakuma, and DHS circuit rides resumed in mid-August 2003 — too late to produce any significant movement of approved individuals to the United States in FY 2003.[49] But resettlement has proceeded in significant volume in FY 2004.[50]

While all these efforts were under way in Kenya, the resettlement NGOs were beginning the process of allocating the previously approved cases to sponsors in the United States, using an approved plan for clustered resettlement in a limited number of US communities. This approach was judged most likely to promote successful integration for a population that would have to overcome significant cultural and educational gaps. The lengthy delays, however, allowed for misunderstanding and resistance to grow in some of the US destination communities among people who were uncertain of what to expect and who sometimes gave public voice to fearful worst-case scenarios that were widely off the mark. These misunderstandings might have been squelched much earlier had those communities begun to receive actual refugees promptly. The cluster resettlement scheme had to undergo some painful readjustments and retreats as a result, although most of those plans remained intact and eventually have proved reasonably successful.[51]

CHAPTER I. ENDNOTES

1 See, e.g., EMPTY SEATS IN A LIFEBOAT: ARE THERE PROBLEMS WITH THE US REFUGEE PROGRAM?: HEARING BEFORE THE SUBCOMM. ON IMMIGRATION, S. COMM. ON THE JUDICIARY, 107th Cong. 22 (2002) (statement of Lenny Glickman, Chairman, Refugee Council USA).

2 The worldwide total of refugees, generally placed now between twelve and fourteen million, is subject to dispute. UNHCR's methodology for counting or estimating refugee populations has serious limitations, and in any event the underlying estimates for many regions of the world apply a definition of "refugee" that is wider than the definition governing the US admissions program, as discussed in Section A5 of this chapter.

3 See GIL LOESCHER & JOHN A. SCANLAN, CALCULATED KINDNESS: REFUGEES AND AMERICA'S HALF-OPEN DOOR, 1945-PRESENT 138-46 (1986).

4 See Sten A. Bronée, The History of the Comprehensive Plan of Action, 5 INT'L J. REFUGEE L. 534 (1993); Yen Tran, Comment, The Closing of the Saga of the Vietnamese Asylum Seekers: The Implications on International Refugees and Human Rights Laws, 17 HOUS. J. INT'L L. 463 (1995). See also text of the Comprehensive Plan of Action, 1 INT'L J. REFUGEE L. 574 (1989).

5 JULIA VADALA TAFT, DAVID S. NORTH, & DAVID A. FORD, REFUGEE RESETTLEMENT IN THE US: TIME FOR A NEW FOCUS 94 (New TransCentury Foundation Report 1979), reprinted in SEN. COMM. ON THE JUDICIARY, 96TH CONG., 2D SESS., REVIEW OF US REFUGEE RESETTLEMENT PROGRAMS AND POLICIES 114, 217 (Comm. Print, 1980) (prepared by Congressional Research Service).

6 Foreign Operations, Export Financing, and Related Programs Appropriations Act of 1990, Pub. L. No. 101-167, Title V, § 599D, 103 Stat. 1195, 1261 (1989), as amended, 8 U.S.C. § 1157 Note (2000).

7 See, e.g., SEAN D. MURPHY, HUMANITARIAN INTERVENTION: THE UNITED NATIONS IN AN EVOLVING WORLD ORDER 145-281 (1996); Sadako Ogata, Humanitarian Responses to International Emergencies, in PEACEMAKING AND PEACEKEEPING FOR THE NEW CENTURY 215 (Olara O. Otunnu & Michael W. Doyle eds., 1998).

8 See VOLUNTARY REPATRIATION, UN Doc. EC/GC/02/5, paras. 1-13 (April 25, 2002) (prepared for 4th Meeting of the Global Consultations on International Protection), reprinted in 22/2-3 REFUGEE SURVEY QUARTERLY 225-28 (2003). See generally UNHCR HANDBOOK — VOLUNTARY REPATRIATION: INTERNATIONAL PROTECTION (1996), available at <www.unhcr.ch>.

9 Resettlement possibilities, of course, are not to be wholly excluded in these circumstances. Sometimes a modest opening for distant resettlement of "residual populations," for example, can provide a critical ingredient enabling agreement on repatriation by a host government and the government of the source country. (The term refers to a small percentage of the displaced population who for some reason are unlikely to find a safe place in the repatriation program — for example, families that derive from ethnically mixed marriages.)

10 See US COMMITTEE FOR REFUGEES, WORLD REFUGEE SURVEY 2003, at 6 (Table 5).

11 UNHCR, THE STATE OF THE WORLD'S REFUGEES: FIFTY YEARS OF HUMANITARIAN ACTION 119 (2000).

12 An account of the tangled process of resettling Somali Bantu refugees from Kenya (initially from a large camp in Dadaab), published in the US Committee for Refugees' monthly periodical Refugee Reports, aptly captures this dynamic:

> Going to America is the holy grail of refugee life. People will cajole, bribe, threaten and kill for the opportunity. Dadaab's other desperate refugees are angry that they have been neglected in this [Somali Bantu] resettlement process. People have been devising schemes and strategies to access the program. When the resettlement interviews began, urban refugees from Nairobi arrived in droves, looking for opportunities to buy ration cards from people scheduled for an interview. . . .
>
> All the interviewing officers were struck by the naivete of the Bantus [when UNHCR verification interviews began]. The majority had never been exposed to resettlement in a way that would influence their stories and responses. In Nairobi, urban refugees pay for coaching lessons before resettlement interviews. They often present stock stories and rehearsed responses, and there is never an empty slot in a family. If a real family member has passed away or is not present at the time of interview, that slot can be sold for as much as $5,000. The Bantus [in contrast] spoke honestly about the people who had passed away or left Dadaab.

Sasha Chanoff, After Three Years: Somali Bantus Prepare to Come to America, REFUGEE REPORTS, Nov. 2002, at 1, 3-4.

13 See generally Rey Koslowski, Economic Globalization, Human Smuggling, and Global Governance, in GLOBAL HUMAN SMUGGLING: COMPARATIVE PERSPECTIVES 337 (David Kyle & Rey Koslowski eds., 2001).

14 See Chapter VI, Section A1.

15 Convention relating to the Status of Refugees, art. 1, done July 28, 1951, 189 U.N.T.S. 137, as modified by the Protocol relating to the Status of Refugees, done Jan. 31, 1967, 19 U.S.T. 6223, T.I.A.S. No. 6577, 606 U.N.T.S. 267.

16 Organization of African Unity Convention Governing the Specific Aspects of Refugee Problems in Africa, art. 1, entered into force June 20, 1974, 1001 U.N.T.S. 45.

17 See David A. Martin, Refugees and Migration, in THE UNITED NATIONS AND INTERNATIONAL LAW 155, 159-62 (Christopher C. Joyner ed., 1997).

18 A proposed Widows and Orphans Act of 2003, S. 1353, 108th Cong., 1st Sess. (2003), appeared to provide such a set of fixed criteria, provided that the woman or child was referred by designated US, international, or nongovernmental organizations. The bill would offer admission as special immigrants in accordance with Immigration and Nationality Act (INA) §§ 101(a)(27) and 203(b)(4), 8 U.S.C. §§ 1101(a)(27) and 1153(b)(4) (2000), but the design and oper-

ation would make it a de facto refugee program. Its beneficiaries would expressly be eligible for domestic refugee assistance under INA § 412, 8 U.S.C. § 1522 (2000). (The bill was not enacted).

19 Bronée, *supra* note 4, at 534-39.

20 See, e.g., Joanne van Selm, *Perceptions of Kosovo's 'Refugees'*, in KOSOVO: PERCEPTIONS OF WAR AND ITS AFTERMATH 251, 255 (Mary Buckley & Sally N. Cummings eds., 2001).

21 See *Uprooted in Cote d'Ivoire Struggle to Survive*, REFUGEE REPORTS, June 30, 2003, at 7-9.

22 See Barry Newman, *Open Door: In a Riskier World, US Recommits to Aiding Refugees*, WALL ST. J., Dec. 11, 2003, at A1. After recounting earlier periods where the focus was on the narrower conception of rescue, the author describes an evolution toward a broader understanding of the concept, including this comment: "'A rescue situation doesn't only mean a guy's got a gun to your head,' says one State Department official. 'It means kids growing up with no schooling. Those kids could be in the United States. . . .'"

23 The US Committee for Refugees devoted its latest issue of the *World Refugee Survey* to the issue of warehousing refugees, recounting numerous examples from around the world, describing the impact of this practice on those affected, and calling for action to end such conditions. US COMMITTEE FOR REFUGEES, WORLD REFUGEE SURVEY 2004: WAREHOUSING ISSUE.

24 Bill Frelick, *Rethinking US Refugee Admissions: Quantity and Quality*, WORLD REFUGEE SURVEY 2002, at 28, 35.

25 See, e.g., CANADIAN COUNCIL FOR REFUGEES, WORKING PAPER ON THE STRATEGIC USE OF RESETTLEMENT (June 2003) (prepared for 2003: UNHCR Annual Tripartite Consultations on Resettlement); Erika Feller, Director, Department of International Protection, UNHCR, Address at the International Conference on the Reception and Integration of Resettled Refugees, Norrköping, Sweden 3 (25 April 2001). Both documents are available at <www.unhcr.ch>.

26 Although resettlement offers were successfully used in this fashion at crucial moments in the Indochina and Kosovo refugee crises, they are likely to succeed for this objective only in highly specialized circumstances and only in the earliest stages of a sudden and massive movement. Immediate receiving states today have become more resistant to resettlement, and are more likely to treat any such offer as a pull factor that will worsen their medium to long-term situations, whatever short-term assistance it may provide.

27 See JOANNE VAN SELM, TAMARA WOROBY, ERIN PATRICK, & MONICA MATTS, FEASIBILITY OF RESETTLEMENT IN THE EUROPEAN UNION 8-12 (Migration Policy Institute, 2003); JOHN FREDERIKSSON & CHRISTINE MOUGNE, RESETTLEMENT IN THE 1990S: A REVIEW OF POLICY AND PRACTICE 7, 20-21 (UNHCR Evaluation Report, Dec. 1994).

28 Foreign Operations, Export Financing, and Related Programs Appropriations Act of 1990, Pub. L. No. 101-167, Title V, § 599D, 103 Stat. 1195, 1261 (1989), 8 U.S.C. § 1157 Note (2000). This provision has been frequently amended since enactment, primarily to extend the expiration date.

29 A companion measure, § 599E of the same Act, *supra* note 28, 103 Stat. 1264, 8 U.S.C. § 1255 Note (2000), has clearly outlived its original rationale and now often leads to unjustifiable access to US resettlement. A full understanding of its genesis helps evaluate its current use. Before the relaxed qualifications of § 599D were enacted, the executive branch had used the parole power as a stopgap measure in order to deal with the unexpected complications that resulted from the sudden change in US application of the refugee standards. In this way, it managed to allow resettlement to the United States for virtually all persons from the Soviet Union who had traveled to third countries in the expectation that they would be included in the USRP. Parole resolved immediate pipeline problems and also smoothed relations with the transit countries (Italy and Austria), but it left the individuals with no clear avenue to permanent resident status in the United States. Section 599E therefore authorized adjustment to permanent resident status for persons from the Lautenberg countries who were paroled into the United States "after being denied refugee status," in the period from August 15, 1988 to a specified end date — which has since been regularly extended in harmony with the Lautenberg sunset extension. A more complete account of the history leading up to adoption of §§ 599D and 599E appears in THOMAS ALEXANDER ALEINIKOFF, DAVID A. MARTIN, & HIROSHI MOTOMURA, IMMIGRATION AND CITIZENSHIP: PROCESS AND POLICY 820-23 (5th ed. 2003).

The new adjustment provision was quite appropriate for those caught in the transition before enactment of the Lautenberg Amendment on November 21, 1989, but it makes little sense now that the relaxed standards of § 599D are being applied in these countries to determine whether the person qualifies for refugee status. To the consternation of some persons interviewed for this project, however, INS (now DHS) administrative practice still applies what is in essence a presumption that denied applicants in the former Soviet Union will be offered parole (and eventual adjustment of status), unless there is a showing of fraud or some other serious disqualification. I heard concerns that this practice is too easily subject to misuse and manipulation, including by criminal rings. Section 599E clearly does not require such ready resort to parole — it simply permits adjustment of status for those who happen to gain parole on the stated basis — and there is no good reason to continue this practice. The DHS should instruct its officers to cease granting parole to denied applicants in this fashion, and Congress should refuse to extend any further the end date that limits the qualification for adjustment under § 599E (currently confined to persons paroled on or before September 30, 2004).

30 See, e.g., DON BARNETT, OUT OF AFRICA: SOMALI BANTU AND THE PARADIGM SHIFT IN REFUGEE RESETTLEMENT 1, 6-8 (Center for Immigration Studies Backgrounder, Oct. 2003) (charging that resettlement is dominated by "a constellation of hundreds of interrelated government funded non governmental organizations (NGOs) pursuing their own institutional interests," including narrow or personal financial considerations).

31 See, e.g., Carrie Teegardin, *Welcome to America: Most US Aid for Refugees Spent on Pay, Office Costs*, ATLANTA JOURNAL AND CONSTITUTION, Oct. 22, 2000, at 1A; Carrie Teegardin,

Atlanta Not Alone in Having Troubled Refugee Program, id., Nov. 5, 2000, at 11A.

32 But see the letter to the President from the two key House chairmen that responded to the consultations with the State Department regarding FY 2004 refugee admissions. It stated:

> While other members of Congress and various refugee resettlement groups repeatedly demand higher ceilings of at least 100,000 refugees resettled, we are not concerned with arbitrary numbers. Rather, we want the Administration to have a resettlement program with integrity that admits bona fide refugees with well founded fears of persecution.

Letter from F. James Sensenbrenner, Jr., Chairman, House Comm. on the Judiciary, and John N. Hostettler, Chairman, Subcomm. on Immigration, Border Security and Claims (Oct. 15, 2003).

33 See, e.g., early versions of amendments proposed by Sens. Sam Brownback and Edward Kennedy and Reps. Christopher Smith and Howard Berman to the 2003 foreign relations authorization bill (on file with the author). Later versions were published at 149 CONG. REC. S9307-08 (July 11, 2003) and id. at H6740, § 229 (July 15, 2003).

34 The final provision to this effect that was enacted as part of the FY 2004 omnibus appropriations bill was scaled back to a more modest mandate for NGO involvement, which is fully consistent with the approach recommended here. Pub. L. No. 108-199, Div. D, Tit.V, § 590(a), 118 Stat. 3, 207 (2004).

35 EUROPEAN COMMITTEE ON REFUGEES AND EXILES & US COMMITTEE FOR REFUGEES, RESPONDING TO THE ASYLUM AND ACCESS CHALLENGE: AN AGENDA FOR CONSTRUCTIVE ENGAGEMENT IN PROTRACTED REFUGEE SITUATIONS (April 2003), text at note 75. Other comparative studies, after examining the experience of the United States and other countries, have noted the ways in which resettlement success stories help shape public attitudes toward all parts of refugee assistance and protection. VAN SELM, ET AL., *supra* note 27, at 118-19; FREDERIKSSON & MOUGNE, *supra* note 27, at 43-44.

36 INA § 207(e), 8 U.S.C. § 1157(e) (2000).

37 INA § 207(b), 8 U.S.C. § 1157(b) (2000). These additions took place in FY 1988 and 1989, both times to account for additional outflows from Eastern Europe and the Soviet Union as the grip of the Communist regimes suddenly weakened, and in FY 1999 to provide for admissions of Kosovar refugees. See Table I-1 in this chapter, and T. ALEXANDER ALEINIKOFF, DAVID A. MARTIN & HIROSHI MOTOMURA, IMMIGRATION AND CITIZENSHIP: PROCESS AND POLICY 1004-05 (4th ed. 1998), and id. 810-12, 816 (5th ed. 2003).

38 Pub. L. No. 96-212, 94 Stat. 102.

39 INA § 203(a)(7), 8 U.S.C. § 1157(a)(7) (1976). This provision was repealed when the Refugee Act of 1980 created a different framework for refugee admissions.

40 See Sen. Comm. on the Judiciary, *supra* note 5, at 12-15.

41 See David A. Martin, *The Refugee Act of 1980: Its Past and Future,* 1982 MICH.Y.B. INT'L L. STUD. 91.

42 *Id.* at 97-99 & nn. 36-38. Sen. Kennedy's 1978 bill had a fixed ceiling of 40,000 refugees, S. 2751, 95th Cong., 2d Sess. (1978), whereas Rep. Eilberg's 1977 version had a ceiling of 20,000, H.R. 7175, 95th Cong., 1st Sess. (1977). Both were subject to modest increases for "emergent" refugee situations.

43 INDOCHINESE REFUGEE REPORTS, Jan. 15, 1980, at 10.

44 8 U.S.C. § 1157(a) (2000).

45 It is sometimes argued, drawing on isolated floor statements pulled from the legislative history of the Refugee Act of 1980, that Congress has already determined that the baseline or target level for refugee admissions should be 50,000 annually, barring some sort of exceptional circumstances. But the history recounted in the text here indicates why such a conclusion is incorrect. The conference committee in fact deleted the baseline number after the first three years of its operation, leaving admissions totals thereafter entirely to the annual consultation process. Some who supported deletion of the 50,000 baseline did so, to be sure, because they hoped that in the long term, following the Vietnamese crisis, admissions would decline to below 50,000 annually. See Martin, *supra* note 41, at 99-100 & n.41. But that wish was clearly not shared by the full Congress. Moreover, the State Department team working with the Congress on the legislation was pleased to support the conference amendment for the opposite reason — because the change would make it easier to sustain a higher admissions number if later policy dictated. (The present author was a member of that team.) The conference committee report says little about the change, and what it says does not suggest a long-term commitment to 50,000 admissions. The relevant passage announces only the conferees' intent that Congress review the 50,000 figure before FY 1983 "and take appropriate action to retain or adjust this figure." REFUGEE ACT OF 1980: CONFERENCE REPORT, H.R. REP. NO. 96-781, at 20 (1980). But no systematic congressional review took place, much less led to a reinstatement of a baseline or default number, at 50,000 or any other level.

In any event, Supreme Court decisions now strongly discourage reliance on comments in the legislative history when interpreting statutes. Instead, the Court insists, primary reliance must be placed on the enacted text. See, e.g., Connecticut National Bank v. Germain, 503 US 249, 253-54 (1992) ("in interpreting a statute a court should always turn first to one, cardinal canon before all others. We have stated time and again that courts must presume that a legislature says in a statute what it means and means in a statute what it says there. . . . When the words of a statute are unambiguous, then, this first canon is also the last: 'judicial inquiry is complete.'") The text in the early bills that provided for a perpetual 50,000 ceiling or benchmark was indisputably removed, to be replaced by the current wording of INA § 207(a). That enacted text does mention 50,000, but it does so only as a baseline for FY 1980-82, and it clearly allowed the President to exceed that ceiling even during that period — a power that everyone knew he would use, given the unprecedentedly high admission needs at the time of enactment. The text sets forth no expectation about numbers thereafter, but leaves that issue entirely to Presidential determination, following consultation with Congress. If the annual PD number is to be brought back to 50,000, therefore, that decision must be made on the basis of current policy — not because of a supposed notion that Congress already solidified such a policy in 1980. Congress deliberately left this issue for future debate and annual decision, based on a careful, contextual assessment of the relevant factors.

46 Several knowledgeable government officials interviewed for this project expressed doubt (sometimes strong doubt) as to whether the United States could successfully launch many initiatives targeting those who have spent long periods in a refugee camp unless there is a statutory change. The needed change would expressly allow inclusion of refugees in groups or categories designated by the President, without individual determinations of a well-founded fear of persecution according to the current legal definition. (Many refer to such a process as "humanitarian track" admissions.) Chapter VII includes a recommendation for such a statutory change.

47 See ANDREW HOPKINS, REPORT ON THE UNHCR P-2 SOMALI BANTU VERIFICATION EXERCISE IN DADAAB (UNHCR Report, Feb. 18, 2002).

48 A helpful account of the background and of many stages of the Bantu resettlement, particularly of the conditions at Dadaab and the hazards confronted in the move to Kakuma, appears in Sasha Chanoff, *After Three Years: Somali Bantus Prepare to Come to America*, REFUGEE REPORTS, Nov. 2002, at 1.

49 See *Refugee Interviews to Resume in Kenya*, US REFUGEE ADMISSION PROGRAM NEWS, Sept 16, 2003, available at <www.state.gov/g/prm/rls/other/24174.htm>.

50 The account here draws on the cited public sources, plus information compiled from unclassified PRM documents.

51 See, e.g., Rick Hampson, *In USA, Somali Refugees See a Reversal of Fortune*, USA TODAY, Aug. 4, 2003, at 1A; Jay Rey, *Brave New World: A Bantu Family from Somalia Has Found a New Beginning on the West Side; Its Arrival, However, Is Greeted in Some Circles with Suspicion and Resentment*, BUFFALO NEWS, July 18, 2003, at A1; Candace Page, *Bantu Find Jobs, Acceptance in Adopted Vermont Homes*, BURLINGTON FREE PRESS, Mar. 22, 2004 at 1A.

Chapter II

Reforming the System for Deciding on Resettlement Initiatives

As Chapter I recounted, the United States finds itself in a new era of refugee resettlement. Not only must we deal with new operational challenges triggered in part by the dangers of terrorism, but we must sustain the admissions program largely out of a host of smaller, short- to medium-term resettlement initiatives. Improvements for operations will be addressed in later chapters. This chapter focuses on the system that provides the precursor to field operations — the system that decides which groups and individuals will receive access to the US Refugee Program. The program is only beginning to come to grips with the full scope of the new access challenges.

This chapter is premised on the underlying stances recommended in Chapter I: that the USRP be expressly mandated to go beyond the narrow version of the rescue principle in identifying possible candidates for admission, that it affirmatively seek to resettle persons whose lives are subject to serious long-term dangers and impairments and not just immediate threats to life, and that it treat the admissions number set in the annual Presidential Determination as a goal, not an optional ceiling. The PD number thus becomes a benchmark for holding the various offices and players in the system accountable and for measuring their performance. Reforming this access system is primarily a job for the Department of State, but it must be done in a way that appropriately draws on the expertise and cooperation of the Department of Homeland Security, as well as the other key partners, particularly the voluntary agencies (and other NGOs) and the Office of the UNHCR.

A. The Scale of the Challenge

It is essential, first of all, to be clear on the scale of the challenge now faced. The next chapter will examine in some detail the priority system used to allocate refugee admission spaces (currently categories P-1 through P-5). But of greater initial importance in assessing the challenges and evaluating the overall access system are the broad functional types of admissions that have been employed in implementing the program since its early days. Even if the current priority system is revised, the program will almost surely still be composed of these generic types of admissions:

- **Individual case referrals.** Individual referrals to the refugee admissions program are usually based on an assessment that compelling protection needs require moving a specified individual or family from the current location. Since the admissions priority system was revised in 1994, these types of referrals, overwhelmingly from UNHCR, have occupied the top category, P-1, which is open to any nationality. P-1 also allows for individual referrals to be made by US embassies, and certain initiatives are under way to enhance the ability of NGOs in the field to generate individual referrals as well.

- **Family-based access.** The USRP strives to keep families together for purposes of both processing and travel, and US law allows for nuclear families (spouse and minor unmarried children) to qualify for admission even if only one parent meets the refugee definition.[1] Even if they do not travel together, nuclear family members of any nationality may later "follow to join" based on a filing by the previously resettled anchor relative, which is normally then processed through consular offices. And the program has also regularly made further room, via priorities P-3 through P-5, for the admission of wider circles of family members through the refugee admission machinery, covering refugees from a specific list of countries (set year-by-year) designated for eligibility in the particular priority category.

■ **Group-based access.** The most visible part of refugee admissions is probably that which focuses on particular groups that are given access to the program under the P-2 processing priority, based on a judgment that the group is of special humanitarian concern to the United States. Group-based access for Vietnamese and for large categories from the former Soviet Union provided a mainstay of the USRP for many years, and broad eligibility categories remain in place for the three nations where in-country processing has regularly been authorized: Vietnam, Cuba, and the former Soviet Union. Additional, more focused P-2 groups have included the so-called Lost Boys of Sudan, Somali Bantu from Kakuma camp in Kenya, and Iranian religious minorities. Groups also sometimes gain access on the basis of a group referral from UNHCR, and are then known as P-1 groups.

All three of these broad categories hold potential for expansion in order to revitalize the program and match up more effectively with genuine worldwide resettlement need, but the third will be the key. Despite initiatives to increase individual referrals from UNHCR, US embassies, and NGOs, such referrals will likely increase only gradually. Adding more countries to the P-3 family list would generate additional admissions, as would needed improvements in the follow-to-join process. But the family admission procedures have encountered a high level of fraudulent submissions. Although program changes in the last two years have gotten a better handle on the problem, none are foolproof, and P-3 expansion will probably take place slowly and produce only modest numbers. This means that enhancing the pace of admissions will have to focus in major part on group designations.[2]

What follows is a very rough illustration of the group designation challenges to be faced, using for illustration purposes a PD number of 70,000 (the

number that has been set in the annual PD for the past three years). For the next few years, it is a reasonable (though quite rough) assumption that individual referrals and family-based access will generate perhaps 20,000 admissions.[3] (See Table II-1 showing admissions by priority for FY 1994-2003 and Table II-2 showing total refugee admissions for family-based categories for those years.) This leaves approximately 50,000 to be derived from other sources. The long-established Moscow and Havana programs can perhaps produce another 10,000. It is not a stretch to conclude, then, that other group-based initiatives will have to produce another 40,000 admissions in order to reach a 70,000 total — roughly 3,000-4,000 admissions per month through group designations (whether US-designated P-2 groups or based on UNHCR group referrals). Ramping up to this level cannot be done overnight. Work needs to begin promptly in order to develop additional candidate groups, complete the detailed further inquiry needed before final designations can occur, select among those so developed, and initiate the preinterview machinery. Six to twelve months might be thought a good allowance of the time needed for this process, from early consideration until a DHS circuit ride, although wide variations can be expected. The time frame can be compressed if conditions are favorable. For example, the 2003 Liberian P-1 group process got off the ground in about three months. But it can also take far longer if conditions prove unfavorable; nearly three years elapsed before the first admissions of Somali Bantu, and closer to four years before sustained processing began.

Moreover, it is not enough simply to designate groups consisting of, say, 3,500 members each month, because clearly not all refugee applicants granted access to the interviewing process will be approved. If we assume a modestly optimistic DHS approval rate of 80 percent, group designations will have to embrace approximately 4,500 per month in order to produce an annual total of all admissions at the 70,000 level. And the predesignation exploratory work will of course have to include groups totaling a still larger figure, perhaps 7,000 per month, because not all initially promising groups will prove to merit access, and others may be placed on hold while the full range of other durable solutions is explored. Few candidate groups on the current horizon contain more than 7,000 members, although there are some exceptions. We can therefore expect to have to designate about one new

TABLE II-I

REFUGEE ADMISSIONS BY PRIORITY, FY 1994 - 2003

Fiscal Year	Priority 1	Priority 2	Priority 3	Priority 4	Priority 5	Visas 93	Priority Unknown*	Total
1994	17,414	75,984	5,000	1,201	4,675	2,560	6,147	112,981
1995	11,003	68,886	4,326	3,436	1,306	2,669	8,348	99,974
1996	9,376	49,507	2,968	3,708	3,263	2,235	5,346	76,403
1997	9,656	41,247	1,471	5,014	6,395	2,683	4,022	70,488
1998	8,912	53,721	3,056	5,444	3,241	1,823	883	77,080
1999	19,235	47,246	8,058	4,946	415	1,614	4,011	85,525
2000	16,730	38,892	9,439	4,279	30	1,743	2,034	73,147
2001	16,146	39,718	9,555	2,193	12	1,669	11	69,304
2002	6,794	17,932	728	287	0	1,361	8	27,110
2003	7,944	12,494	5,714	938	1	1,331	0	28,422
Total	123,210	445,627	50,315	31,446	19,338	19,688	30,810	720,434
%	17	62	7	4	3	3	4	100

* Data transferred from Refugee Data Center records did not always include priority information.
Source: Bureau of Population, Refugees, and Migration, June 2004.

TABLE II-2

REFUGEE ADMISSIONS FOR FAMILY-BASED CATEGORIES, FY 1994 - 2003 (P3 - P5 AND VISAS 93*)

FY	Family	Total	% of Total
1994	13,436	112,981	12
1995	11,737	99,974	12
1996	12,174	76,403	16
1997	15,563	70,488	22
1998	13,564	77,080	18
1999	15,033	85,525	18
2000	15,491	73,147	21
2001	13,429	69,304	19
2002	2,376	27,110	9
2003	7,984	28,422	28
Total	120,787	720,434	17

* The historical family admissions picture includes the Lautenberg caseload from the former Soviet Union (part of P-2), which has been largely based on family filings by a wide range of relatives. Those totals, not included here, have declined fairly steadily from over 43,000 in FY 1994 to below 9,000 in FY 2003.
Source: Bureau of Population, Refugees, and Migration, June 2004.

group each month, on average, using either the P-1 group referral process or the P-2 category.

B. PRM's ROLE

1. Overview

The State Department's Bureau of Population, Refugees and Migration (PRM) has introduced improvements over the past few years that further this pipeline development process, such as a reporting matrix that pulls together the key information on potential target groups in a standard format to facilitate comparisons. But the group identification and designation process is not currently oriented toward the necessary volume. Some persons interviewed for this report worried that there is little of the sense of urgency in PRM about group development that is needed under today's conditions — although others disputed this characterization. Several persons complained that the actual selection criteria and the precise decision mechanism for getting a group on the approved P-2 list are obscure. As a result, some of the groups under discussion have been kicking around for years, without discernible progress toward a clear go or no-go decision.

Several persons interviewed, including many in government positions and in PRM itself, lamented the current state of relations between the PRM Admissions Office and the resettlement NGOs, believing that much could be done from both sides to overcome this divide. NGOs, some suggested, need to nurture a more complete understanding of the obstacles and complications that have affected the program over the past two years, and curb the tendency to read bad faith into outcomes that prove disappointing. But PRM could also do much to help revive the spirit of public-private partnership that was a hallmark of the program, treating the volags as allies and fostering ways to improve transparency and communication. A healthy partnership includes candid and ongoing two-way critique. Such give-and-take — frank, robust, even harsh — is a legitimate part of the democratic decision-making process, and PRM should not take offense when criticism is voiced.

A few examples of communication difficulties are worth describing. Cooperative working groups, involving PRM and NGOs (and often other government players) were initiated a few years ago.

The group that dealt with fraud issues worked well and produced a useful report, whose recommendations are now largely being implemented.[4] Its operations were widely commended. But other working groups did not go well, and most fell into disuse. I heard from many people about one particular meeting of the "Rest of the World" working group (so labeled to distinguish it from the group focused on Africa). The meeting was attended by PRM staff, regional bureau officers, and NGO representatives. The NGO staff came to the meeting intending to present ideas for eligible group initiatives and to work through the advantages and disadvantages of each. The meeting was apparently conducted in such a way, however, that an initial NGO recommendation was immediately met by a strong comment from a State Department officer at the meeting, setting forth reasons why such an initiative would not work — in a fashion that was perceived by the NGOs as an intended conversation-stopper instead of a mutual effort to examine pros and cons. Some participants felt that the regional bureau officers had been brought to the meeting precisely in order to knock down the ideas the NGOs were going to offer. Accounts from the State Department side, while agreeing that the meeting went badly, attributed the problems more to clumsiness in meeting design, perhaps a misunderstanding of the best ways to foster effective communication, and particularly NGO unwillingness or inability to address in detail the hard and detailed questions of logistics, regional politics, magnet effects, and fraud concerns that officials regularly have to confront. From the viewpoint of those who put the meeting together, the presence of the regional bureau officers was meant to assure the availability of area expertise, in order to help all participants truly engage these hard questions. Many officers find it frustrating that, in their estimation, the resettlement NGOs are quick with their criticisms without fully addressing these sorts of issues.

For PRM to push the NGOs to engage on such questions is quite legitimate. Indeed, it is imperative that NGOs shoulder their own responsibility for making the public-private partnership effective, and to do so they need to wrestle realistically with political and logistical barriers outlined in Chapter I, Section A, just as PRM must do on each occasion. But if that was the objective of that particular meeting, a more detailed agenda or even advance submission of more precise questions for the NGOs to prepare to address, with a clearer indication of the format of the meeting, might have been more productive. And the context has to make clear that all parties are present to seek and shape the most feasible options, not simply to parade difficulties or squelch proposals.

Involving NGOs more completely in the design and field implementation of certain initiatives could also be beneficial. For example, I heard from stateside NGO representatives who had offered support when they were initially told of a planned training session in Nairobi for NGO personnel (mostly from assistance-focused NGOs), to enable them to make NGO referrals of highly jeopardized individuals for processing as P-1 refugees. The persons making the comments were then disappointed that the later parts of the training initiative were developed without the input they had offered to provide. Although a thorough evaluation of this ongoing NGO referral initiative has not yet been completed, several people both inside and outside government offered impressions that the results have been disappointing. Perhaps it could be more successful, several ventured, with greater input from NGOs more closely familiar with resettlement. Of course, the unfortunate ongoing tensions between resettlement-focused NGOs and assistance-focused NGOs, for which PRM is not responsible, may also have contributed to these difficulties.[5]

Joint PRM-NGO working groups are now being revived — a welcome and useful step. PRM should make sure that meeting agendas and operating rules provide for a productive give-and-take. The exact methods, of course, will depend on the subject matter and the state of development of the initiative or operation being discussed. But more use of meetings designed largely to have State Department personnel listen actively to NGO ideas, without a need for immediate and definitive governmental response, might be useful. There will be adequate time away from the meeting for government players to hash out their fully considered positions, perhaps then scheduling one more round of interaction and comment on a more fully formed position before it goes final. Such a procedure could improve the sense of full partnership and involvement, even if the government position remains unchanged in the final outcome.

This is a key attitudinal point — and it has some application to both government and NGO players.

The Admissions Office often gives the impression that it views the acceptance of input on a wider scale as tantamount to surrendering control over the program's decisions or implementation to the NGOs. There need be no such equivalence. PRM properly asserts authority to decide in the end how the program should run and what new initiatives to undertake. But input can produce ideas that deserve acceptance on the merits. And even if the agency largely sticks with its original approach, the dialogue can produce useful refinements and tweakings — and a better sense of why the original approach is judged best. Moreover, NGOs would be much happier with a framework that invites their suggestions in a candid and ongoing way, even if their advice on a particular matter is not followed. A respectful disagreement is better than a feeling that one's views were not even invited or considered.

For this working relationship to function well, however, NGOs also must approach their dealings in this spirit, prepared to accept that governmental players will sometimes decide to reject or greatly modify an NGO proposal. NGOs are sometimes too quick to treat an honest and reasoned disagreement (or a negative decision by someone in the State Department chain of command, which must then of course be defended by PRM) as mere stonewalling or unresponsiveness on the part of government players. Going the extra mile to work through all such issues with their executive branch partners directly, instead of resorting readily to congressional pressure, can do much to improve the sense of partnership.

It must be acknowledged, however, that fostering effective communication requires considerable staff time and energy, commodities that remain in short supply. Augmenting the limited staffing of the PRM Admissions Office, discussed in this section, would open up better possibilities.

Resolving differences among the various bureaus and agencies involved in refugee processing away from public meetings is also important. I heard accounts of finger-pointing toward other government agencies or offices in public meetings, or occasional open displays of sharp intragovernmental differences. These not only hampered relations with NGOs, but they also sometimes made it difficult to reach constructive resolution among government players. The last two and a half years have been times of great difficulty for the resettlement program, producing unusual strains for all involved. Even in quieter times, however, the program will work best if such differences, when they exist, are fought out and resolved in internal forums.

2. FOR THE FUTURE

A clear sense that the PD number is a target rather than a ceiling, as recommended in Chapter I, could both energize PRM's scouting for eligible resettlement initiatives and fortify the Bureau during the interagency discussions that have to take place before new resettlement initiatives are approved. This does not require that PRM become an indiscriminate cheerleader for any resettlement proposal that may be advanced by the NGO community — a concern some expressed in interviews for this project. It is admirable and indispensable that the Bureau maintains its own critical perspective in evaluating such suggestions. Nonetheless, PRM's Admissions Office has to be the component in the decision-making system that gives the benefit of the doubt to resettlement, as a counterweight to the negative arguments that will readily appear from other governmental or international quarters. PRM also has to be the part of the system that maintains a global perspective on resettlement, to help assure that particular initiatives are not simply picked off and squelched one-by-one.

The group designation process requires obtaining preliminary information on candidate populations; identifying their needs and the conditions of life in the current first-asylum or in-country situation; assessing the political landscape and the impact that a new resettlement initiative would have on the target population, host and neighboring governments, and on others who might migrate in response; identifying other features or steps that might minimize adverse impacts (such as a prior registration or UNHCR verification exercise); estimating the likely interview success rate if resettlement is offered; and eventually clarifying logistical needs and ways to meet them (such as safe interview sites). NGOs can be of real assistance with many of these stages. The annual admission recommendations in the Refugee Council USA (RCUSA) volume can provide a useful starting point, although the sheer sweep of those recommendations may blunt their impact. Specific NGO missions, without direct government involvement, have also produced detailed reports that triggered

real PRM interest and additional steps to investigate resettlement possibilities. Such NGO reports or suggestions have been most effective along these lines when they engage in detail with the hard questions about obstacles and limitations like those outlined in Chapter I, Section A. Moreover, UNHCR's nascent group referral process holds promise in assisting along these lines, although it will probably require a few years (and successful pilot implementation) before that mechanism will produce significant volumes of referrals. See Chapter VI.

But even with such assistance, managing all these access-development tasks sets a highly ambitious agenda for a unit the size of the PRM Admissions Office. Through much of FY 2003, it functioned with approximately twelve permanent officer positions, plus five refugee coordinators posted to field offices globally whose primary duties focused on admissions (one each in Accra, Nairobi, Cairo, Havana, and Ho Chi Minh City). The program unit in headquarters devoted to overseas operations had only four officers, although its work has been augmented in various ways by the three officers on the domestic programs side of the house (whose primary tasks involve monitoring the resettlement agencies operating under reception and placement grants from the State Department), and by certain other arrangements. Nonetheless, the tasks assigned to these officers cover a huge range, leaving relatively little time for the crucial group-development work. For example, they must help deal with logistical difficulties that arise during a DHS circuit ride, help answer congressional inquiries, and address individual problem cases, including inquiries from family members whose relative in a camp is stuck somewhere in the process. And many of them have worked on nights or weekends over the past year to help do vital, but largely clerical, tasks entailed in the new security screening process (the preparation of cables notifying the field of the results of the screening, an indispensable step in clearing persons for the final stages of admission). Some temporary staff have now been added, primarily to handle these security-related functions, and three new officer positions are in the works.

Even with these additions, however, this staffing level is insufficient for the new era of refugee resettlement. Additional officer time must be freed up to focus on group development, and also for better communication with the office's public and private partners. An addition of five officer positions to the Admissions Office would not be out of line, in view of the vastly changed landscape of refugee admissions as compared to the previous decade. These additional officers should not be hired on as specialists doing only group development, however. It is salutary for Admissions Office staff to share in many parts of the resettlement work, from individual problem solving to wide-scale group scouting to monitoring of domestic resettlement, so that they gain a complete picture of the resettlement process. The Department should also find more efficient ways to handle security screening tasks, freeing admissions officers from those duties.

Enhanced PRM staffing, with a shift in outlook as outlined above, should help energize the group-development process, and it will give PRM the capacity needed in order to sustain the quality of decisions on resettlement initiatives. It will not serve the cause of the refugees, nor provide credit to the program, if sloppy decisions are made in the service of a new drive to increase resettlement numbers. The objective is not simply to drive the numbers upward, but to use the humanitarian resource of resettlement spaces to maximize the world community's response to genuine refugee needs. The office needs to have enough potential initiatives under consideration at all times so that the refugee program can afford to be selective, while still sustaining a steady flow at the needed level.

RECOMMENDATION II-1: PRM, as the lead office in the process of group designation, must develop a sense of mission about adding one or two new groups to the pipeline development process each month. PRM must impart energy and vision to this mission, in a way that will promote added efforts on the part of the other players in the process, both governmental and non-governmental. It must seek innovative ways to accomplish the various functions involved. The Admissions Office staff should also expand in view of the very different requirements in this new era of refugee resettlement. Without abandoning its own critical perspective on admissions proposals, the Admissions Office must come to think of itself as the component in the decision-making system that gives the benefit of the doubt to resettlement, so as to serve as a counterweight to negative arguments that will readily appear from other governmental or international quarters.

C. THE INVOLVEMENT OF THE REST OF THE DEPARTMENT OF STATE

If the burden of meeting the President's target in this new resettlement era is seen as falling solely on PRM, the target probably will not be met. Approval of new P-2 groups (and indeed acceptance of a UNHCR group referral) must be cleared more widely within the Department of State. In particular, such approval generally requires the assent or acquiescence of the appropriate regional bureau. It must also have genuine support from the DHS. Persons interviewed for this project recounted marathon efforts by some within PRM during FY 2002 to propose and develop new group initiatives, only to meet with resistance of varying degrees from the regional bureaus or the DHS, and sometimes from UNHCR. Resistance took some or all of the following forms: security concerns about the refugee populace, skepticism about the logistics of processing (including safe interviewing sites), warnings about pull factors, or dire predictions about the reactions of host governments or their neighbors. The point is not that these concerns were illegitimate or unworthy. Instead, I was told, they were often seized on early in the process as complete trumps of any further consideration — blocking PRM's efforts either to probe the concern more thoroughly or to develop additional strategies, in cooperation with the objecting office, that could overcome the problem. The possible disruptions and imponderables deriving from a new resettlement initiative tend to loom large for desk officers or ambassadors, too few of whom have historically felt a real responsibility for bringing admission totals up to the level set in the PD (and perhaps are not as attuned as PRM to the underlying humanitarian needs and objectives). If the numbers fall short, that outcome has often been seen as essentially PRM's problem, not the Department's.

These last comments overgeneralize, of course, and there are important counterexamples. In fact, many successful resettlement initiatives owe a great deal to vigorous support by the ambassador posted to the first-asylum country or to an officer in a regional bureau in Washington.

But the key point is that this outlook, this feeling of an immediate responsibility for making full use of the humanitarian resource that annual refugee admissions numbers represent, must come to be more widely shared within the Department under today's conditions. A more focused and better staffed PRM can help, as could a clear directive from the Secretary of State stating that the PD number is a goal, not simply a ceiling, and that all offices are charged with helping to meet that objective. But bureaucratic processes respond only sluggishly, if at all, to exhortation. Short- to medium-term institutional or procedural changes may also be useful in order to make sure that such views become deeply instilled in the actual operations needed to restore the refugee admissions program.

D. Suggested procedure for deciding on group initiatives

Clearly many possible institutional changes could contribute toward these ends, and none offers a sure-fire solution to the difficulties identified in this report. Nonetheless, institutional innovation can provide a change in atmosphere and perhaps cut through entrenched stalemates. I offer one possible framework here.

1. Refugee Admissions Committee

The Department of State was faced with a somewhat comparable need for institutional and attitudinal change in the 1970s, when human rights was introduced as a systematic foreign policy priority. At that time, the need for such change derived from a major new policy thrust, whereas now the challenge is essentially to meet a continuing policy objective but in significantly changed world conditions — marked by both greater operational hazards and the end of predictable large-scale multi-year resettlement flows. Nonetheless, there are enough points of similarity between the two challenges to make the earlier experience instructive.

In the 1970s, not only had President Jimmy Carter directed the Department to give more prominence to human rights, but more concretely, Congress had passed several statutes specifically mandating human rights considerations in decisions on foreign aid, including economic and social assistance, military assistance, and US votes in the international financial institutions. In order to be sure that these mandates were followed, and also to develop a consistent set of policies and criteria for implementing them, the administration decided that many of the key decisions, especially on multilateral loans, would be made at periodic meetings involving

all potential players. The meetings therefore included the regional bureaus, the human rights bureau, other interested units from the Department, and representatives of other departments with a stake in the issue, particularly the Treasury Department. Because these sessions were chaired by the Deputy Secretary, Warren Christopher, the body came to be known as the Christopher Committee.[6] Representatives of all the regional bureaus were expected to attend each session, in order to help facilitate an accurate comparison with earlier decisions and thereby to develop a more consistent set of criteria and standards. Their steady involvement (even at meetings where no proposal from their region was at issue) was also intended to assure that a full understanding of those criteria would be worked back in to each party's internal deliberations in the future. The process also assured that a final decision was reached in a timely fashion, because the meetings concentrated attention and forced action.

An adapted version of this model, a Refugee Admissions Committee to be chaired by the Assistant Secretary for Population, Refugees, and Migration, could bring benefits, at least as a transitional measure to be used for a few years while all concerned gain familiarity with the requirements of this new era of admissions. Each regional bureau would be asked to designate a senior officer for regular attendance, as would other appropriate offices, such as the Bureau of Democracy, Human Rights, and Labor (DRL). Representatives of the DHS and the National Security Council should also be invited to participate. Additional officers would attend specific meetings as needed, based on their own expertise or responsibility regarding a particular nation or situation slated for consideration in detail. Committee meetings should be placed on a firm schedule set well in advance, meeting no less often than bimonthly — as an action-promoting timetable. If agreement can be worked out in advance among the relevant bureaus and officers, then the meeting could simply hear a report on the plans, including an account of the most difficult issues and how they were resolved. This would be instructive for all involved, providing a growing sense of consistent criteria that are relevant in designating a group, and of the range of creative steps that can be taken to overcome obstacles.

The committee could also be called into session quickly if needed to consider an urgent group resettlement need. Alternatively, if wide agreement among all relevant bureaus to designate a particular group is achieved between meetings, the committee may want to have a supplementary procedure for such additions without having to convene a special session or waiting until the next regular meeting is scheduled.

2. REFUGEE ADMISSIONS COMMITTEE PROCEDURES

The committee would of course need to develop and refine its own procedures in light of experience, but a clearer structuring of the decision process could be quite useful for all involved. I recommend using three categories for group consideration: potential groups, candidate groups, and designated groups.

PRM would prepare a list of potential groups, casting a fairly wide net and working with counterparts in the appropriate regional office. Some judgment and discretion are necessary in compiling even this preliminary list, of course, but extensive investigation would not be expected, and the existence of disadvantages or concerns, even if they initially seem fairly significant, should not be used at this point to knock a group off the list of potentials. Each committee meeting could begin by considering this list, in order to identify those that are appropriate to raise to the next level as candidate groups.

Candidate groups are those that are seen as reasonably promising for a resettlement initiative, though they need not be problem-free to be moved to this list. Inclusion as a candidate would mean that the group is appropriate for more intensive investigation, usually including field visits. The field inquiry team should include the DHS and could also involve NGO representatives, UNHCR, IOM, and other players as appropriate. This investigation is meant to develop more detailed information about the characteristics of the proposed group, including camp conditions, the level of risk or harm its members face, the political impact of a resettlement decision, obstacles to a successful program, and steps that might be taken to overcome the obstacles. For example, the candidate group might be located in an area seen as relatively unsafe for DHS interviewing. The field inquiry would examine, perhaps in cooperation with the embassy security officer, whether changes could be made to facilities in the area where the refugees are located, in order to

reach a satisfactory level of safety. Alternatively, the team could explore possibilities for moving the population to another site for processing, as occurred with both the Liberians in Cote d'Ivoire and the Somali Bantu in Kenya. Or if the main problem is the risk of a magnet effect, the team could determine whether existing registration records or a new UNHCR verification might provide an adequate basis for limiting the resettlement program to persons who had already been in first asylum since a stated date. Field inquiry may find that only a subset of the candidate group is appropriate for resettlement. In order to avoid generating unrealistic expectations among refugees in the area, decisions to name a candidate group should not be publicized, and the inquiry team should strive to work behind the scenes and without advance publicity of the purpose of its visit. This investigative procedure would fit very well with efforts PRM is already launching for "targeted response teams," usually including both NGOs and government officials (and some involvement from UNHCR or IOM), which have begun to do detailed field investigations of this general type.

Any proposal by UNHCR for a group resettlement referral (so-called P-1 groups) should be immediately included on the candidate list, and enjoy a presumption of support, although it would remain for the US government to decide for sure whether and to what extent to accept the referral. Further investigation can perhaps be more limited for such submissions, but such proposals should still come to the committee for a final decision before the group is approved for resettlement to the United States.

The results of the field investigations and other inquiries regarding candidate groups would be reported to the next Refugee Admissions Committee meeting, and would provide much of the basis for choosing which candidate groups would actually be designated for priority resettlement — the final stage in the group-development process. Once a group is designated, the logistical steps for actual resettlement would be put into motion. PRM would make arrangements for preliminary processing (by an overseas processing entity (OPE)) and eventual medical screening and transportation. The DHS would be asked to prepare a schedule of circuit rides and to work with the embassy to resolve other preliminary issues, such as final approval of interviewing sites. And the resettlement volags would be notified so that they could begin preparing reception and placement plans as necessary.

Obviously, some candidate groups will prove, upon investigation, not to be good possibilities for resettlement, and the committee can then make a firm decision not to proceed. Or the committee may decide to postpone decision on certain groups, awaiting other political or logistical developments. For these reasons, there will always be attrition as groups move from one level to the next. It will be essential to assure that there are enough potential groups and candidate groups in the works at any given time to produce designations on the scale needed to meet the target, even allowing for attrition and postponements.

3. ADVANTAGES

The committee would provide a structure for considering resettlement options in a comprehensive and consistent fashion. The current diffuse process, wherein proposals circulate separately, sets up a dynamic of discussion and negotiation primarily involving only PRM and the regional office at issue (and on some occasions the DHS as well). This setting risks undervaluing the positive features of the proposed resettlement and may give undue weight to the disadvantages, allowing the initiatives to be more readily disapproved or delayed one-by-one. In contrast, the Refugee Admissions Committee process would facilitate — even require — disciplined comparative judgments. It would help assure that all participants remain mindful of the program's positive humanitarian mission and of its ultimate target numbers, even while giving close scrutiny to the disadvantages and obstacles affecting any particular group. Participants in the meetings who are skeptical about resettling a certain population may find their doubts diminished when they learn of steps taken to overcome similar disadvantages initially encountered with regard to another group in a different region. Even when doubts cannot be wholly eliminated, this comprehensive approach would allow an informed comparative choice of those groups that present the fewest concerns and disadvantages.

Dealing with group initiatives through the committee would also facilitate well-calibrated adjustments throughout the fiscal year, going further down the list of promising candidates if necessary in order to assure a more even flow. The committee would be

a forum, in other words, for keeping track of the pipeline and admissions progress to date, making its new decisions in light of that information. It would afford a better framework for building up to and then sustaining a steady pace of admissions throughout the year, minimizing the current year-end rush.

4. ASSURING TIMELY COMPLETION OF THE FULL PRESIDENTIAL DETERMINATION PROCESS

Finally, other related tasks, especially preparation of the annual admissions consultation document to be transmitted to Congress, might work more smoothly if they are tied in to the regular meeting schedule of the committee. Final clearance of the consultation document often bogs down in disputes over recommended numbers, groups, or wording, delaying consultation meetings and helping to push the issuance of the Presidential Determination a few days or weeks into the next fiscal year. Delays have serious operational consequences that seem insufficiently appreciated by some players in the process, including congressional offices. If no PD is in place by September 30, all refugee movement must halt and future flight bookings can be made only at risk of having to pay for unused spaces. Several valuable weeks can be lost. A healthy admissions program should not countenance these significant inefficiencies.[7]

The objective should be to prepare a document in time to assure completion of the full consultation process before Congress's August recess. That timing would allow final deliberations on the congressional feedback, plus the preparation and signing of the PD, by early September, making sure that operations can continue without break. Instead of allowing debates over the document to cause such delays, the document could be scheduled for firm resolution at a stated meeting of the committee, ideally in late spring (to permit whatever further interagency clearances are needed). A fixed date of this kind could help foster early compromise among competing camps, but if agreement is not reached, the dispute could be crystallized for discussion at the meeting and, if still not resolved, for preparation of the papers needed for resolution at a higher level.

RECOMMENDATION II-2: The Department of State should establish a Refugee Admissions Committee, to meet no less often than bimonthly. In a multilevel decision process, the committee

should consider lists of potential groups and select candidate groups for more thorough investigation. After the investigation, which could involve field visits by targeted response teams that include representatives of NGOs, the DHS, and perhaps UNHCR and IOM, the committee will ultimately designate groups for priority resettlement, at a rate needed to meet the PD target and to sustain a reasonably steady flow of admissions. The committee should also play a central role in the adoption of the annual congressional consultation document. It should schedule its deliberations so as to assure that the document is prepared in a timely and complete fashion that will enable consultation with Congress before its August recess and signing of the Presidential Determination by early September.

CHAPTER II. ENDNOTES

1   INA § 207(c)(2), 8 U.S.C. § 1157(c)(2) (2000) (covering spouse and unmarried minor children of the principal refugee applicant).

2   One respondent to an early draft of this report suggested that it is mistaken to think of gearing up the program to designate many more groups, often in widely dispersed locations. The USRP has worked best, he suggested, when it had to deal with only a few groups and could concentrate resources for long-term, steady processing. Therefore, we should seek out fewer group designations, not more, and try to concentrate them — aiming for perhaps four to six source countries with ten to fifteen subgroups involved.

Although the respondent is correct about his assessments of past operations and what might make for easier program management, I disagree with this suggestion for two main reasons. First, in today's conditions, open-ended long-term programs of the kind advocated generally attract both more migration and expanded fraud. Host countries are increasingly resistant to such arrangements, particularly as they harbor concerns about the true durability of any resettlement country's commitment. If problems arise or the latter country's priorities shift, those host countries would be the ones left with any residual population. Even if the United States wanted to find a half dozen such long-term resettlement sources, it is unlikely that host countries would permit it. They are much more likely to bless only the resettlement of smaller, distinct, finite groups. Second, the proposal risks losing sight of the primary reasons for a refugee admissions program. The point is not to generate numbers, but to do our best in meeting genuine humanitarian needs. To be sure, all resettlement programs are untidy and cannot match up reliably with target populations strictly on the basis of need or of an assessment of who has endured the greatest past suffering. But we should be reluctant to abandon the aspiration to develop a system that addresses genuine need, simply because such a system would present greater management challenges.

Similar concerns arise with respect to what initially seems a very different proposal by another respondent, meant to address the problems of uneven pipeline flow and frequent shortages of travel-ready cases. He argued for a "full access" system, which would augment the current limited access system with the following arrangements. Nationals of specified countries (a fairly lengthy list), provided they were registered as refugees with UNHCR, would be allowed to ask in writing for US resettlement consideration. Those letters would go to the locally based NGO processing agency and be screened by its caseworkers according to preset criteria, as time permitted, for conditional access to the program. Final access to resettlement, of course, would require ultimate DHS approval following an interview. This pool of persons would be drawn upon as needed to maintain a steady processing pipeline and travel flow, including a "full-time, non-fluctuating" DHS interview schedule, to fill gaps not being evenly met by the processing of persons in the P-1 through P-3 categories. Though this proposal would address legitimate processing issues, it raises serious concerns about feasibility. The expectations generated by such a process would almost surely produce a magnet effect — leading to keen resistance from host countries. This system could also greatly complicate the work of processing agencies and UNHCR, both in volume and expectations. It is better to try to fix the problem of uneven processing through a direct effort to designate more groups on a more regular basis.

3   This figure is somewhat below the totals for these categories in most of the last eight years (since the current priority system was implemented — and not counting the two years since the September 11 attacks), but not far below. The higher totals in some of those years reflect large-scale emergency programs such as Kosovo (1999), or other factors not likely to be repeated. Moreover, although family admission totals moved up significantly from 2002 to 2003, the current anti-fraud screening makes it unlikely that family totals will readily return to their pre–September 11 levels.

4   Memorandum from Joseph D. Cuddihy to Kelly Ryan, et al., Recommendations Paper from Fraud Working Group (Aug. 11, 2003) (attaching report submitted by coconvenors of the working group, Joe Martin of the Refugee Office of the DHS Bureau of Citizenship and Immigration Services and Anastasia Brown of the US Conference of Catholic Bishops).

5   For many years, all refugee-related NGOs convened together under the auspices of a broad umbrella organization called Interaction, which now includes a total of approximately 160 US organizations involved in international development and humanitarian action. In 2000, differing perspectives resulted in a split-off that has divided resettlement-focused NGOs from those whose major role relates to assistance. Refugee

resettlement NGOs grouped together, along with some additional advocacy organizations, to form the Refugee Council USA (RCUSA), whose website describes its role in this way: "The Refugee Council USA serves as the principal consultative forum for the national resettlement and processing agencies as they formulate common positions to conduct their relations with the US Government and other partners, and support and enhance refugee service standards." RCUSA currently has twenty full members, some of which also are members of Interaction (because those member organizations also perform overseas refugee assistance). Several persons interviewed for this project, in both governmental and nongovernmental circles, expressed regret or sorrow about the split. Some felt that RCUSA, with its narrower focus on US resettlement, was not as well positioned to address the difficult questions that arise in the overseas setting and that must be resolved before a resettlement initiative can be launched. When all the organizations were combined under the Interaction umbrella, these individuals stated, the NGOs were more likely to wrestle with the trade-offs and hard questions that government officials must regularly confront before launching a resettlement initiative.

6   See SANDY VOGELSANG, AMERICAN DREAM, GLOBAL NIGHTMARE: THE DILEMMA OF US HUMAN RIGHTS POLICY 207-08 (1980).

7   Chapter VII sets forth a proposed legislative amendment that would ameliorate the most damaging operational consequences of such delays. But even if such a change is made, the entire program will continue to function best if PDs, including their allocations of admissions numbers, are issued well before the beginning of the fiscal year.

CHAPTER III

THE PRIORITY SYSTEM FOR ACCESS TO THE ADMISSIONS PROGRAM AND ARRANGEMENTS FOR URGENT CASES

The priority system structures access to the US Refugee Program. Falling within one of the operative priorities permits a person to apply, to be processed for consideration, and usually to be interviewed by a DHS officer, but it does not guarantee approval. The DHS officer still must find that the person meets the refugee definition, is not firmly resettled, and is not excluded by any applicable ground of inadmissibility (many grounds are waivable for refugees).[1]

The current priority system replaced an earlier scheme that had largely been shaped by the Indochinese resettlement experience. Although it did reserve its first priority for cases of "compelling concern/interest," the former system based most categories on ties to the United States of various types, including prior employment by the US government or by US companies or foundations, certain US educational ties, and family members already in the United States.[2] In 1994, the Department of State announced a significant reshaping of the system, effective for FY 1995, based in part on a recognition that US ties were of declining significance in identifying threatened persons, given the wider range of refugee situations then under consideration. The new system was expressly designed "to reflect the US intent of providing resettlement to those most in need, relying to a greater extent on UNHCR to refer such individuals to our program."[3]

This chapter describes the priority system and then considers proposals to change its overall shape or the use of certain categories within it. It concludes with a review of arrangements for urgent cases.

A. OVERVIEW OF THE PRIORITIES

The five current priorities are known as P-1 through P-5. This section describes their history and operation.

1. THE P-1 CATEGORY: UNHCR AND EMBASSY REFERRALS

P-1 cases may be of any nationality and are based on referrals from either UNHCR or a US embassy. The focus of the P-1 category is compelling cases, but official descriptions of this priority usually go on to list specific factors that may support a decision to refer. Many of these parallel the factors given prominence in the *UNHCR Resettlement Handbook*.[4] The following is a typical list, although the formulations sometimes vary slightly:

■ persons facing compelling security concerns in the country of first asylum
■ persons in need of legal protection because of the danger of refoulement
■ persons in danger because of threats of armed attack in the area where they are located
■ former political prisoners or persons who have experienced persecution because of political, religious, or human rights activities
■ women at risk
■ victims of torture or violence
■ physically or mentally disabled persons
■ persons in urgent need of medical attention not available in the first-asylum country
■ persons for whom other durable solutions are not feasible and whose status in the place of asylum does not represent a satisfactory long-term solution

In its early years, P-1 operated mainly as a vehicle for individual referrals, primarily coming from UNHCR. But the system as designed also allowed UNHCR to refer groups that met the standards of this priority. At various times, the Office did refer a few groups for US resettlement, such as specific groups of Benadir and Barawans from Somalia in 1996 and 1997.[5] By the turn of the century, however, that UNHCR group referral practice had declined, fading from the memory of many persons involved in the admissions system (who by then associated group access solely with the P-2 category), to the point that the 2003 UNHCR referral of a P-1 group of vulnerable Liberians in Cote d'Ivoire was widely regarded as a novel development. But that referral amounted instead to a revival of an earlier practice, not a novelty.

2. THE P-2 CATEGORY: GROUPS OF SPECIAL HUMANITARIAN CONCERN

P-2 is for groups of special humanitarian concern to the United States who are designated by the US government for resettlement processing. Specific categories from the former Soviet Union, Cuba, and Vietnam, processed inside their countries of origin, have consistently been designated as P-2 groups, and other categories have been added at various times. These have included the so-called Lost Boys of Sudan, certain Burmese ethnic leaders and political activists, and mixed-marriage families from Bosnia (along with a wider list of victimized groups from Bosnia). For FY 2004 the congressional consultation document listed these additional P-2 groups: Somali Bantu in Kenya, Baku Armenians in Russia, and Iranian religious minorities, primarily in Austria.[6] It also stated that other groups were under consideration, and some have been added during FY 2004, including Meskhetian Turks in Krasnodar, Russia, certain Hmong refugees in Thailand, and a specific population of roughly 2,000 Vietnamese in the Philippines.

The history of this priority is instructive. As of the 1994 change in the priority system, P-2 was not expected to be the major or exclusive vehicle for group admissions, because continuing P-1 group referrals from UNHCR were anticipated. P-2 instead was adopted primarily to allow for the admission of groups that are covered by US law and policy but for which UNHCR involvement or referral could not be expected. For example, UNHCR's authority normally extends only to per-

sons who are outside their country of nationality.[7] For historical reasons, however, growing out of US experience with the Cuban Freedom Flights and the Vietnamese Orderly Departure Program, the Refugee Act of 1980 authorized US processing, as refugees, of persons not yet internationally displaced but who face persecution in their country of residence.[8] UNHCR would lack the legal authority to screen such persons in their countries of nationality. Therefore, such "in-country refugees" from the former Soviet Union, Vietnam, and Cuba have been dealt with through the P-2 category. They comprised a high percentage of US refugee admissions during the 1980s and 1990s.

Later, as political or financial limitations on UNHCR's potential involvement in other refugee situations became apparent, PRM began to use P-2 more widely. Certain Bosnian groups were designated in 1997, for example, under the P-2 framework, based in part on the initial rationale that these were persons whom UNHCR would have referred, if it had sufficient resources for full engagement there. The Bosnian group designations were quite specific, such as persons in ethnically mixed marriages or former detainees who had been held on account of ethnicity or political or religious opinion.[9] The designations were specific because this part of the USRP used an "open access" model. That is, Bosnians who believed that they fit one of the P-2 group specifications could present themselves directly to the processing agency. Obviously they still had to pass the initial screening and INS adjudication of their claim to refugee status before being approved for resettlement. But access to the process did not depend on a prior official notification or appearance on a specific registration list; individuals could take the initiative to start the process. Today's P-2 designations for Baku Armenians, Meskhetian Turks, and Iranian religious minorities in Vienna also follow the open access model. Open access can work because these specific groups are rather narrowly or specifically defined or because other factors (such as limited permission to travel to Austria) impose constraints on the potential universe of applicants.

As PRM began to make wider use of the P-2 category, it then developed another model as well, sometimes called a "circumscribed group" model. Such a group designation commonly requires not only a finding of common characteristics that indicate a risk of persecution, but also a registration or other way of obtaining a definitive list of persons, in advance of group designation. This practice started with a specific group of Burundian and Rwandan families of mixed marriages between Hutus and Tutsis, located in the Mkugwa camp in Tanzania, and fully registered by UNHCR.[10] Later, PRM added P-2 designations, based on a consolidated registration or verified list, for Sudanese Somalis in Dadaab camp in Kenya, the so-called Lost Boys of Sudan, Ogoni refugees in Benin, and Hmong Lao in Thailand. The circumscribed group model is seen as necessary in these circumstances in order to avoid overwhelming the processing agencies, to defeat attempts at fraud, and to minimize any magnet effect. PRM officers indicated that they had felt it important to have a solid way to "draw the circle" — i.e., to assure themselves of ways to identify the intended beneficiaries definitively — before announcing any designation. This model amounts essentially to the finite group approach discussed in Chapter I — which is likely, as that chapter discussed, to be of increasing importance in the conditions under which refugee resettlement must function in the twenty-first century.

3. CATEGORIES P-3 THROUGH P-5 AND VISAS 93: FAMILY-BASED ACCESS

P-3 through P-5 are based on family relationships to persons in the United States, but these priorities are made available only to specific nationalities. P-3 includes spouses, minor children, and parents, whereas P-4 and P-5 apply to more distant relatives.[11] The nationality must be on the list at the time that the anchor relative in the United States files the affidavit of relationship (AOR) that starts the process going. For most of the time that these priorities have been in use, anyone lawfully resident in the United States (including citizens, lawful permanent residents, persons having refugee or asylum status, and certain parolees) could file the necessary documents to initiate resettlement for a relative, if that nationality was covered by an operative priority. For FY 2004, however, this privilege has been limited to persons initially admitted to the United States as refugees or asylees. This latest restriction has been explained on the basis that the US government will have sufficiently complete family information only for those categories of anchor relatives — information needed to provide a good basis for checking the validity of the claimed family relationship.[12]

In addition to the P-3 category, a provision added by the Refugee Act of 1980 keeps families together by providing categorically that the spouse and minor unmarried children of a refugee are entitled to derivative refugee status themselves, even if they do not have an individual risk of persecution.[13] (Such derivative relatives may be of any nationality.) This provision works straightforwardly when families move together from a refugee camp to their new home in the United States. It has raised more complications, of both process and proof, when a spouse or child uses this provision to "follow to join" the principal refugee, as the Refugee Act specifically permits. As Section E and Chapter V explain in greater detail, the follow-to-join provision for spouses and children is implemented through a process known as Visas 93, often handled by consular officers through procedures that differ markedly from the normal refugee admissions machinery. Because the Visas 93 procedure is unfamiliar to many consular officers, delays or misunderstandings often arise. P-3 eligibility, for the nationalities listed in a given year as eligible for that priority, overlaps a fair amount with the Visas 93 process. Both provisions cover spouses and unmarried minor children; P-3 differs in that it also includes parents of the principal refugee. Although P-3 requires each relative to satisfy the refugee definition independently, while the Visas 93 process does not, P-3 is often favored by refugees and the volags that assist them because the procedures are seen as more reliable and familiar.

P-4 and P-5 have not been made available since the end of registration for the Bosnia P-4 program in November 1999. P-3 was made available for only four nationalities in FY 2003, and nine in FY 2004, although it has been open to as many as eighteen in the past. Reductions in the list of eligible nationalities in later years derived in significant part from concerns about fraud (discussed in Section E of this chapter).[14] Actual P-3 admissions for any given year, however, typically include a wider array of nationalities, because eligibility is governed by the nationality list that applied at the time the AOR was filed. An AOR provides only access to the process, not a guarantee of admission. The DHS still must find that each person to be admitted under P-3 individually satisfies the refugee definition, or is the spouse or child of an accompanying relative found to be a refugee. Many persons who fit P-3 through P-5 might also be eligible, now or after the anchor relative naturalizes, for immigration in one of the family preference categories of the regular immigrant admission system. Backlogs in that system usually make the refugee route advantageous, however, if the applicant can demonstrate a well-founded fear of persecution.[15]

B. BROAD RESTRUCTURING OF THE PRIORITY SYSTEM?

Dissatisfaction with the priority system usually focuses on the relatively limited use of P-2 group designations (which is addressed in Chapter II) and on the limited list of nationalities eligible for P-3. Many people argue for a universal P-3, available to all nationalities. Other critics suggest that too much reliance in the overall system is placed on UNHCR's role in referring refugees (for P-1 admissions) — a gatekeeper role for which, they argue, UNHCR has not been adequately staffed or supported. They want to see a greater push for embassy referrals and a wider referral role for NGOs. Some consider that the P-1 category is too diffuse, including a wide range of different types of potential refugees that would better be separated for admissions planning purposes. If it were divided so as to create a wider array of categories, they assert, the priority system might better allow for giving precedence to the truly urgent case. And some critiques call for a complete revamping of the priority structure. This section considers proposals for broad restructuring. Later sections then move on to review specific suggestions for each of the primary functional categories: individual, group, and family processing.

1. THE FRELICK PROPOSAL

Bill Frelick, who has extensive experience in refugee issues and is currently Director of the Refugee Program for Amnesty International USA, proposed a thoughtful restructuring of the priority system in testimony before the Senate Subcommittee on Immigration in 2002.[16] Frelick's proposal begins by noting the unevenness of the list of factors that govern the existing P-1 category. That list covers a wide variety of situations, some far more compelling than others. He proposes regrouping them with closer attention to their relative urgency, as well as introducing new priority categories based on some factors not directly addressed in the current system.

Frelick would pull together the most urgent refugee cases in countries of first asylum as a new P-1 category, still to be based on UNHCR or embassy referral. These would be the first three subcategories in the list set forth in Section A1 of this chapter, plus persons in urgent need of medical attention (the eighth factor listed). P-2 would be a new category, although one that is similar to categories used in the pre-1994 system: persons whose fear of persecution is based on actual or imputed association with the US government or US nongovernmental entities. P-3 and P-4 would also be break-outs from the current P-1 factor list. P-3 would be for women at risk in the first-asylum setting, and P-4 would cover physically or mentally disabled refugees and survivors of torture or violence. Frelick's P-5 would be what is essentially our current P-2 category, State Department designated groups of special humanitarian concern, selected based on specific group circumstances. P-6 would become what is essentially today's P-3, close family members, but open to all nationalities. And P-7 would be for long-stayer refugees whose situation in the country of first asylum does not amount to a satisfactory durable solution. He lists specific factors to consider in making that determination.

Frelick has subdivided the list and paid close attention to the ordering because he intends these categories to be true priorities: it is more important to use admission spaces for his P-1 refugees than for P-2s, and so on, and admissions must take that hierarchy into account. Significantly, his P-7, long-stayers, is meant to be a category that comes into play in order to assure use of PD admission slots that would otherwise go unused — and there have of course been such unused slots, sometimes in large quantities, throughout the history of the program. If a given year appears unlikely to make use of the full allotment for persons in the first six priorities, he suggests, then the United States should process long-stayers so as to make full use of the PD resource. He is aware of the difficulties of initiating resettlement in the midst of a long-term refugee situation, and he offers specific steps to minimize resentment by those not chosen and to reduce any pull factor.

2. EVALUATION AND RECOMMENDATION FOR MORE MODEST REVISION

Frelick's proposal is a worthy effort to retool the priority system to respond better to real humanitarian need, and the system he proposes would certainly be workable. I recommend making more modest changes in the overall priority system, however. In my view, the major difficulties in the current system do not result from the priority system as such. Numbers have gone unused, for example, not because of the lack of a P-7 category that can serve as a reserve pool, but because of difficulties with the decision-making structure and a failure to treat the PD number as a target. These problems are addressed directly by the recommendations in Chapter II. Moreover, even if we agreed to fill unused slots with long-stayers, we would still face difficult decisions about just when to trigger that resettlement (Frelick does not contemplate that we wait until the final quarter of the fiscal year to see how large a shortfall is looming) and above all, which long-stayer situations to focus on. Making those decisions will inevitably require group-based determinations by those in charge of the USRP, not unlike what is now required for the current P-2 process. Although it is definitely wise to look more systematically at protracted refugee situations as the source for significant admissions in this new resettlement era, this objective is best accomplished by incorporating it into an established group designation process, as outlined in the previous chapter.

Frelick's ranking of the relative urgency of current P-1 factors (as reflected in the different break-out categories) makes sense, but it seems unlikely that there will often be situations where we must choose the higher ranking categories to the exclusion of the lower. The mechanism will still be individual referrals, if not from UNHCR, then from a US embassy or, under expanded arrangements, from NGOs or other partners. Increasing the overall system's capacity for individual referrals could proceed without explicitly subdividing the different subcategories of P-1. Also, giving priority to admission of persons who are persecuted precisely because of their ties to the United States is a worthy objective, but that factor can be accommodated within the individual referral system. It might be wise to add that consideration explicitly to the P-1 list — presumably a factor that is more likely to be acted upon by US embassies than by UNHCR. If identifiable groups are targeted for persecution because of such US ties, that fact would also constitute a strong argument in favor of P-2 designation, which of course can be so linked, on a case-by-case basis, without any change in the overall priority system.

Frelick's proposal does helpfully point out a major disconnect between one of the P-1 factors and virtually all the rest. The factor that is based on lack of another durable solution combined with an unsatisfactory situation in the country of first asylum (the final factor in the list set forth in Section A1) presents less of the immediately compelling short-term risk that characterizes most of the other entries on the list. Moreover, such a characteristic is less likely to apply to isolated individuals, but instead will probably be shared by a larger populace. That is, it is more likely to lend itself to a P-1 group referral. UNHCR is working to develop a new set of procedures that will facilitate systematic use of group referrals on a larger scale in the future (see Chapter VI), and a great many of these are likely to derive from the comparable no-other-durable-solution category used by UNHCR in its own resettlement referral system.

I would prefer to use this functional insight and implement only a modest revision in the priority system. At a time when the refugee admissions system is going through several other significant changes, there are advantages to keeping the priority system as stable and straightforward as possible. We essentially have operated with three broad functional sources of refugee access: individual referrals, group decisions, and family-based access. These correspond roughly, but not precisely, to the current P-1, P-2, and P-3 categories. We should bring those correspondences more completely into line, by treating all group-based admissions under the P-2 category and employing for all a systematic group decision mechanism, one version of which is outlined in Chapter II. When UNHCR refers a group, as it may well do with increasing frequency over the coming years, that referral should then be given prompt consideration for inclusion as a priority group within the USRP. Any such UNHCR group referral should ordinarily come to the Refugee Admissions Committee with considerable momentum for approval.[17] But there should be a deliberate US decision process for deciding whether we want to participate in that resettlement effort (as opposed to, say, leaving a certain situation primarily for other resettlement countries). That decision should be worked into the same procedures that will come to be used on a more frequent basis for the traditional P-2 group decisions. Hence we would cease using the terminology of "P-1 groups," instead coming to recognize that P-2 groups could originate from different sources — the familiar US-initiated group designation or a UNHCR referral.

Beyond this, I agree with Frelick that we now have little need for the current P-4 and P-5 categories as such. Such factors — more distant family relationships to persons resident in the United States — have been sparingly used and do not deserve their own priority designations. Nonetheless, these relationships may in limited circumstances remain of importance. For example, the United States has sometimes felt called upon to respond to a large refugee flow (such as from ex-Yugoslavia or Afghanistan), but under circumstances that make it clear that resettlement can address only a small fraction of the overall need. In these settings, we may occasionally want to employ family ties to US residents (more distant than those relationships covered by P-3) as an access factor, probably just one among many factors, that can help select a manageable resettlement pool out of a potentially enormous and overwhelming refugee population. But we do not need separate priority categories for these purposes. Such qualifications can be worked into the description of the precise group given priority access under the P-2 process.

RECOMMENDATION III-1: The priority system should be revised modestly, so that P-1 becomes the priority for individual referrals from UNHCR, US embassies, or, in some circumstances, other referring entities; P-2 covers all decisions for designated groups; and P-3 remains the category for close family members of US residents. P-4 and P-5, now covering more distant family relationships, should be removed as priorities, although those same family connections might sometimes be characteristics used in specific P-2 designations. UNHCR group referrals should be worked into the group designation process under P-2, and should cease being thought of as P-1 groups. Such UNHCR referrals should generally enjoy additional momentum for approval as an access category. PRM should consider refining the list of factors for P-1 referrals accordingly, as well as adding a factor for persons facing persecution that is based on their real or imputed ties to the US government or US entities. PRM should also regularly post on its website a list of P-2 groups currently being given access to the US system.

C. INDIVIDUAL REFERRALS

1. UNHCR REFERRALS

P-1 admissions derive primarily from UNHCR referrals. This system has worked reasonably well, although a few reforms would be worthwhile. The main complaints I heard about individual referrals were that there are too few of them. This theme has been particularly urgent in the past two years of low overall admission totals. Some have blamed the 1994 redesign of the priority system for the problem, believing that it unwisely gave too much of a gatekeeping role to UNHCR without assuring that the latter was funded and staffed at a level that could keep admissions at historic US levels, as the Soviet and Indochinese programs phased down. Nonetheless, it should be noted that the 1994 changes did not necessarily require that most admissions come through UNHCR. P-2 has always played a significant role in sustaining a large-scale program, and PRM's use of the P-2 category has adjusted over time in light of limitations affecting UNHCR, as described in Section A2.

PRM has provided the UNHCR protection division with several million dollars worth of additional resources for referrals in recent years, eventually insisting upon performance criteria based on actual referrals produced as a result of the enhanced funding.[18] UNHCR has added staff for these purposes and has increased its output of individual referrals. It has also made increasing use of a cooperative deployment scheme with the International Catholic Migration Commission (ICMC) that was first established in 1998. Through these arrangements, the ICMC maintains a roster of persons with expertise in various phases of resettlement work, including refugee identification, claim verification, case processing, and the best interests determinations (BIDs) needed before unaccompanied minors are assigned for resettlement. UNHCR can call upon them as needed for assignments of several months' duration. As of December 31, 2003, 114 persons were on the roster, 43 of them deployed to the field.[19]

PRM should keep up the pressure for the system to continue growing its capacity, including use of cooperative deployments from the ICMC or other NGOs. The individual referral process at UNHCR can be quite cumbersome, often involving an individual refugee status determination (RSD) based on lengthy individual interviews, followed by the completion of a multipage resettlement registration form (RRF). Some UNHCR field offices have experimented with a streamlined process, particularly using abbreviated forms for resettlement referrals to the United States. Although there are trade-offs to be made, UNHCR should consider further streamlining, at least on a selective basis.[20] A one-size-fits-all model of individual referrals may not be appropriate. Some countries in Europe accept UNHCR referrals based on the dossier only, without doing their own separate preadmission interviewing. For those countries, the elaborate UNHCR investigation and paperwork may make sense. But, for interview-based systems like that of the United States, which inevitably include their own separate and thorough inquiry into refugee status and other qualifying characteristics, UNHCR could simplify its process.

PRM should also continue to support ongoing UNHCR reforms that are meant to enhance quality control and consistency in the standards for individual referrals. I was told of situations where some offices are more likely to refer troublesome or pushy refugees from a first-asylum situation, simply in order to be rid of the hassle, without much attention to the merits of the individual's case for resettlement. The UNHCR individual referral system must reliably focus on individually worthy cases, according to the criteria set forth in the UNHCR resettlement manual. UNHCR is aware of this issue, and has been developing new measures, such as greater use of regional resettlement hub offices, that are improving quality-control monitoring and overall performance.[21]

2. US EMBASSY REFERRALS

Although US embassies have not produced a high volume of referrals, this mechanism should certainly remain available as a source for P-1 admissions. The Department of State should include in the initial training of foreign service officers more systematic instruction on refugee and humanitarian programs generally and on the specific opportunity and procedures for referrals of this type. It should also improve and simplify the annual State Department instruction cable regarding embassy referrals.[22] The current procedures are daunting, very likely to deter an embassy officer who might initially learn of a local refugee in danger for whom

US resettlement seems appropriate. Creative thinking needs to go into mechanisms that could make it easier for embassy officers to watch for, and then act speedily on, the cases of qualifying refugees who come to their attention. With some simplification of existing processes, embassy officers would be in a better position to act on urgent cases informally brought to their attention by NGOs. Nonetheless, one should not expect more than modest increases in referrals from embassies, which are already stretched thin by their other responsibilities.

3. NGO REFERRALS

Some people have proposed to expand possibilities for NGO referrals, looking to this mechanism in part as a potential source for a significantly increased volume of admissions. The International Rescue Committee (IRC) developed an NGO referral system several years ago that referred a modest number of individual Afghan refugee cases in Pakistan (mostly women at risk), and the Hebrew Immigrant Aid Society (HIAS) has such a program in East Africa. PRM also initiated a pilot program for enhanced NGO referrals with a two-day training session in Nairobi in early 2003, targeted at the staff of assistance-focused NGOs who are regularly present in refugee camps or settlements. These initiatives are worthwhile, and PRM should systematically evaluate the experience under each of them, in order to refine the system and carefully deploy it elsewhere. In particular, persons interviewed suggested that a less cumbersome procedure than the one set up as part of the Nairobi training would be more likely to produce better results. If the paperwork required is too extensive, busy NGO personnel in the camps will be deterred from triggering the process.

Although a refined and more widely deployed system for NGO referrals would be worthwhile, it is important to be realistic about what the program can expect to accomplish through this mechanism. In fact, it was not until after many months of interviews for this project that I came to appreciate that persons speaking about NGO referrals may have two quite different kinds of programs in mind.

One model, which was used at certain stages in the Indochina program, I was told, gave voluntary agency representatives a rather extensive and proactive role in going out to find refugees, but according to carefully defined criteria set out by the

State Department. Such a model can generate significant numbers of refugee admissions, but it would appear to work well only in conditions where there are reasons not to worry greatly about a magnet effect or where the criteria employed can be readily applied based on accessible documents or other objective factors. Such an NGO role would probably have to be accomplished by special NGO staff (probably affiliated with an OPE) designated specifically for admissions purposes; it is not at all realistic to add this function as a kind of sidelight to be carried out by NGO staff who work primarily on assistance. For the reasons set forth in Chapter I, however, today's refugee situations are unlikely to lend themselves to this kind of approach, because in most of them concerns about magnet effects, fraud, and exaggerated resettlement expectations loom large — for host governments and for many other players, often including NGOs and UNHCR. This first model, despite its important historical antecedents under somewhat different circumstances, should not be seen as a promising method for improving today's refugee admissions program. But it could remain on reserve in the program toolbox, to be used if circumstances generate a large-scale resettlement initiative for which such an approach is appropriate.

The second model is more in line with the IRC Afghan program, or the recent pilot project in Nairobi. Such programs are meant to draw, discreetly and carefully, on the contacts NGOs already have in refugee settlements in order to find particularly vulnerable cases who could then quietly be moved to safety in the United States. The premise is that the NGO's other work, not expressly resettlement-oriented, places its staff in a better position than UNHCR or US personnel to learn of such vulnerable persons. In order for this model to operate discreetly, it cannot involve any significant deployment of new personnel, and certainly not any who are expressly designated as resettlement staff. Many people interviewed for the project, including several NGO representatives, emphasized — vigorously — that NGO assistance staff in camps must not be put in a position where they become known as a kind of ticket to admission to the United States. In many first-asylum settings, hunger for resettlement possibilities is so great that knowledge of such a role might leave the NGO staff besieged with supplicants, interfering greatly with their primary operational work, and sometimes even generating security or crowd management problems. (The desire to avoid this risk, perhaps more than cumbersome paperwork, may account for the apparently low usage of the Nairobi pilot referral system.) For these reasons, referral programs of this type will at best involve modest numbers of refugees, although they can help the refugee program meet a highly important objective: identifying persons quietly facing acute dangers who might otherwise be overlooked.

Under today's conditions, the individual referral role for NGO staff is best done under the second model. It will be able to focus only on those in the most urgent need to escape from dangers in the camp or settlement, and the NGO function must remain discreet, almost covert. NGOs do have a role in helping to facilitate access decisions on a larger scale, but that should come through their involvement in the group designation process, as discussed in Chapter II and in the following section of this chapter.

RECOMMENDATION III-2: PRM should press UNHCR to continue expanding its individual referral capacity, possibly streamlining the referral process for US-destined cases, and enhancing its mechanisms for quality control and consistency. Procedures for embassy referrals of P-1 cases should be simplified, and State Department training should better equip embassy personnel for this role. PRM should systematically evaluate the past experiences with NGO individual referral schemes, so that the process can be refined and made available elsewhere. Such referrals will ordinarily be done quietly by NGO personnel present in the camp or settlement for other reasons, and can be expected to produce only modest numbers, because they will focus on urgent, compelling cases.

D. GROUP ACCESS

Chapters I and II addressed many key questions surrounding the process of deciding on the groups to be granted priority access to the USRP, recommending an attitudinal and institutional framework for improvements. An additional word about NGO roles, initially discussed in Chapter I, Section B1, is appropriate. NGOs perform a considerable service in recommending group initiatives to the Department of State, and they have provided highly valuable information sources for these purposes for several years. Publications like the *World Refugee Survey*, produced by the US Committee for Refugees, as well as the human rights reports of some other organizations, provide well-organized accounts that can be of great assistance in identifying potential groups for access to the US program. The most focused NGO resource of this type, however, consists of the annual recommendations volumes produced by the Refugee Council USA, the umbrella organization for the resettlement volags.[23] Each year they provide details, region by region, of needy refugee populations, and make specific recommendations for enhanced individual access or P-2 designation, as appropriate.

No official sanction, such as legislative authorization, is needed for this process. RCUSA and others should continue to provide this type of detailed nonofficial input, which should be of assistance in preparing and refining the list of potential groups for consideration by the recommended Refugee Admissions Committee. More visible demonstrations of a departmental intention to examine these suggestions seriously, coupled with an effective and sustained increase in the use of the group designation process — which is decidedly needed anyway (and is occurring in FY 2004) — should decrease the momentum for enshrining this initial NGO process in legislation. Further, RCUSA will maximize the impact of its recommendations to the extent that they openly deal, in close detail for each specific refugee situation, with the trade-offs, barriers, and obstacles that government players must confront, as sketched in Chapter I, Section A. (It could be expected that such considerations would sometimes result in the removal or postponement of specific resettlement proposals.)

Once a potential group has been chosen as a candidate group, NGOs can play a highly useful but focused and selective role as part of the investigatory process contemplated before a decision on final designation. PRM's current efforts to establish targeted response teams, teams assigned to undertake a field visit to look in detail at particular populations who might be appropriate for a resettlement initiative, seem to afford a useful model. The teams are meant to be composed of governmental experts as well as NGO representatives who have particular knowledge of the targeted country or population, coupled with familiarity with the resettlement program, and who would be available for service, sometimes on fairly short notice.

Those teams should also include a representative of the DHS. Until now, the DHS (like its predecessor the INS) has tended to want to leave the group designation process to the Department of State. It then takes up its role only after designation has occurred. I was told that this reticence traced in part to the diffuse process for group designation. The DHS did not want to be fingered as the source of denial of a group designation, when all it might have done was to suggest certain problems or obstacles — objections which it often did not see as fatal to a proposed designation. But if the process becomes more clearly defined, as suggested in Chapter II, a DHS role should fit far more comfortably. The Department of State would take responsibility for developing the list of potential groups to bring to the Refugee Admissions Committee. Only after a formal decision to name a candidate group would the DHS be asked to play a role in the future investigation and development of possible plans for resettlement.

Such a DHS role at the stage of investigating a candidate group is needed to assure ample consideration of operational issues and means of addressing them, *before* a final designation is made. Under past practice, I heard of several instances where rather significant problems affecting the DHS role had not been spotted until the circuit ride team arrived to begin interviews — resulting in damaging inefficiencies. Sometimes these had to do with operational issues, like the quality and identity of translators, or the adequacy of arrangements for site security. Other times the overlooked issues were legal questions. For example, a common issue for Colombians has been whether payment of ransom to retrieve a relative from paramilitary kidnappers should be considered "material support" to terrorists, which would render the person inadmissible to the United States. And with regard to Liberians, an issue arose over whether those who had married Ivorians were "firmly resettled" in Cote d'Ivoire, and therefore ineligible for the refugee program. Not all such operational and legal questions can be spotted in advance, and some capacity to respond quickly in the midst of a DHS circuit ride will always be required. But any gain in advance preparation can make for better use of resettlement resources.

Moreover, DHS involvement at this stage can help provide a better estimate of the approval rates likely once interviewing begins — which can be useful to assure that all players share realistic expectations about the program and to allow better planning for the later stages of the process. Approval rates have proven a sore point in interagency dealings over the past few years, but my interviews suggest that this usually resulted from an inadequate understanding of the roles and perspectives among the various players in the process. (See Chapter V, Section A4.) Including the DHS on the investigatory team considering a candidate group will go a long way toward providing better understanding of this factor, and also toward educating PRM and NGO staff about the realities and constraints of the DHS's role. This process can also bring advantages in the other direction. The DHS will thereby learn in more detail about the perspectives of PRM and the NGOs regarding the group, and the DHS member may be better able to convey the real level of need presented by the refugee situation back to all the potentially involved bureaus in DHS headquarters — thereby expanding support for efforts to facilitate the process at every stage where DHS is involved. DHS participation in the field investigatory and preparation process should help assure a full buy-in and commitment by the DHS when the decision is made to move ahead with admissions.

RECOMMENDATION III-3: The Department of State should give close attention to NGO suggestions, including the annual RCUSA recommendations report, when developing the potential group list. Concomitantly, NGOs should work to address more concretely the trade-offs, barriers, and obstacles that would affect any resettlement initiative — and that sometimes counsel against undertaking it. No legislative sanction is needed or desirable with regard to that sort of input. Once a group has been chosen as a candidate group, further investigation of group needs and characteristics should take place. It will often prove advantageous to proceed through a field mission by a targeted response team, which should ordinarily include NGO representation and one or more participants from the Department of Homeland Security.

E. FAMILY-BASED PRIORITIES, INCLUDING ISSUES OF PROCESSING BOTTLENECKS AND FRAUD

As noted in Section A, family reunification has been a constant and enduring value in modern US immigration law and policy, and US law provides that the spouse and minor unmarried children of a refugee, if accompanying or following to join that person, may be admitted without having to meet the refugee definition independently.[24] This applies to refugees of all nationalities, and does not require further specific authorization through the priority system. Thus the nuclear family may be kept together even if only one parent has become the target of persecution. This provision becomes somewhat more problematic in follow-to-join cases, wherein the principal refugee files only after admission to bring the spouse and minor children. The reasons derive largely from problems with the process, known as Visas 93, used to handle follow-to-join cases.

If that process worked smoothly, one would probably see far fewer applicants trying to use the P-3 process, because a major part of the eligible P-3 pool overlaps with the class of persons who could use Visas 93. In fact, because P-3 applicants must independently satisfy the refugee definition individually, at first glance there would appear to be significant incentives to use Visas 93. But that has not been the experience. For any nationality to which P-3 applies, the P-3 process has been favored over Visas 93. In any event, a well-designed P-3 process remains a real need, because some of those eligible could not use Visas 93 — primarily parents of the anchor relative. In addition, there is no derivative status to a Visas 93 admission. To appreciate the significance of this limitation, consider, for example, an unmarried teenage daughter of a previously admitted refugee who gives birth (perhaps as a result of a sexual assault) before she can travel as a Visas 93 beneficiary. Because she is a derivative relative, rather than someone qualifying for refugee status in her own right, the law does not permit her to bring her child as part of this process.[25] The P-3 category provides a possible means to keep such a mother and child together, although she would then have to show independently that she meets the refugee definition. (And when P-3 is not available, PRM and the DHS normally find another way to assure that the family stays together.)

The P-3 program has encountered a significant amount of fraud. Although new measures in place for the past couple of years provide improved means to detect and deter fraud, the prior experience soured many government players on the whole category. The following sections explore these issues, leading toward recommended improvements for both the Visas 93 and P-3 processes, so that both can be used more readily. They also evaluate a frequently voiced proposal to adopt a universal P-3 category — that is, to open the P-3 category to persons of any nationality, and not limit it to a specified list of countries of origin.

I. THE VISAS 93 PROCESS FOR IMMEDIATE FAMILY FOLLOWING TO JOIN

A person already admitted to the United States as a refugee under INA § 207 who wishes to bring in his or her spouse and minor unmarried children begins the process by filing a Form I-730 with the Nebraska Service Center of the DHS, accompanied by proof of the family relationship. Once the I-730 is conditionally approved, it is sent via the National Visa Center to the overseas post where the family members are expected to complete the rest of the process. DHS officers often tend to refer to these as I-730 cases, because the Form I-730 provides their main initial contact with such applications. But the State Department refers to them as Visas 93 cases, a sometimes confusing nomenclature.[26]

In a few locations, Visas 93 work is handled by those involved in the general refugee processing procedures, including preparation of the case by an OPE and often adjudication by a DHS officer. As will be discussed in Chapter V, such case preparation is the bread-and-butter work of OPEs, and they are expert in the overall refugee admissions process. Such expertise helps the Visas 93 process work efficiently in those locations. But in posts where such processing is not employed, Visas 93 processing often does not proceed smoothly. These types of cases are a relatively exotic form of application, and many consular officers, as well as the local-hire staff who often play a key role in consular processing, are not familiar with the specialized steps needed to complete them. The cases are dauntingly labor-intensive, meaning that the consular officer may have to postpone work on several of the more familiar types of visa applications in order to process one Visas 93 case. As a result, Visas 93 applications may simply be laid aside, lan-

guishing for many months on a desk in the consulate. Moreover, consular officers may have difficulty arranging for the needed interview with the family members, because the family members living in a refugee camp may not be able, at least not without special clearances, to travel to the consular post. Delays and uncertainty over the Visas 93 process have often led volags to counsel their clients trying to bring in spouse and minor children to use the P-3 process, if it is available for their nationality.

PRM has taken steps to address these problems with Visas 93, including assigning an officer in headquarters to spend a major portion of her time troubleshooting, helping to get delayed cases unstuck, and walking consular officers through the process. The staff of the Refugee Processing Center in Arlington (a contract unit that manages the basic data processing system for the refugee program), also spends a fair amount of time assisting consular officers or local-hire staff to work through these cases. PRM has also worked for more coverage of Visas 93 in the consular training program. But these cases remain a problem, and more should be done. At the very least, Consular Affairs should incorporate Visas 93 training more thoroughly into the normal consular training course, and the *Foreign Affairs Manual* (FAM) section dealing with these cases should be updated.[27] It would also be good to route approved I-730s through the Refugee Processing Center (or at least assure inclusion of full tracking data in the Worldwide Refugee Admissions Processing System (WRAPS)), so that PRM could better monitor such cases and act promptly when processing bogs down in particular locations or for particular cases.

One source of confusion could be reduced if the DHS would agree to change its I-730 form, so as to signal better to the consular officer who will eventually process the case the distinctive requirements in Visas 93 cases. This particular confusion arises because the Form I-730 is used for two related, but in the end importantly different, types of cases — to bring in both the family members of persons who gained status in the United States as a result of an asylum claim under INA § 208 and the family members of persons admitted as refugees under INA § 207. The State Department labels the former Visas 92 cases and the latter Visas 93. Visas 93 cases count fully as refugee admissions in the annual totals and therefore occupy one of the admission spaces made available by the PD. Visas 92 family members (spouses and children of asylees) do not. Most importantly, Visas 93 cases benefit from the special treatment and subsidies that the US system provides for refugees, while Visas 92 cases do not.

Visas 92 cases therefore look a lot more like the normal kind of case a consular officer might handle. The individual applicants are responsible for completing the medical examination at their own expense, making their own travel arrangements, and paying for their air tickets. But in Visas 93 cases, the US government pays for the medical examination and obtains the ticket through the International Organization for Migration (IOM). The government advances the cost of the ticket, but in the form of a loan that must be repaid over time after resettlement in the United States. Hence in Visas 93 cases, the consular officer must take additional steps quite different from all other consular cases — arranging for the medical exam through or in cooperation with IOM, obtaining the ticket, getting the individual to sign the loan note, and also initiating the process that will result in the required sponsorship assurance from one of the resettlement volags in the United States. (Chapter V explains these distinctive processes in greater detail.)

Using wholly different DHS forms for the two types of cases would therefore be beneficial. Alternatively, the DHS might at least issue a revision to Form I-730 that would signal to the consular officer more prominently just which of the two types of cases is involved. Furthermore, for Visas 93 cases, a larger "official use only" box could provide spaces for the consular officer to check off completion of the distinctive steps that are to be completed at government initiative (and usually expense): medical exam arrangement, sponsor assurance, IOM contact for the ticket, and the loan note. Although these would be unusual changes to make on a DHS form, they are worthwhile in this setting, precisely because the Visas 93 procedures have proven to be so daunting for consular posts that see them infrequently. The high importance of reuniting a resettled refugee with his or her spouse and minor children would justify such relatively unusual steps.

A more ambitious change to the process, suggested to me during the interviews for this project, might provide a more broadly applicable and reliable fix. The basic problem is that Visas 93 cases are shoe-

horned into the consular caseload, whereas most of the process follows instead the distinctive procedural contours that have evolved for refugees — quite different from the normal consular routine. It would be better to use the refugee-specific procedures, to the greatest extent possible, for the Visas 93 cases. This would mean processing by an OPE and adjudication (ordinarily) by a DHS officer (with the concomitant changes in budgeting). Of course, Visas 93 cases could crop up anywhere in the world, and are not necessarily confined to the major refugee processing sites. Thus some additional circuit riding, for both OPE staff and the DHS, would be required — often to service a rather small caseload. Some allowance would probably still have to be made for consular processing where a caseload is so small as to make OPE and DHS travel there impractical.

RECOMMENDATION III-4: The Visas 93 process needs to work reliably and efficiently, because it serves a vital function: reuniting a resettled refugee with his or her spouse and minor children. At the least, Visas 93 training should be a regular part of consular training, and the State Department should adopt additional procedures (possibly including a greater monitoring role for WRAPS) to assure that such cases do not languish. The DHS should also either revise the Form I-730 or develop two separate forms for Visas 92 and Visas 93 cases, so that the form will better guide the consular officer through all the distinctive steps needed for Visas 93 cases, owing to their inclusion in the special benefits of the overseas refugee program. The DHS and PRM should also consider arrangements that could take most Visas 93 work from consular officers and have it handled through standard OPE procedures, with ultimate adjudication by the DHS.

2. P-3 PROCESSING

The P-3 category is available for spouses, minor unmarried children, and parents of persons resident in the United States. As noted, it is an access category, not a derivative benefit. This means that such persons can get access to a DHS interview, but must independently satisfy the refugee definition.[28] Historically the process began with the filing with a local volag office of an affidavit of relationship (AOR) by the already admitted anchor relative. The volag office then typically forwarded the affidavit on to the overseas processing location near the site where the family members were located. For many years different volags used their own diverse affidavit forms, and efforts on the part of the volags to verify the family information set forth in the affidavit were uneven. As the volume of P-3 filings grew, government officers involved in the process began to suspect a significant amount of fraud. (The extent of fraud varied by refugee situation, and people interviewed for this project speculated that the variances trace to some extent to cultural differences and perhaps more to whether or not good civil records systems existed, recording births and marriages for the refugee population at issue.) Access to US resettlement is a highly prized commodity. It is likely that some of those committing fraud used the P-3 process to help more distant relatives or acquaintances who may have been quite needy in their own right — even if not technically eligible for P-3. But the scale of the fraud appeared to go beyond that, and some of the misrepresentation was much more cynical, involving the buying and selling of access. The requirement that all P-3s meet the refugee definition might help screen out non-needy impostors, persons not at risk of persecution, but that process too has hardly been foolproof. Some INS officers pushed for reforms for many years, suggesting especially that new AORs be checked against family tree information gathered by the processing team around the time of the principal alien's interview and now contained in his or her INS file, known as the A-file.

Those suggestions did not get far[29] until the September 11 attacks brought heightened attention to all the vulnerabilities of the refugee admission system. At that time, the INS set up a Refugee Access Verification Unit (RAVU) to manage a verification process that would apply to all future P-3 admissions. This screening is separate from, and in addition to, added screening for national security purposes. It is not directly targeted at the kinds of terrorist dangers that September 11 revealed. Instead, September 11 merely provided the impetus to tighten up many parts of the admissions system, and it invited close attention to long-pending suggestions for building better means to respond to fraud in the P-3 process.

RAVU verification involves obtaining the A-file of the anchor relative and checking the currently claimed family relationship against the family information submitted at the time of the initial application. If discrepancies appear, denial or revo-

cation of approval is likely. But the process generally allows the anchor relative an opportunity to submit additional information, often including DNA testing at his or her expense, to explain the variances and offer more solid proof of the relationship.

All P-3 cases that had not yet traveled to the United States as of September 11, 2001, were subjected to the new verification process. This meant that a significant number of persons who thought that they had been approved for admission saw their cases reopened and their approvals suspended. Notifications of discrepancies were sometimes delayed, as were notifications of final revocation of admission approval. Therefore, many refugees who thought they had been fully approved for resettlement in the United States found themselves in limbo for months, and a great many for years. These limbo cases have received a good deal of media attention, often confusing the issue and blaming the delays and disappointments solely on security screening rather than antifraud review. The inordinately lengthy delays affecting these persons once approved for resettlement have attained special prominence in the strong criticism the program has incurred since September 11. Final resolution of these cases and speedy notification of the results must be given a high priority.[30]

Despite these rocky patches in the initial implementation of RAVU, the basic process is sound and much needed. Fraud has been a genuine problem that should be addressed systematically. NGOs agree fully with this position, although many suggest that the prevalence of fraud often reflects the depth of need in the refugee camp. They urge that tightening up on fraud be matched with other efforts to expand access to the refugee program. That idea is fully consistent with the general approach recommended in this report, but one must be realistic about the impact of expanding other forms of access. Even in the best of scenarios, there will still be enormous demand or desire for US resettlement that will go unmet. Temptations to commit fraud will still be substantial. Hence the program must definitely continue to make use of available tools to deter and detect falsehood. In the absence of good civil records, which is the case with many refugee situations, the A-file information (i.e., the family tree information developed when the principal alien applied to the program) may provide the best possible documentary handle on the issue. Of course, there can be innocent explanations for discrepancies, particularly for applicants from societies that are less oriented toward linking important events to clock and calendar. The system needs to make allowances for these problems, and provide genuine opportunities to explain family tree variances.

Other antifraud steps, some initiated before the September 11 attacks, have also been implemented in connection with the P-3 category. They include the development of a standard AOR form and instructions that must be used by all volags. The instructions now include a prominent warning about the penalties for submitting false information as part of the process. AORs may no longer be sent directly to the overseas processing location from a local volag office, but instead must be sent to the national volag, which is called upon to review the information for quality control and to report anomalies to the DHS. The RAVU process is now done up-front, before a P-3 case is cleared for interview by a DHS circuit ride team. Thus, in marginal or uncertain cases, DHS interviewers can be equipped with the RAVU information to use in exploring family relationships during the circuit ride interview.

The NGOs have been supportive of most of these steps, reserving, of course, the right to criticize particular aspects of implementation. The most successful of the post–September 11 PRM-DHS-NGO working groups was the one dealing with fraud issues. It came up with nineteen specific action suggestions, transmitted in the spring of 2003, many of which are in the process of implementation.[31] The DHS also has its own Operation Fair Refuge, with an action plan containing additional steps in the process of exploration or implementation. Continued vigilance and continued evolution of antifraud measures will be necessary, because entrepreneurs in the camps will continue to seek ways to defeat current measures. Situations have already been discovered where persons have planted dummy family members when reporting family trees during their own refugee interviews, so as to lay the groundwork for a later fraudulent family admission that would not be detected using current RAVU techniques. I was told that in a few instances, RAVU-cleared families were found to be composed entirely of unrelated individuals. As a general matter, however, the DHS's antifraud framework is now sufficiently institutionalized and sufficiently aware of the dynamic nature of

antifraud efforts that it should be able to find reasonable counters to new fraudulent techniques. The DHS is also considering making the AOR, with revisions, into a full-fledged government form. Such a step would be worthwhile, because it would probably strengthen the ability to apply criminal punishment to those who commit fraud in such a filing (although one should not expect a dramatic impact).

The ultimate safeguard in checking most claimed family relationships would of course be DNA testing.[32] It is currently in use in a limited fashion, largely in connection with anchor relatives' efforts to overcome a RAVU denial based on discrepancies in family information.[33] But it might be possible to use it more widely, as a far more effective deterrent and obstacle to fraud. One well–thought-out and detailed proposal that I received during the interviews would call for DNA testing for all refugee cases (save solo applicants) as a routine part of the medical examination required before travel. Once the mandatory use of such a procedure became known, the proponents explained, it would put certain kinds of "refugee brokers" and fraud rings out of business, and would end the nascent practice of claiming false relatives during the initial family tree interview so as to defeat RAVU screening. The proponents of this proposal also pointed out that it would carry genuine protection benefits for large numbers of innocent refugees, because it would largely shield them from intimidation by criminal syndicates pressing them to add impostors to their applications.

The major drawback to this proposal, of course, is cost. DNA testing currently costs about $300 per case, although the price has declined steadily over recent years.[34] Proponents therefore suggested alternatives to across-the-board DNA testing. For example, DNA testing could be employed on a random sample basis for a stated percentage of cases. Particularly if the sampled percentage is reasonably high, this prospect might increase the risk of detection enough to deter some organized fraud — although to a lesser extent than the main proposal. (Some were skeptical that it would deter the worst refugee brokers, who could still claim that most of their clients would get through.) Alternatively, if measures could be developed for adequate preservation, DNA samples could be taken routinely as part of every medical examination but tested only upon a later determination that such a step is necessary or advisable. (Taking a sample is a simple and inexpensive procedure, whereas the testing requires more expensive laboratory work.) Publicizing this step and what it means as a possible benchmark for judging later family filings could also help deter family fraud. Or across-the-board testing could be triggered at a particular site or for a particular population when other objective indicators of fraud, such as the RAVU rejection rate, reach a preset benchmark level.

These proposals for wider use of DNA testing carry considerable merit, and should be pilot-tested in selected locations. There will probably come a point when DNA testing costs decline sufficiently that it will make sense to include such testing in the medical exam for all family cases. Some NGOs have expressed skepticism about wider use of DNA procedures. But if such a change could greatly reduce the concern about fraud in refugee family cases, it might well make possible far wider use of the P-3 category. Nonetheless, there remain some important ethical and logistical issues to address before launching wide-scale DNA testing. Some test results could have a traumatic or tragic impact on the persons involved, such as a revelation that a child raised since infancy as part of the family unit is actually not related. Or a DNA test that reveals that a child was actually the product of a previously unknown adulterous relationship could trigger spouse or child abuse. An IOM paper helpfully considers the various possible roles of DNA testing in family reunification cases, including discussion of logistical and ethical constraints and cautions.[35]

RECOMMENDATION III-5: Review of family cases by DHS's Refugee Access Verification Unit (RAVU), which includes checking asserted family relationships against earlier family information in the anchor relative's A-file, has been a highly worthwhile development. RAVU also provides an institutional location for ongoing innovations to respond to what will inevitably be new schemes and patterns of fraud. The DHS should continue to work cooperatively with PRM and the NGOs in developing such refinements, and PRM should make the affidavit of relationship, with revisions, into an official government form. The DHS and PRM should also pilot-test wider use of DNA testing and should closely consider the costs and benefits of routine DNA testing as part of the medical examination all refugees must pass, particularly as testing costs decline. Ongoing improvements in the safeguards against fraud should permit an expansion in the availability of P-3 admissions.

3. A UNIVERSAL P-3 CATEGORY?

Many in the NGO community have long supported a universal P-3 category — that is, making P-3 access available to family members of US residents who prove that they are refugees, no matter what their nationality. These calls became more urgent after September 11, 2001, as usage of refugee admission numbers declined steeply. Why not, the proponents have asked, use those admission slots more aggressively for family members, at least until P-1 and P-2 admissions rebound? Instead, these proponents noted, the trend has run in the other direction. Eighteen nationalities qualified for P-3 in FY 1999, but the list declined to four in FY 2003. (For 2004, however, the list has rebounded to nine nationalities.)

These are worthy questions, but a bit of perspective is helpful. Although it would seem shocking to allow only a limited group of refugees to reunite with their families, and to parcel out those numbers based on nationality, in fact the situation is not nearly so stark. We do have a highly important universal family reunification provision for the spouses and unmarried minor children of refugees — the Visas 93 program. This is not limited by nationality and is available to the closest family members of all refugees. The call for a universal P-3, therefore, is a call for universal access by refugee parents of US residents, who are not eligible for Visas 93. (And perhaps the call also reflects a strategy that might allow a higher number of spouses and minor children to avoid the processing problems that have often beset the Visas 93 program.) Reunion of adult US residents with refugee parents can be important, but it is less compelling than the forms of family reunification covered by Visas 93. Some government officials I interviewed also thought that the admission of parents was more vulnerable to fraud than some other categories — not so much because of fraud regarding the parent (for whom DNA testing could potentially identify impostors), but because parents often have remarried by the time of the interview and have a whole new stepfamily to bring in as derivative relatives — a stepfamily that lacks a blood relation, and perhaps even an acquaintance, with the anchor relative who filed the AOR. Opportunistic marriages could result, perhaps at the instance of refugee brokers in refugee settlements.

PRM tries to balance multiple objectives in setting the P-3 nationality list. The Admissions Office of course understands the value of family reunification, but on the other side lie concerns about fraud and also — less widely recognized — the desire to assure that qualified P-3 applicants can receive timely processing in a program whose reach is manageable. DHS circuit rides, with the necessary preparation by an OPE, are costly to schedule and perhaps not worthwhile if only a handful of cases await processing in a particular location. One way to identify nationalities likely to yield significant numbers of bona fide P-3 applicants is by consulting the UNHCR document on resettlement need for the coming year. For the last several years, therefore, PRM has determined the composition of the P-3 nationality list based largely on those nationalities with the greatest need for resettlement overall, as identified in this UNHCR document.[36] No set projection of numbers from UNHCR provides a minimum cut-off, but in general nationalities would not be considered for inclusion absent identified resettlement need numbering in the hundreds. PRM in the past has also experimented with different formulae. The FY 1999 list of eighteen nationalities derived from an effort to incorporate a complicated multifactor matrix in which UNHCR projections played a more limited role.[37] Unfortunately, that expansion triggered such a large number of new filings, including a high percentage of claims that proved fraudulent but could only be weeded out by a time-consuming process, that PRM sought ways to create more restricted lists in following years.[38]

Shortening the nationality list may have been an understandable step to take before other and more targeted antifraud measures were in place. But it is much better to target fraud directly, rather than simply disqualifying large categories that may contain hundreds of genuine applicants. The system has now equipped itself far better for that task, largely but not exclusively through the RAVU process — strengthening not only its current review procedures but also its role as an institutional home for ongoing antifraud innovations. These improvements should be seen as setting the stage for expanding the P-3 nationality list, at least until such time as the other priorities are positioned to fill more of the admissions slots made available in the annual PD.

In fact, it may be worthwhile, at least on a test basis for a year or two, to implement a universal P-3

category, if only to provide solid data about just what such a system might accomplish and about what logistical difficulties it would spawn. Several NGO personnel with whom I spoke were convinced that such a step would generate thousands of new, valid refugee admissions. PRM personnel and some others were far more skeptical. They believe that the current formulas, although they could be tweaked to add a few more nationalities to the P-3 list, already result in P-3 processing in the main locations where significant numbers of family members could be expected to apply. New admissions, they thought, might only number a few hundred, and at a high logistical cost. A universal P-3 could spark unrealistic expectations that would go unmet because processing teams could not realistically be deployed to low-density locations.

Several NGO representatives with whom I spoke, sensitive to concerns about fraud, expressed support for a kind of compromise on these issues, one that would still allow a cautious form of a universal P-3. They referred to a processing change introduced in FY 2004, of which many NGOs have otherwise been critical. This is the restriction on the categories of persons who may apply for family members through P-3: for FY 2004, only persons initially admitted to the United States as refugees or asylees can file an AOR. (Before that, virtually any lawful US resident could file.) The rationale is that better family tree information exists in these anchor relatives' files, which can serve as a useful check against false filings. Although these NGO representatives would have preferred a universal P-3 category using the old filing rules, they would find the new restrictions on those who can file far more acceptable if refugees of all nationalities became eligible for admission.

When I discussed this possibility later with some PRM officers, they expressed a wary interest, but they still worried about stale cases and about processing capacities if there is such expansion. As we talked through these problems and possible remedies for them, I concluded that a viable pilot test of a universal P-3 category might best be constructed on the basis of the NGO representatives' tentatively voiced compromise, but with two additional constraints. First, to avoid stale cases, there should be a time limit between the refugee or asylee anchor relative's admission and the time when the AOR is filed. For an initial pilot trial, this period might appropriately be longer than what one would expect if a universal P-3 category became a regular part of refugee admissions.[39] After all, in the first year, filing would be possible for several persons whose family members (or at least whose parents) would not have had any earlier chance to qualify, because their nationality was not on an earlier list. Hence the lateness of the filing would be based on prior ineligibility, not lack of interest. Thus the pilot test might allow filing within, say, three or four years of the principal relative's admission. Second, publicity for the expanded program should make it clear that some applicants in low-volume locations may find that their cases cannot be scheduled for interview at all, or that they might have to wait several years until enough cases accumulate at that location to make the dispatch of processing teams worthwhile.

That proposal, a prudently constrained version of a universal P-3, merits serious consideration. Trying a universal P-3 on these terms for two or three years would enable a full assessment of what the impact might be, both on processing and on numbers. It should afford as well an opportunity to measure the risk of fraud through false stepfamilies or other devices. If the risks are unacceptably high or the logistical problems significant — or if P-1 and P-2 numbers independently expand to the point of using a far higher percentage of the annual refugee admission spaces — then the P-3 category could later be scaled back.

RECOMMENDATION III-6: Now that anti-fraud capacity has significantly improved, PRM should continue expanding the list of nationalities for whom P-3 access is available. It should also give serious consideration to implementing a carefully designed universal P-3 category for a few years on a trial basis, at least until the other priorities come closer to using all available admission spaces. This universal program, however, should use the AOR filing restrictions implemented in FY 2004 (permitting filings only by those persons admitted to the United States as refugees or asylees). Additionally, it should allow filings only within a stated number of years after the principal relative's admission, and should warn explicitly that cases in low-volume locations may not be processed, or may have to wait many months or years for processing. Such a pilot test should be carefully monitored for problems with either processing or fraud.

4. FUNCTIONAL FAMILY RELATIONSHIPS

Interviews for this project produced many comments that the refugee program should make better provision for functional family relationships in the chaotic aftermath of refugee flight. For example, in a conflict like that in Liberia, orphaned children may be picked up and cared for by distant relatives or by neighbors. This relationship may be established in the country of origin before the flight or only in the refugee settlement. Sometimes it leads to very close ties, functionally the same as family affinities, between the children and their caretakers. In many settings the caretakers refer to themselves as foster parents, but rarely are such relationships formalized through legal procedures. In this context, it can be traumatic for all concerned if only a part of the functional family unit is approved for resettlement in the United States. Some therefore suggested that the concept of family to be used in the refugee program should be broader. Foster children should be treated like blood children so as to keep the functional family unit together during resettlement.

The impulse behind this suggestion is unassailable. Resettlement should not add family separation trauma for those who have already suffered such separation once before, through the death of their actual parents or children. The system currently takes account of such a situation through the case composition rules that go some distance toward accommodating this need. They provide:

> For humanitarian reasons, other family members [besides the spouse or unmarried minor children] may be presented to DHS as part of the same case if they resided together prior to flight, continue to reside in the same household, and are part of the same economic unit as the PA [principal applicant]. Such add-on family members may be assigned the same priority as the PA but must establish their own individual claims to refugee status.[40]

These guidelines cover many of the functional family situations of concern here, especially since I was told that "other family members" for these purposes can include in practice so-called foster children who lack blood ties, as long as the other qualifications are met.

But because the rules invariably require residence together both before and after the flight, they will miss the situation of those children taken in to another family only in the refugee settlement. Some have urged that coresidence or dependency, such that the members all form part of the same economic unit, should be sufficient even if it occurs only in the refugee camp.[41] When I inquired about making such a change, DHS officials explained that such a rule would be too open to fraud. Requiring that the persons in question have shared life together in both settings provides opportunities for questioning about both locations that is more likely expose outright impostors. If impostors only had to present consistent stories regarding camp life, it would be easier to carry off the fraud. These officers candidly acknowledged that the existing rule will unfortunately bar from being considered as part of the same case some persons who have formed genuinely close family-type affections through perhaps many years of life together in the refugee camp. They pointed out, however, that the others might be able to gain access to the program anyway in their own right, particularly when group designations are the source of access. If that occurs, case allocation procedures covering ultimate sponsorships in the United States can often be used to make sure that the functional family members wind up in the same destination community to restore the family unit, and may even be used to assure that they travel together.

This concern is real and worthwhile, but I have not found a solution that is superior to the current arrangements without opening up unacceptable chances for fraud. PRM and the DHS should nonetheless keep this issue active and continue searching for better methods that might enable keeping functional family units of this type together.

F. URGENT CASES

1. GENERAL CONSIDERATIONS

The popular image of refugee rescue often includes spur-of-the-moment efforts to pluck people from danger and move them swiftly to the state of refuge. The reality of most resettlement is quite different — understandably, in view of the complexity of the system and the many moving parts that must be put in motion and kept in synchrony. Nonetheless, the system can sometimes gear up for extremely urgent action for large groups, as happened with the Kosovo crisis of 1999.[42] Such a

mobilization of course requires a very high degree of political commitment, running all the way to the very top levels of the US government, and so will perforce be infrequent.

But small-scale urgent cases crop up more often, involving an individual, a couple, or an extended family placed in immediate and life-threatening danger. The volume still is quite low, but the need can be acute. Part of the impulse behind the creation of the current P-1 category was to allow better for timely action to deal with these kinds of urgent individual cases. Unfortunately, as the program has developed, and particularly with the additional screening added after September 11, 2001, it is very hard to get the USRP to act with the speed needed for these isolated individual cases. UNHCR officials reported numerous occasions where cases of this type were referred to the United States but where the process took so long that UNHCR turned instead to other resettlement countries that are better equipped to act speedily, such as the Netherlands or the Nordic countries, or occasionally Canada.

I discussed this issue during several interviews. One opinion voiced during the conversations was that perhaps this is not a wholly bad situation — but instead marks out a healthy division of labor. The United States is quite good at running a high-volume program, a kind of aircraft carrier among the fleet of resettlement nations. But this means it cannot turn quickly to deal with smaller scale urgent issues. Nations with smaller programs, especially ones that can accept cases based only on a review of a UNHCR-prepared dossier, are the PT boats of the resettlement world, and they should be deployed for these purposes. Others acknowledged the difficulties the United States faces, but insisted that we should restore the capacity to move very quickly in a limited number of urgent cases — and that we should especially have this capacity for rescuing persons who have been placed in immediate danger precisely because of actions they took in support of US objectives or policies. They pointed out that even after September 11, we do sometimes move quickly for such purposes, as in the widely reported case of Mohammed al Rehaief, the lawyer who was protected by the United States because of his role in assisting US forces to find the wounded US soldier Jessica Lynch in the early days of the Iraq conflict.[43]

Today such cases are usually handled through the mechanism of parole, which is discretionary permission to establish physical presence in the United States, but without a formal admission.[44] Parole permits such presence without regard to the usual screening and inadmissibility requirements. And in principle, because parole does not count as an admission, the individual can be removed more easily if disqualifying acts or traits later come to light that were missed in the foreshortened review that preceded his or her evacuation. In practice, however, it is very hard — nearly impossible — to remove someone paroled in these circumstances (when there are indications of threatened severe harm in the home country), even if derogatory information is discovered later. For this reason, preparole review or screening, even if compressed or unorthodox, has remained quite important. Parole also has several drawbacks for the individual. Most importantly, it gives the person no clear immigration status in this country, and in most cases no direct avenue toward qualifying for lawful permanent residence. (Parolees in these circumstances may well qualify for asylum upon application filed after their arrival here, but success is not guaranteed.)

In reality, people paroled in these urgent circumstances are being brought to the United States as resettled refugees. It would make abundant good sense to treat them, as much as possible, within the framework of the refugee program, with its established immigration status, provisions for both private and public assistance, and direct avenue toward permanent resident status. What I learned during interviews about the steps needed to achieve governmental approval of urgent paroles led me to believe that it would be no more difficult to put together a similar set of waivers and urgent decisions in order that such persons could qualify as refugees under INA § 207. The program at various times has set up expedited procedures for particularly urgent cases. These should be revisited, updated, and revised for use in the post–September 11 environment. They will still be invoked only in a small number of cases, probably below 100 per year.

RECOMMENDATION III-7: PRM and the DHS should work together to restore the capacity to act in a matter of days or weeks to approve and resettle as § 207 refugees persons who are in grave and immediate danger and whose cases are referred by UNHCR or a US embassy. This procedure for urgent action cases should replace the use of parole to the greatest extent possible. Such cases will be exceptional and the volume of such cases can be expected to be quite low, thus making such special arrangements feasible.

2. PROPOSALS FOR A UNIVERSAL IN-COUNTRY DESIGNATION

As it happens, some urgent cases have to do with persons still within their countries of origin. Such persons cannot meet the Convention refugee definition, which requires that a person be outside the country of origin before qualifying as a refugee, and so they cannot be referred by UNHCR. But their need may be no less acute. If such cases arise in one of the three countries normally listed in the PD as approved for in-country processing, then inclusion in the refugee program is possible. Some have recently suggested a new approach to in-country designation in order to make provision for this kind of urgent case on a wider scale. They propose that the President designate all countries for in-country processing, although specifying in some fashion more limited criteria to make it clear that this will be invoked only in exceptional circumstances. Others have argued that such a universal in-country designation is not legally authorized.

In my view, such a designation could be done in a fashion that is consistent with the statute. INA § 101(a)(42)(B)[45] authorizes in-country refugee determinations "in such special circumstances as the President after appropriate consultation [with Congress] may specify." To date, the "special circumstances" specifications have been done by means of limiting this access to a short list of countries, although the PD typically does further state that such admissions shall be available only for those "otherwise qualified." Other guidance then spells out more precise criteria that govern access to the in-country program. But nothing in the statute requires geographic limitations as the way of honoring the "special circumstances" requirement. Nonetheless, the "special circumstances" requirement must be honored in some fashion. A Presidential specification that covers all countries would have to limit the reach of in-country processing in some other significant fashion. If all that is contemplated is a handful of in-country urgent cases, then it should be quite possible to spell out limiting criteria in the PD, in a manner that would be legally sufficient.[46] Whether such a universal specification would constitute wise policy is a closer question. Fuller exploration of the policy disadvantages is necessary before taking that step.

RECOMMENDATION III-8: The President has the legal authority to designate all countries for in-country processing, provided that other precise limitations confine its effect, thus honoring the **"special circumstances" requirement of the statute. Such a designation would hold advantages for a handful of urgent cases each year, involving the rescue of individuals from immediately dangerous circumstances in their country of nationality. But a full exploration of possible drawbacks should be undertaken before deciding on such a step.**

CHAPTER III. ENDNOTES

1 INA § 207(c)(1), (3), 8 U.S.C. § 1157 (c)(1), (3) (2000).

2 See DEPARTMENT OF STATE, PROPOSED REFUGEE ADMISSIONS FOR FISCAL YEAR 1994: REPORT TO THE CONGRESS 18-19 (Sept. 1993).

3 DEPARTMENT OF STATE, PROPOSED REFUGEE ADMISSIONS FOR FISCAL YEAR 1995: REPORT TO THE CONGRESS 19-21 (Sept. 1994). What we now know as P-2 (groups of special concern to the United States) was initially set forth, in the 1994 announcement, as a subset of P-1. In order to provide greater clarity on the differences between the system for UNHCR or embassy referrals and the group identification process, the priority description was modestly reorganized in 1995 (effective in FY 1996), by splitting off current P-2 from P-1 and renumbering the remaining categories accordingly. DEPARTMENT OF STATE, DEPARTMENT OF JUSTICE, AND DEPARTMENT OF HEALTH AND HUMAN SERVICES, REPORT TO THE CONGRESS ON PROPOSED REFUGEE ADMISSIONS FOR FISCAL YEAR 1996 18-19 (July 1995). At that time, the priority system took essentially its current shape, although of course the nationalities or precise groups offered access under each numbered priority (save P-1, which is not limited by nationality) have changed over time.

4 See UNHCR, RESETTLEMENT HANDBOOK: DIVISION OF INTERNATIONAL PROTECTION Chapter 4 (rev. ed. 2002).

5 DEPARTMENT OF STATE, DEPARTMENT OF JUSTICE, AND DEPARTMENT OF HEALTH AND HUMAN SERVICES, PROPOSED REFUGEE ADMISSIONS FOR FISCAL YEAR 1999: REPORT TO THE CONGRESS 8 (June 1998).

6 DEPARTMENT OF STATE, DEPARTMENT OF HOMELAND SECURITY, DEPARTMENT OF HEALTH AND HUMAN SERVICES, PROPOSED REFUGEE ADMISSIONS FOR FISCAL YEAR 2004: REPORT TO THE CONGRESS 7 (Sept. 2003).

7 See Statute of the Office of the United Nations High Commissioner for Refugees, UNGA Res. 428 (V) (Annex), para. 6 (Dec. 14, 1950).

8 INA § 101(a)(42)(B), 8 U.S.C. § 1101(a)(42)(B) (2000). See David A. Martin, *The Refugee Act of 1980: Its Past and Future*, 1982 MICH.Y.B. INT'L L. STUD. 91, 101-04.

9 DEPARTMENT OF STATE, DEPARTMENT OF JUSTICE, AND DEPARTMENT OF HEALTH AND HUMAN SERVICES, *supra* note 5, at 15.

10 Id. at 21.

11 P-4 covers married sons and daughters, siblings, grandparents, and grandchildren. P-5 covers uncles, aunts, nieces, nephews, and first cousins. Department of State, Department of Justice, and Department of Health and Human Services, *supra* note 3, at 20.

12 I was also told that a growing proportion of P-3 cases, before this restriction was imposed, involved filings by beneficiaries of diversity visas — that is, persons who win one of the 50,000 spaces provided annually as a result of a visa lottery. INA § 203(c), 8 U.S.C. § 1153(c) (2000). Because such persons could have brought their spouses and minor children with them at the time of admission under the lottery (see INA § 203(d)), this increase apparently raised suspicions about this use of P-3, although the 2004 limitation on those who can apply for P-3 family members was never expressly justified to me on this ground.

13 INA § 207(c)(2), 8 U.S.C. § 1157(c)(2) (2000).

14 See DEPARTMENT OF STATE, DEPARTMENT OF JUSTICE, AND DEPARTMENT OF HEALTH AND HUMAN SERVICES, PROPOSED REFUGEE ADMISSIONS FOR FISCAL YEAR 2001: REPORT TO THE CONGRESS 6 (June 2000).

15 If the person can qualify as an immediate relative of a US citizen (spouse, minor unmarried child, or parent) — a category to which no quota limits and hence no backlogs apply — then he or she must ordinarily use that route rather than gain admission as a refugee. 8 C.F.R. § 207.1(d) (2004); 9 FOREIGN AFFAIRS MANUAL (FAM), Appendix O, § 204. Under the regulation, this restriction may be waived "in the public interest," however, and in recent years, when it was clear that many refugee admission numbers would go unused, the INS and the DHS have allowed a blanket waiver.

16 *Empty Seats in a Lifeboat: Are There Problems with the US Refugee Program?: Hearing Before the Subcomm. on Immigration, S. Comm. on the Judiciary*, 107th Cong. 40 (2002) (statement of Bill Frelick, Director of Policy, US Committee for Refugees). The proposal also appeared in Bill

Frelick, *Rethinking US Refugee Admissions: Quantity and Quality,* 2002 WORLD REFUGEE SURVEY 28.

17 That is, most of the time the committee should look favorably on promptly accepting the UNHCR referral and designating the group as a P-2 group for purposes of access to the US admissions process. Actual admissions, of course, would still come only after individual DHS interview and approval.

18 See JOANNE VAN SELM, TAMARA WOROBY, ERIN PATRICK, & MONICA MATTS, FEASIBILITY OF RESETTLEMENT IN THE EUROPEAN UNION 113 (Migration Policy Institute, 2003). The US demand for a higher level of resettlement referrals also helped strengthen the momentum for UNHCR to complete the development of group referral procedures, described in greater detail in Chapter VI.

19 UNHCR-ICMC RESETTLEMENT DEPLOYMENT SCHEME: UPDATE FOR TRIPARTITE RESETTLEMENT MEETING (March 17, 2004), available on the UNHCR website, <www.unhcr.ch>. A similar cooperative arrangement for temporary deployment of skilled protection officers, known as the Protection Surge Capacity Project, has been worked out with the International Rescue Committee. Launched in July 2001, it is largely funded by PRM. The IRC's description may be found on its website, at <www.theirc.org/index.cfm/wwwID/555>.

20 The more elaborate procedures were developed and have been perpetuated in part as a way of helping to deter or detect integrity problems in the UNHCR resettlement system. See Chapter VI. Streamlined procedures, to be sure, would make it easier to disguise fraud or other manipulation — but it should be possible to find an alternative to current UNHCR arrangements that would be less cumbersome, while still retaining adequate checks and balances for integrity purposes.

21 VAN SELM, ET AL., *supra* note 18, at 11-12.

22 Department of State, How a Post Can Refer Cases to the Refugee Admissions Program, State 326248 (Nov. 24, 2003) (unclassified cable).

23 See, e.g., REFUGEE COUNCIL USA, US REFUGEE ADMISSIONS PROGRAM FOR FISCAL YEAR 2004: RECOMMENDATIONS OF THE REFUGEE COUNCIL USA (May 2003).

24 INA § 207(c)(2), 8 U.S.C. § 1157(c)(2) (2000). Persons admitted in this way are often called derivative relatives, because they derive their eligibility for the program from the characteristics of the principal alien, who is often called the anchor relative. The specified family relationship must have existed at the time that the anchor relative was admitted to the United States. A further administrative limit requires that the application for follow-to-join cases must be filed within two years of the principal's admission as a refugee. In contrast, most other follow-to-join provisions in the immigration laws allow such benefits without time limit. The two-year limitation was explained to me as a function of the special benefits and public assistance that apply to refugees. After two years the principal alien should be better established — and should then be able to use normal immigration provisions to seek the entry of close family members. See also Procedures for Filing a Derivative Petition (Form I-730) for a Spouse and Unmarried Children of a Refugee/Asylee, 63 Fed. Reg. 3792, 3793 (1998) (explanation accompanying final rule adopting

this limitation). The two-year limit can be waived for humanitarian reasons, such as a situation where the family members were missing or unreachable for a lengthy period. 8 C.F.R. § 207.7(d) (2004).

25 It is hard to conceive of a legitimate policy reason for barring the entry of mother and child in these circumstances, but this outcome stems from the particular wording of INA § 207(c)(2). See 63 Fed. Reg. 3792, 3794 (1998) (rejecting a suggestion, lodged in response to a proposed regulation, that derivatives of derivatives be allowed admission, on the basis that such a change is foreclosed by the wording of the statute). A technical amendment should be adopted to remedy this situation. Replacing "paragraph (1)" the first time it appears in INA § 207(c)(2) with "this subsection" would appear to cure the problem.

26 The precise reference of "Visas 93" is to a type of cable used as part of the processing, to communicate between the consular post and State Department headquarters. Technically, persons admitted as refugees do not receive US visas, INA § 211(c), 8 U.S.C. § 1181(c) (2000), but instead receive a different form of travel authorization from US officials that permits them to board the aircraft and apply for admission at a US port of entry. Also, the Form I-730 is used for two types of cases that look quite similar for the DHS processing center's purposes, but quite different to a consular officer, for reasons described in the main text to follow below. It covers both the family members of persons who gained status in the United States as a result of an asylum claim under INA § 208, 8 U.S.C. § 1158 — called Visas 92 cases by the State Department — and the family members of persons admitted as refugees under INA § 207, 8 U.S.C. § 1157 — Visas 93 cases.

27 9 FAM, Appendix O, Part 1700.

28 Small exceptions to this generalization exist for derivative relatives of a qualifying P-3 who accompany that P-3 for admission purposes. For example, if a P-3 wife meets the definition, her minor children in the interview room with her need not be found to have a well-founded fear of persecution. Similarly, if a P-3 father qualifies under the definition, the DHS need not make a separate refugee status determination with regard to his accompanying wife. INA § 207(c)(2), 8 U.S.C. § 1157(c)(2) (2000).

29 I was told that some version of this type of checking against A-file information actually existed in the early years of the Indochina program, and was done by the joint voluntary agency staff that was responsible for initial refugee processing. But any such systematic checking process had disappeared by the 1990s.

30 See, e.g., Mary Beth Sheridan, *Terrorism's Other Victims: Refugees Cleared to Join Family in US Stuck in Limbo After Attacks,* WASH. POST, Dec. 2, 2001, at C1; Rachel Swarns, *US Security Backlog Strands Many Refugees in Camps Abroad,* N.Y. TIMES, June 4, 2003, at A10; Anastasia Hendrix, *Post– 9-11 Delays Hurt US-bound Refugees: Security Checks Leave Immigrants in Dangerous Limbo,* SAN FRAN. CHRONICLE, Nov. 30, 2003, at A1. Although most of these backlogs have now been overcome at the screening stage, not all notifications of negative results had been delivered to the applicants at the time of my major interviewing in fall 2003. Sometimes this further delay resulted from UNHCR or host country concerns

about the notification process, particularly when RAVU screening resulted in a high percentage of revocations for once-approved cases. Some notifications were therefore delayed so that a comprehensive notification plan could be developed in order to deal with expected public-order problems in the camps. Such caution is understandable, but some notification plans seem to have languished for far too long. It is important that all final notifications in these cases be completed.

31 Memorandum from Joseph D. Cuddihy to Kelly Ryan, et al., Recommendations Paper from Fraud Working Group (Aug. 11, 2003) (attaching report submitted by coconvenors of the working group, Joe Martin of the Refugee Office of the DHS Bureau of Citizenship and Immigration Services and Anastasia Brown of the US Conference of Catholic Bishops).

32 Obviously such testing applies directly only to claimed blood relationships and could not verify an asserted marriage. Where there are offspring in the family, however, their DNA results could provide relevant evidence (with adequate allowance, of course, for adoptions and stepchild relationships).

33 See PRM to Allow DNA Testing for Refugee Family Reunification, REFUGEE REPORTS, May 2003, at 9.

34 This is not the true measure of the net per capita cost, however, because implementation of such a system should be offset by savings deriving from likely reductions in other antifraud measures, particularly in resources now devoted to catching and prosecuting fraud after admission.

35 JACKIE TAITZ, EXPLORING THE USE OF DNA TESTING FOR FAMILY REUNIFICATION (IOM publication, Dec. 2001).

36 See, e.g., UNHCR, UNHCR PROJECTED GLOBAL RESETTLEMENT NEEDS 2004 (June 2003).

37 See State Department Expands Family-based Refugee Processing for Africans, REFUGEE REPORTS, Sept. 1998, at 7-9.

38 See DEPARTMENT OF STATE, DEPARTMENT OF JUSTICE, AND DEPARTMENT OF HEALTH AND HUMAN SERVICES, PROPOSED REFUGEE ADMISSIONS FOR FISCAL YEAR 2001: REPORT TO THE CONGRESS 6 (June 2000).

39 In an ongoing program, the two-year limitation on filing I-730s in follow-to-join cases (Visas 93) would seem to provide a logical benchmark.

40 Department of State, FY 2002 Refugee Admissions Processing Guidelines, State 43737, para. 24 (March 6, 2002), (unclassified cable).

41 See, e.g., COMMISSION ON IMMIGRATION REFORM, US REFUGEE POLICY: TAKING LEADERSHIP 46 (1997).

42 See Kosovo: Outpouring of Misery, REFUGEE REPORTS, March/April 1999, at 1; Here Come the Kosovars, id., May 1999, at 1; Citing Kosovo as "Example of U.S. Leadership," State Department Proposes Increasing US Refugee Admissions, id., July/August 1999, at 1.

43 See, e.g., Jerry Seper, Iraqi Lawyer Who Saved Pfc. Lynch Granted US Asylum, WASH. TIMES, April 30, 2003, at A15.

44 INA § 212(d)(5), 8 U.S.C. § 1182(d)(5) (2000).

45 8 U.S.C. § 1101(a)(42)(B) (2000).

46 For example, the PD could designate persons within their countries of nationality or habitual residence who face grave threats of immediate harm, as determined by the chief of the US mission to that country.

CHAPTER IV

THE ROLE OF THE DEPARTMENT OF HOMELAND SECURITY

I nterviews for this project raised several issues concerning the role of the Department of Homeland Security (DHS) and its predecessor, the Immigration and Naturalization Service (INS). This chapter recounts and evaluates those criticisms and suggestions. Some of these issues are well on their way to resolution, such as a better under-standing of security requirements at interviewing sites — now generally resulting in timely deployment of DHS interviewing teams. Further improvements that respond to nearly all the identified problems would be advanced greatly by a change that the DHS has initiated, but that is on a slower path toward implementation than many observers would like. That step is the creation of a more central-ized and specialized refugee corps within the DHS to handle interviewing and related tasks.

A. THE NEED FOR A BETTER STRUCTURE TO RESOLVE DEPARTMENT-WIDE REFUGEE AND IMMIGRATION POLICY

The INS was abolished in March 2003 and its functions were transferred to three separate bureaus of the new DHS. The Bureau of Citizenship and Immigration Services (USCIS) inherited the services and adjudication functions of the INS. These include most responsibilities relating to the refugee program, which are principally handled by the Office of Refugee, Asylum and International Operations. The INS's enforcement functions were combined with those of the Customs Service and then divided between two bureaus, according to whether the function related primarily to border or interior enforcement. Border enforcement, includ-ing inspections of persons arriving at ports of entry, is handled by the Bureau of Customs and Border Protection (CBP), interior enforcement by the

Bureau of Immigration and Customs Enforcement (ICE). Both of these enforcement bureaus report to the Under Secretary for Border and Transportation Security (BTS), who also oversees, among other programs, the Transportation Security Agency. That Under Secretary, like the Director of USCIS, reports directly to the Deputy Secretary of the Department.

This split of responsibilities, coupled with the lengthy and sometimes confusing transition to the new Department, has caused problems when guid-ance or policy concerning the refugee program needs to be cleared within the DHS beyond USCIS — that is, on issues seen as having an enforcement component or impact. I heard of several instances wherein PRM sought approval of such items, but months passed without a definitive response from the DHS. As a result, no guidance or policy could be issued, field staff were on their own, and public spokespersons had to avoid commenting on the question. On many of those occasions, the officers in the DHS with whom PRM has principal contact apparently had forwarded a proposed response to other DHS offices in timely fashion, but some kind of deadlock emerged, and there was no readily available mechanism within the DHS for resolving it or forcing action being delayed by a single office.

This situation reflects a wider problem besetting immigration functions within the new department: there is no central location for determining overall immigration policy on issues that transcend the somewhat artificial enforcement-services split or for forcing offices to act so that a timely response is given. Several matters, not just affecting refugee policy or operations, have been bogged down in this fashion. On questions of overall immigration policy, some commented of the DHS that there is "no one home" or "there is no there there." These comments clearly exaggerate, but the issue is real. The DHS needs to move promptly both to resolve the pending specific requests and to create a central structure, probably under the auspices of the Deputy Secretary (though other frameworks are certainly possible), for decisive and timely decisions on matters that affect all three immigration-related bureaus — or all four of the relevant DHS units, if one is to count BTS as yet another player.

Sometimes the problem is not delay or drift. I heard of some instances where the speaker believed that needed steps had been blocked by DHS opposition originating from the enforcement units. Some State Department officers felt that this problem was especially evident in getting clearance on the consultation document that must be sent to Congress each summer as a prerequisite to issuing the annual Presidential Determination. One described DHS's role as ranging "from difficult to intractable." In this and in some other instances, some felt that DHS officials who were opposing gave insufficient attention to the real needs of a forthcoming refugee program that can meet the President's objectives. That is, they felt that enforcement personnel were exaggerating risks and underplaying advantages, discounting the views of those in USCIS with more direct responsibility for refugee matters — and that no adequate higher-level mechanism existed within the DHS to resolve the clash of positions. The enforcement objection could therefore turn out to be a de facto veto, but without an adequate department-wide airing of the question.

Some of these problems simply reflect growing pains for a new department, and it appears that improvements have occurred as time has passed. But sore points remain. A crucial example is the DHS policy that limits refugee flights to no more than thirty-five persons per plane, so that the DHS can assure that port-of-entry inspectors can fully complete their expanded clearance, review, and documentation responsibilities. Such a temporary limit was quite understandable when it was initially imposed in the months after September 11, 2001. But it imposes significant costs and complications on refugee processing and movements — costs incurred primarily by players other than CBP, which is in charge of inspections. The DHS is aware that practices need to be altered in order to permit larger planeloads, and I began hearing in late summer 2003 that the issue was nearing resolution. Highly detailed proposals have been written and reviewed, but proposed pilot testing of a solution was delayed at the last minute, and as of June 2004, there is still no definitive decision on how to proceed. Meantime, the overall program continues to be saddled with the inefficiencies that this policy imposes. Prompt resolution is imperative.[1]

To overcome problems of this sort may require a more active policy-setting and dispute-resolution role by the office of the Deputy Secretary of the DHS, because that is the official who is the immediate superior of both the immigration services and immigration enforcement units.[2] When I discussed this idea for a greater role for the Deputy's office as part of the initial interviews for this report, some DHS officers thought the suggestion far too bold, taking insufficient account of the vast range of responsibilities that the Deputy Secretary of the DHS already shoulders. I certainly appreciate the competing claims on that official's attention, and I do not suggest that resolving immigration deadlocks should occupy much of his personal time or crowd out more important issues. But it is wholly possible to provide for this role in the Deputy Secretary's office (or even the Secretary's) in ways that are realistic given his other responsibilities.

The parallel experience of the Department of Justice before the 2003 reorganization could be quite instructive in this regard. Since 1940 the Attorney General had carried overall responsibility for virtually all immigration functions, with the exception of those assigned to the Department of State (principally relating to visas and portions of the refugee program). Specific Justice Department oversight of policy and coordination of the immigration-related departmental units was the responsibility of the Deputy Attorney General (DAG) throughout much of the past twenty-five years.[3] The DAG also carried responsibility, of course, for a vast array of other sensitive and important functions, including much of federal law enforcement — an agenda probably just as crowded as that facing the Deputy Secretary of the DHS. And yet that immigration coordination role was manageable because the DAG was assisted by a small staff, reporting directly to him or her, that specialized in immigration issues. Typically a senior attorney, with the rank of Associate Deputy Attorney General (ADAG), led that team — often a highly seasoned and bright individual who did not necessarily have a background in immigration matters. The ADAG would be assisted by one to four attorneys or officers who did have considerable background in the immigration field, usually including past service in the INS or other related experience. At various times these latter officers held the title of counselor or special assistant to the DAG. The ADAG served as the principal eyes and ears of both the DAG and the Attorney General, to assure that immigration policy decisions were made in timely fashion and that policy was consistently implemented, to help identify and overcome conflicts among units on particular issues, and to raise matters to the principals of the Department when necessary for ultimate decision on highly important policy matters. Above all, this small staff helped assure that immigration issues did not simply drift without resolution. Most deadlocks could be resolved without the Deputy's direct involvement, however. The ADAG's personal attention was usually enough to force the agencies or officers involved to meet, hash out the issues, and reach some accommodation, without requiring resolution by higher officials, because it was clear that this relatively senior official could speak authoritatively, on most occasions, for the DAG. This latter attribute, clarity about the ADAG's clout and authority, was critical to his or her ability to force action and enforce deadlines.

There is nothing magical about the particular staffing structure employed by the Department of Justice, and the DHS could choose other workable arrangements. But some such central monitoring, coordination, and oversight capacity for immigration policy, probably attached to either the Secretary's or the Deputy Secretary's office is highly necessary, especially given that immigration responsibilities formerly under the unified responsibility of the Commissioner of the INS are now split among three separate bureaus. Whatever structure is adopted, no time should be lost in addressing this ongoing need.

RECOMMENDATION IV-1: The DHS should place a high priority on developing a system for prompt resolution of internal disputes over immigration- and refugee-related guidance and policy, a problem that arises when a given issue holds implications for both enforcement and services. The system must assure that services-related perspectives are given a full airing and are not drowned out by concerns emanating from DHS enforcement offices. Such a system will likely

require a far more active policy and coordination role in this realm for the office of the Secretary or Deputy Secretary, the only officials who have direct authority over both the enforcement and services units of the DHS. The Department should also move promptly to resolve currently pending matters for which a decision or clearance has been requested by other departments.

B. ISSUES AFFECTING INDIVIDUAL ADJUDICATIONS

I heard from both NGOs and State Department officers about inconsistent standards applied by different INS or DHS officers or circuit ride teams. Two successive teams interviewing the same refugee population might have widely variant approval rates. And particular officers on their own have sometimes insisted that they should begin applying the refugee definition with greater rigor than had been practiced by other officers. In response to this problem, the DHS has taken useful steps to improve the consistency of its adjudications. Each circuit ride now has a team leader who reviews all proposed decisions for quality-control purposes and consistency. For large teams, more than one such leader is appointed; the intention is to have one team leader for every six to eight officers.

Overcoming inconsistency is rendered difficult by the indeterminacy of the underlying refugee standard, which requires a finding that the individual has suffered past persecution or has a well-founded fear of persecution on account of race, religion, nationality, membership in a particular social group, or political opinion.[4] This broad standard leaves room for varying applications to particular fact situations as they are presented in the interviews, and oscillation between strictness and generosity in its application in the refugee admissions program has been a problem since the adoption of the Refugee Act of 1980.[5]

It makes sense to use a generous interpretation of the standard in the overseas program, even though the government should continue to use a more strict approach in asylum adjudications involving persons who have already reached US soil. This difference in emphasis is appropriate because the United States remains in full control of the volume of overseas admissions in any case. To be more precise, for asylum applications in the United

States, the only real control on the volume of ultimate admissions as asylees is the refugee definition. Those who meet that test almost always receive asylum; those who do not may be removed from the country. In the overseas program, the United States can apply a variety of other screening tools (such as the precise limitations on access categories) to assure that admissions do not exceed a preset level. That is one basic function of the priority system, which essentially allows the application of these other screening criteria, plus a kind of metering of volume, before the case is presented for a DHS officer to test the person's claim against the refugee definition. Further, the refugee populations covered by an access priority have been selected for the USRP based on a broad policy decision that they are generally in need of protection and of special attention by the United States. For these reasons, a generous interpretation of the definition in the overseas setting makes functional sense. This study found that the DHS generally agrees with this conclusion and strives to incorporate a generous application of the definition into its overseas operations. Contrary to the impression held by some NGO representatives, the DHS officers who have responsibility for this function are generally in tune with this approach. But ongoing vigilance to assure consistency is needed, particularly while circuit ride teams remain largely composed of temporary-duty officers. An officer new to the refugee interviewing function, particularly one whose normal job is as an asylum officer, might easily begin his work by applying the strict interpretation more common in the asylum process.

A related problem surfaced in the interviews done for this project. Much of the refugee adjudication interview must perforce be taken up with questions directed to the issue of whether the applicant has suffered past persecution or has a well-founded fear of persecution on account of one of the five listed grounds. Interviewing officers, who are responsible for completing a stated number of adjudications each day, often expressed the wish that they could spend less interview time on the definition and more time asking questions that relate to identity, including family composition, and to possible inadmissibility, such as drug dealing, or security risks — issues that have properly assumed higher importance in the wake of September 11. (The guidelines for daily interview completions were reduced after the terrorist attacks, precisely to allow more attention to identity and inadmissibility questions.) Given

that the US government has already made important decisions to favor admission of the population at issue (embodied, for example, in the P-2 designation or the priority enjoyed by persons referred by UNHCR), several field officers would prefer a system that allowed them to use more accessible objective criteria to determine initial refugee eligibility, thus freeing up interview time for the other questions.

Not all refugee situations will lend themselves to this approach, but USCIS could draw more thoroughly on information available through its Resource Information Center (initially developed primarily to assist in asylum adjudications) in order to provide more precise training and guidance (perhaps for certain populations in the form of rebuttable presumptions) that might facilitate more efficient and consistent application of the refugee definition. Detailed training on the particulars of conditions in the country of origin could be particularly profitable. (These suggestions are discussed more thoroughly in Chapter V, Section C2.) The importance of using the interview for these security-related functions also suggests that carefully crafted statutory revisions should be considered, in order to enable DHS officers to decide on basic eligibility through the use of more accessible or objective criteria — an issue addressed in Chapter VII, Section F. Such a statutory change could also help minimize the inconsistency problems mentioned in the previous paragraph.

RECOMMENDATION IV-2: The DHS should continue to use and refine existing quality-control measures to assure consistency in refugee adjudications, properly applying a generous interpretation of the refugee definition in overseas processing. It should also give ongoing consideration to other measures, such as detailed training on conditions in the country of origin, as well as guidance on specific situations that should be presumptively regarded as justifying a finding of a well-founded fear of persecution. Such steps would both advance quality control and consistency and also free up interview time to address questions of identity and inadmissibility, including security concerns.

C. Deployment of Circuit Ride Teams and the Security of Interviewing Sites

One of the strongest complaints about DHS actions in the wake of September 11 related to its stance regarding the security of interviewing sites. Some proposed resettlement initiatives in FY 2002 were squelched because the INS believed it unlikely that secure interviewing sites could be found. Many in PRM believe the low totals for that year resulted primarily from the INS's unwillingness to deploy to very many interviewing sites. This reluctance caused consternation in many circles because the possible sites usually already had a number of foreign nationals present, including UNHCR officers and NGO personnel, often including many Americans. Some charged that the INS (later the DHS) was being overly sensitive about security risks.

Those charges are unfair. A sizeable team of US government officers, posted to a particular location for six to eight weeks, offers a far more exposed and tempting target for terrorist action than do NGOs or even UNHCR. (Recent attacks on humanitarian personnel in many countries, however, including the murder of a UNHCR officer in Afghanistan in November 2003,[6] have muted this overall criticism about the DHS's security concerns.) Moreover, DHS adjudications officers are there precisely to make decisions, some of which will be negative and will therefore create disaffection and anger among the surrounding population. In these settings, extra care about officer safety and security is thoroughly justified — indeed imperative.

But such care can certainly be applied while sustaining an active and vigorous refugee program, as later events have shown. Although there were some misunderstandings over INS site security requirements in FY 2002, as of now the requirements are well understood, the regional security officers (RSOs) of US embassies in the processing countries have grown familiar with the needs, and a good cooperative relationship has developed in most locations. As a result, site selection and site strengthening (installing metal detectors and stronger doors, for example, and assuring adequate exits to be used in case of emergency) now proceed fairly routinely, and this issue has essentially been resolved. The DHS has a full schedule of circuit rides for FY 2004 and recently has been able to find or help develop approvable sites in the areas that PRM wants to target.

There remains a significant ongoing issue, however. Most group resettlement initiatives in this new refugee era will come from first-asylum areas that present dangers — such a feature is inherent in the nature of refugee flight but is compounded in a time of heightened terrorist activity. Thus the DHS needs to continue exploring creative strategies that will permit interviewing even in such circumstances. Greater use of seasoned officers who are deeply familiar with security procedures, for example, could permit deployment in circumstances that might be inappropriate for temporary-duty personnel. Enhanced training on security for both permanent and temporary staff might also help lower the deployment threshold. (Both these improvements would follow once the proposed refugee corps is fully in place, as discussed in the next section.) PRM has sometimes in the past wound up moving refugees to safer locations in order to permit DHS interviewing. It is obviously more cost-effective, whenever possible, to find ways to move the DHS to where the refugees are already located — or else to use modern technology to outflank the problem altogether.

Several persons interviewed suggested the use of technology, particularly video connections, that might enable US officers to interview persons who are in remote sites while the officers remain in the capital city or another secure location. In this scenario, OPE personnel would make sure that the proper documentary information is available to the officer and would also be in place at the remote location to manage logistics and to help applicants overcome whatever discomfort they may feel about the technology. Some officers I interviewed expressed skepticism of such a system, believing that certain qualities of face-to-face interviews should not be sacrificed, or that refugees in these circumstances may never feel sufficiently comfortable to reveal their full stories. These are reasonable concerns, but should not torpedo this idea. If such a video system can be deployed, the loss of direct contact is probably outweighed by the additional capacity to reach those refugees who may be most critically in need of resettlement, precisely because they are located in the most dangerous sites. Most officers were enthusiastic about the possibilities of such technological innovations, while still noting major logistical challenges, including protection of confidentiality when such information is being sent out over the airwaves. Also, some refugee camps are so primitive that creating the appropriate communications links may prove impossible. But there doubtless are sites where using the equipment is technically feasible, and advances in technology will offer expanded possibilities over time. DHS headquarters has been considering potential use of video equipment, among many other technological improvements.

RECOMMENDATION IV-3: The DHS should continue its cooperative work with PRM and embassy security officers to bring about the timely creation of secure sites for interviewing refugees designated for access to the program. It should also place a priority on developing new techniques that can expand the range of possible deployments, because a large number of circuit rides to potentially hazardous locations will be needed in the current era of refugee admissions. Better security training of deployed officers and more use of experienced officers permanently assigned to refugee responsibilities, for example, will help lower the deployment threshold. The DHS should also continue and enhance its active exploration of video hookup possibilities that could enable effective interviewing, when necessary, from a remote location, taking full account of confidentiality and other concerns.

D. THE REFUGEE CORPS

Significant improvements to the asylum adjudication system came about in 1990 when the INS created a specialist corps of asylum officers.[7] Inspired in part by this history, the DHS announced in 2003 agreement in principle with the idea of creating a refugee corps within USCIS. Without such a corps, circuit rides are largely dependent on temporary-duty assignments of other DHS personnel, importantly including asylum officers and some DHS attorneys. Although many of these officers prove to be quite effective in the task, others find it difficult to adjust to the rigors of life in a developing country. Using temporary-duty officers compounds training problems and can make it difficult to assure consistency in the quality of interviews and the standards applied in judging the applicant. Delays in deployment are also far more disruptive without a permanently assigned corps. Unforeseen developments, whether it be flooding in a camp or new security

alerts affecting the country of deployment, can require last-minute rescheduling of planned circuit rides. Even if the delay is only a few weeks, many of the temporary staff cannot so easily reshuffle the plans of their normal unit to be absent at a time different than the one originally planned for, and so may have to drop out.

For all these reasons, the idea of a dedicated refugee corps has gained wide support. USCIS recently took some key steps toward creating such a corps. In February 2004, it proposed a new regulation that would increase overall fees charged to persons applying for most immigration benefits (fees are not charged to applicants for refugee admission or for asylum). The proposed rule explicitly included in the fee calculations an additional charge that will provide the funding necessary for creation and maintenance of a refugee corps.[8] That rule took effect as a final rule on April 30, 2004, retaining the provision of funding for the corps.[9] The DHS has also spoken publicly of initial plans to staff the corps with eighty officers, who will be recruited over a period of two years, but further detailed plans have not been publicly announced. The basic notion, however, is to recruit officers who will be based mostly in Washington DC, but who are willing and able to be deployed abroad roughly half the year, often on short notice. I was originally somewhat skeptical that there would be enough business for the corps in Washington during the time officers will spend there, but was ultimately persuaded that such availability is needed to assure performance of necessary headquarters tasks. When not deployed to the field, many refugee corps officers would work in the Refugee Access Verification Unit (RAVU), described in Chapter III, or perhaps work on other antifraud projects. They would participate in policy development, beef up quality-control measures, and also help develop better training materials and backup information on country conditions that could make the work of field teams far more effective.

Some additional suggestions offered about the corps during interviews for this project might be useful — and so far as I know, have not been finally decided. For example, some part of the corps could perhaps be based productively in overseas DHS offices or refugee hubs. Further, the DHS might not want to use the corps to the complete exclusion of temporary-duty assignments, particularly of asylum officers, whose own training is relevant to the task and who often value the opportunity for this kind of variety in their work. Including too many of such relatively inexperienced persons on a circuit ride team presents the difficulties outlined in the initial paragraph of this section. But using them as only a small percentage of deployed forces might carry advantages, both for morale and for flexibility. (A staffing level of eighty officers for the refugee corps, as publicly announced, will almost surely require some regular supplementing through temporary assignments, drawn primarily from asylum officer ranks.)

These and other design issues will of course be resolved before the refugee corps is fully deployed. But these are details. An institution like the specialist refugee corps is greatly needed for this new era of refugee resettlement. DHS deserves credit for adopting these plans in a time of budgetary stringency, and should press ahead with recruitment and staffing as soon as possible — precisely because the consistent use of well-trained veteran officers offers so many advantages in overcoming the USRP's problems identified in this report. Full-time refugee officers are likely to reach more consistent outcomes and to provide for both better-quality interviews and better-quality decisions. They can receive more extensive training on security measures and safe practices, which should enable USCIS to lower the deployment threshold in hazardous circumstances. They are more mobile, and will be ready on short notice if needed to respond to an urgent refugee

situation. The development of the corps can also be the occasion for reviewing other management arrangements and controls, so as to assure vigorous and proactive guidance from headquarters, and to make sure that field implementation is fully in line with decisions made in Washington (reportedly a problem at times in earlier years). Moreover, the added officer time made available during stateside deployment can be used to improve policy development, training, informational preparation for effective questioning of a newly designated refugee population, quality-control, and antifraud measures like RAVU.

Recommendation IV-4: The DHS should move ahead as soon as possible with deployment of an expert refugee corps. This is exactly the kind of creative institutional change needed to handle the demands of admission processing when most future admissions are likely to derive from a multitude of disparate groups located in far-flung and often dangerous sites, to be handled by circuit rides rather than permanently stationed staff. Having a corps of full-time and experienced refugee officers should alleviate a great many of the problems that other players have raised in the past with DHS performance, and the concept has wide support throughout the government and among NGOs. The DHS should resolve the remaining design questions promptly and begin deployment as soon as possible.

Chapter IV. Endnotes

1 This issue is discussed in greater detail in Chapter V, Section C7, which points out that real improvement could be accomplished through rather simple short- to medium-term changes, while acknowledging that certain operational and statutory complications make the choice of an optimal long-term solution more complex. But the point is this: action should be taken promptly, either to choose a long-term strategy and commence implementation or to act on a short-term solution while more thought is given to long-term resolution.

2 More activist interdepartmental dispute resolution under the auspices of the National Security Council may also sometimes be called for, but it would be far preferable to avoid the need for such action through improving the decision-making structure within the DHS. For one set of suggestions on better departmental structuring for these purposes, including the creation of a centralized immigration policy unit within the Deputy Secretary's office, see DAVID A. MARTIN, IMMIGRATION POLICY AND THE HOMELAND SECURITY ACT REORGANIZATION: AN EARLY AGENDA FOR PRACTICAL IMPROVEMENTS 9-11 (MPI Insight, April 2003), *reprinted in* 80 INTERPRETER RELEASES 601, 608-09 (2003).

3 At various times the Associate Attorney General, the third-ranking official within the Department, filled this role instead, but the basic staffing patterns described in the text were still deployed to make oversight and coordination function effectively.

4 INA § 101(a)(42), 8 U.S.C. § 1101(a)(42) (2000).

5 Some of this history is recounted in T. ALEXANDER ALEINIKOFF, DAVID A. MARTIN & HIROSHI MOTOMURA, IMMIGRATION AND CITIZENSHIP: PROCESS AND POLICY 820-28 (5th ed. 2003).

6 See Pamela Constable, *Aid Agencies Cut Presence in Southern Afghanistan: Withdrawals Follow Killing of French UN Worker*, WASH. POST, Nov. 20, 2003, at A28; Mark Turner, *Aid Workers Seek to Shake Off "Agents of the West" Tag: UN Humanitarian Staff Fear that a Worldwide Movement is Emerging that Characterises Them as Legitimate Targets*, FINANCIAL TIMES (LONDON), Apr. 30, 2004, at 22.

7 See Gregg A. Beyer, *Establishing the United States Asylum Officer Corps: A First Report*, 4 INT'L J. REFUGEE L. 455, 467-85 (1992); Gregg A. Beyer, *Affirmative Asylum Adjudication in the United States*, 6 GEO. IMMIG. L. J. 253, 274-82 (1992).

8 69 Fed.Reg. 5088, 5089 (2004).

9 69 Fed.Reg. 20528 (2004). Some commenters criticized the decision to fund the corps through a surcharge on other immigration application fees, and a reasonable case can be made for funding of this national humanitarian commitment through appropriated funds. But new appropriated money will probably be quite scarce for the next several fiscal years, and it is at least a welcome sign that the Department has now fully committed itself to creation of the corps and has put in place a solid funding mechanism to support early deployment.

Chapter V

Operational Issues and an Overview of the Resettlement Process

Interviews for this project raised many operational issues and produced a host of suggestions for more detailed operational improvements. The most important are addressed in this chapter. The chapter opens with a description of the typical processing pattern for the resettlement of refugees as part of the US Refugee Program, from initial access through arrival in the US destination community. Variations on this pattern exist for certain specific refugee situations, but the basic description helps place into context the recommendations that will follow.

A. The Basic Process

The USRP's system for refugee access, case preparation, screening, interviewing, placement, and travel has evolved over several decades to accommodate shifting demands and requirements. Although the system constitutes an impressive achievement and admirably meshes the efforts of government officers, NGO representatives, and international organization personnel, its evolution has left us with highly complex machinery. I found during interviews for this project that even some persons deeply involved and expert in certain parts of the process may have only a dim conception of other key elements. Occasionally affirmative misunderstandings about what goes on in another part of the process have led to operational confusion, exaggerated expectations, or even anger or accusations of bad faith. A modest measure of operational improvement could be achieved simply by assuring that persons who play key roles in any part of the process are trained or briefed on the operations of the other actors and the constraints they face.

The basic stages of the process are presented in the schematic shown in Figure V-1, and are explained in the balance of this section.

I. Access

As indicated in Chapters II and III, access to the USRP is in three basic forms: individual referrals, group-based access, and family-based access. Individual referrals come primarily from UNHCR, which in most instances has already prepared an elaborate file on the individual, based on fairly extensive interviewing. The file may contain either a UNHCR Refugee Status Determination (RSD, finding the individual to be a refugee under the 1951 Convention or other applicable standard) or a Resettlement Registration Form (RRF, a lengthy document with abundant additional information obtained during a UNHCR interview), or both.[1] US embassy referrals and, in limited circumstances, NGO referrals may also provide individual access to the program.

Group-based access typically results from the State Department's designation of a group under the P-2 process, but may also derive from UNHCR referral of a group. In those cases, PRM usually arranges for an Overseas Processing Entity (OPE) to set up shop at the location where the group members are expected to apply. A prima facie showing of group membership then becomes the basis for access to the next stages of the process, via the OPE. (Exactly what is required to make such a showing, perhaps including certain kinds of UNHCR credentials or other identity documents, is more clearly spelled out in the detailed procedures implementing the P-2 designation.) For a P-1 group referred by UNHCR, access may at least require that the person's name appear on a list of group members pre-

FIGURE V-1

US REFUGEE ADMISSION PROCESS

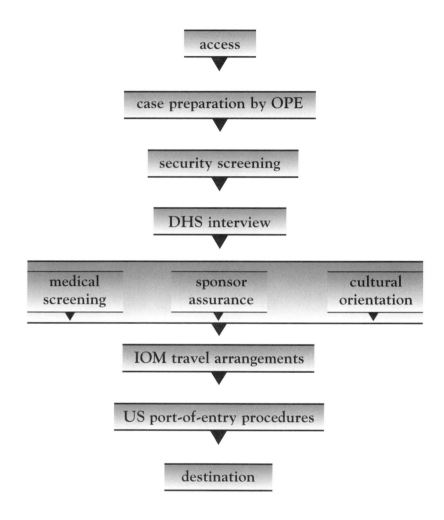

pared by UNHCR. But such group referrals typically will lack the detailed individual workups commonly prepared by UNHCR staff for individual referrals.

Family-based access (today the P-3 category) ordinarily depends upon proper submission of an Affidavit of Relationship (AOR) by the family member who is already resident in the United States. AOR transmittal was once a decentralized process that involved a local volag office's idiosyncratic affidavit form sent directly to an overseas processing location. Today there is a greater degree of uniformity, along with additional safeguards against false or manipulative filings. The procedure now requires the use of a standard AOR form (albeit not an official US government form). Further, for the last several years, PRM has required that AORs be submitted through the national headquarters of one of the recognized resettlement volags, who are obligated to review the submission before sending it on for processing and to report anomalies to the relevant immigration agency, now the DHS. Beginning in late 2001, the government also began to require that family cases all go through the additional antifraud checking provided by the RAVU. As of August 2002, the Refugee Processing Center (RPC) in Arlington, Virginia, receives the AORs and sends all family cases for RAVU clearance first, before transmitting the case on to the OPE. AORs that do not clear the RAVU are usually sent back to the volag by the RPC. RAVU review involves, at a minimum, checking the affidavit against the immigration file of the individual who signed it. If the family relationships claimed in the current filing do not match those described at the time that the filer gained his or her own status (or other immigration benefits) in the United States, the AOR may be rejected or else sent back with a request for more information to explain the discrepancy.

2. OPE CASE PREPARATION

Overview and background. For decades, access to the refugee program typically has not meant access directly to an INS or DHS examiner who passes on the person's eligibility. Instead it has meant access to a processing staff or organization, separate from the US government but funded by it, which performs certain basic screening and prepares the necessary documentation. The documentation summarizes personal and family information as well as key elements of the individual's case, to be used during

the DHS interview and for purposes of ultimate reception and placement. These organizations, formerly known in many locations as Joint Voluntary Agencies (JVAs), are now called Overseas Processing Entities.

Both terms require some explanation. In the 1950s and 1960s, when refugee processing focused primarily on East Bloc refugees transiting through western and central Europe, separate voluntary agencies each ran their own resettlement operations in the primary processing or transit locations. They tended to divide up the caseload according to ethnic background or other characteristic that was the particular organization's focus — or perhaps according to other criteria worked out with the US government. One way or another, escapees would find their way to the proper location for assistance in preparing their cases for INS interviews.[2] After gaining INS approval, the refugee would then normally be resettled by the domestic side of the same volag that had helped with the processing in Europe.

When the refugee program had to gear up in the mid-1970s to handle sudden massive outflows from Indochina, the State Department judged that it would be inefficient to do this type of work through its own direct-hire staff or to set up multiple volag operations in each new processing location. Hence it pioneered the concept of the joint voluntary agency operation. The State Department decided to enter into a cooperative agreement with a single organization selected (usually by the volags themselves) as the JVA in each location to do the initial case processing, as well as to perform certain other functions needed to meet the extensive organizational demands posed by the original outflow. But it was also decided that refugees thus processed would be eligible for placement with any of the resettlement volags in the United States and would not be considered the property of the one volag that had the JVA contract. An allocation process was refined, to take place after INS approval, in order to assure a fair sharing among domestic resettlement volags of the refugee population approved by the INS.

As the refugee program changed and began to process a wider variety of nationalities, sometimes in locations with much smaller volumes, arrangements for processing were diversified. Personal services contractors were hired by embassies for this work in some locations, and direct-hire staff did the initial processing work in Havana. In addition, the International Organization for Migration (IOM) began to seek JVA-type work, and it ultimately secured the agreement for such processing in several locations, including Cairo and Moscow. IOM is an intergovernmental organization and not a voluntary agency. With these new processing arrangements, PRM eventually changed the nomenclature to Overseas Processing Entity or OPE, a term that can cover a JVA or IOM playing this processing role, as well as the other possible scenarios.

OPE processing. In some locations, initiation of the OPE process is highly structured. For example, in the recent Abidjan program, a P-1 group referral, UNHCR supplied a list of individual names that it would present for processing. The initial list went to the Refugee Processing Center in Arlington, Virginia, which imported the names into WRAPS, the data-processing system for the refugee admissions program, thereby creating the initial electronic case file. UNHCR then brought the individuals by bus to Abidjan (if they were not already living there), timed to coordinate with the availability of the electronic files to the OPE. In other circumstances, the RPC's processing of an affidavit of relationship (AOR) leads to the creation of the electronic file and eventually a notification to the prospective refugee to come at a stated time for an interview with OPE personnel. In still other situations, the process can be somewhat more open to a spontaneous application process by persons who believe they meet the access criteria of a P-2 designation. Some will then be filtered out of the process by the OPE, before presentation of the case to the DHS officer. And other patterns are also possible.

OPE processing can be highly labor-intensive. It generally involves three stages, although the stages can be compressed or combined, particularly in circumstances involving a highly literate or sophisticated caseload. With other populations, the separate steps may be spread over several days.

During the first or intake stage, OPE staffers typically take a photograph and do a preliminary interview to capture or verify basic identifying information. Today in almost all locations they work with a computer file for the applicant and family that is part of the refugee program's relatively new WRAPS. The OPE usually also checks its own records to make sure that the individual has not already been processed and rejected. (Some earlier rejections, depending on the grounds, would not necessarily preclude a new filing, but the OPE must make this determination).

The second stage is called form-filling. More detailed biodata are collected, importantly including family information, compiled in a comprehensive family tree. Not only does this process help verify the identity of the individual being interviewed, but it also collects basic information that can be crucial for later determinations regarding the eligibility of family members who might apply for future refugee resettlement. The family tree prepared at this stage generally serves as the basis for any future antifraud screening — if the current applicant does resettle in the United States and then later applies for the admission of a relative as a P-3 refugee.

Getting accurate family information can require great patience and persistence by the interviewer, because many refugees come from cultures that do not place emphasis on exact birthdates and because family composition can be quite complex, particularly in societies with high infant mortality or an acceptance of polygamy. I witnessed one OPE interview in Africa where a refugee applicant, who could not read or write, was unable to give dates of birth for her husband, children, or siblings — a fairly common situation for members of that refugee group. In this situation, the interviewer carefully asked for her to name the children in the order of birth and to provide as much information about the timing as possible. Importantly, the interviewer pressed to assure that the applicant also listed any children or other relatives who had died, in order to make sure that the family tree was as complete as possible (and perhaps to help guard against a later false claim by someone pretending to be a child who was in fact deceased). Many NGO representatives and others stressed to me the vital importance of preparing a detailed and painstaking family tree at this stage (or even better, at the stage of initial registration in a refugee camp — see Chapter VI, Section C). The form-filling interview, which often involves working through an interpreter, can consume many hours. On the other hand, in those situations where more reliable family documentation is available, or even access to official civil records covering the applicant population, this stage can go more quickly.

The third stage is usually called casework. Here a different interviewer typically questions the applicant to capture the full particulars of the refugee claim and to record it in the file that will be presented to the DHS officer. This too may require considerable skill and up to several hours of time, because refugees often have only a dim idea of which parts of their background are salient for the specific purposes of the DHS refugee determination. OPEs generally assign this part of the case preparation process to expatriate staff, to help protect sensitive information. But OPEs cannot always assure that their staff will speak the language of the refugee population. Consequently, the training, deployment, and monitoring of interpreters remains a challenging issue in many locations. OPEs vary in the degree to which they consider themselves to play a prescreening or gatekeeping role. Many will refuse to forward to the DHS clearly ineligible cases, or they will advise individuals in these circumstances that their cases are ineligible and urge them to withdraw, but the limited sampling represented in my interviews for the project suggests that the threshold for such an action can vary greatly. In most cases of doubt, OPEs record carefully the information supplied by the applicant and pass it on for DHS decision.

The WRAPS system now serves as a key tool in the work of the OPEs. WRAPS gradually replaced earlier separate OPE systems and then in 2002 replaced the Refugee Data Center, which was managed by the International Catholic Migration Commission and served primarily to provide linkages for domestic resettlement operations. All of the major refugee processing locations except Havana now use WRAPS, and deployment in Havana is expected within the next year. WRAPS is managed by the RPC, a private organization under contract with the Department of State. Its director, however, is a highly experienced State Department officer. There were several glitches in the transition from the former data systems to WRAPS, provoking still-heated comments from some of the NGO representatives I interviewed in late 2003. Most of the transitional problems have been overcome, however, and RPC leadership is committed to solving the rest, although it must prioritize its work on the various fixes in successive releases of revised software. Many volag and OPE personnel are impatient for those revisions, especially to the family tree format, which is widely viewed in the field as unusable. Nonetheless, they recognize that WRAPS, particularly when the transition and the most pressing software revisions are com-

plete, provides needed automation, streamlining, and standardization that facilitate their daily work and can help generate required reports of various types.

Case composition. The OPE bears primary responsibility for case composition and interview scheduling, using fairly complex guidelines set by the DHS (originally the INS) but included in the periodic refugee processing guidelines cables from PRM.[3] For efficiency purposes, as well as for humanitarian reasons, it is important to keep family members together. Immediate family members (spouse and minor unmarried children) are entitled to admission on a derivative basis if the principal applicant qualifies as a refugee, without review of the family members' claim to refugee status. But it is also efficient for wider family groups to be interviewed together in some circumstances, either because the extended family insists on traveling together or so that the interviewer can resolve more readily any anomalies in claimed family relations. Because of these interviewing guidelines, which can vary from site to site, one DHS interview session can contain as many as a dozen persons, including several adults who must each satisfy the refugee standard individually. For that reason, the DHS officer must allow adequate time for separate inquiry into that question for each such person. Another OPE responsibility, however, is to separate out groups that do not meet the composition or interviewing guidelines, and also to be vigilant not to present unaccompanied minors for consideration until other required procedures have been followed. For example, each such minor is now required to have received a "best interests" determination (BID) by a child welfare professional supporting resettlement for the child, and the file is supposed to reflect adequate efforts to trace parents — so as to avoid child-trafficking or other manipulation of the system. DHS officers indicated that case composition and interview scheduling often give rise to some of the greatest tensions between the OPE and the DHS.

3. SECURITY SCREENING

For many years, the procedures have required that all refugees be checked against the State Department's CLASS (Consular Lookout and Support System),[4] but new security measures adopted in November 2001 strictly require documentation in refugee files that such checks have been completed before the case can proceed. Further, since September 11, 2001, additional names and negative information, drawing on a wider array of data sources, are gradually being added to CLASS. CLASS checks are based on name and date of birth. A CLASS check is now done efficiently via WRAPS, triggered as soon as the OPE has acquired the basic individual information needed to perform the check, and the result is also recorded in automated fashion. Most cases clear this check and can then be scheduled for the remainder of the process.

A positive response from CLASS (a "hit") does not necessarily mean that the person is inadmissible. Some hits may reflect information, such as a visa refusal years earlier, that would not necessarily disqualify the person from admission now as a refugee. Moreover, an apparent match with negative information may prove on inquiry not to relate to the actual individual now applying for refugee admission. For that reason, a CLASS hit often requires the fingerprinting of the individual, to enable more precise checking. IOM or embassy personnel usually take the fingerprints, which are then transmitted back to the United States for further screening. Often the person can then be cleared, but in some circumstances additional inquiry based on the information may be required during the DHS interview. Because of confidentiality requirements, in such cases the hit information is transmitted to the OPE in a sealed envelope. The OPE then includes that envelope in the case file that the officer will use during the interview, and only the DHS officer may unseal the envelope. A similar physical transmission process is required for certain other security-related hits and negative information developed by the RAVU antifraud process.

The other major element of security screening consists of what are called security advisory opinions (SAOs). This procedure has been used for decades for selected categories of individuals seeking admission to the United States, and is not by any means confined to refugees. SAOs became a major problem for the refugee program after the September 11 attacks, because new procedures implemented in November 2001 required SAOs for a far wider range of individuals, sometimes based on nationality and sometimes on other criteria. Moreover, the new procedures required SAOs for refugees in the covered categories after September 11 even if they had already been approved for admission to the United States (and so were expecting to travel imminently). The SAO processing machinery was swamped by all the new demands, which primarily derived from wider changes in the visa screening program, and a great many refugee cases languished as a result.[5] Through 2002, it was often difficult for sponsors or family members (or even PRM officers) to identify exactly where a case was stuck. After a very difficult period, however, SAO procedures have now been improved and given adequate resources, so that new cases are now reliably cleared within forty-five days of submission, if no negative information is located. Most cases that stalled in 2002 have now also been located and cleared, although work still proceeds on some of that old caseload.

The SAO process involves requesting additional agencies, including the Federal Bureau of Investigation and Central Intelligence Agency, to check their databases for information on the individual, based on name and date of birth. (The procedures include a check of similar names and nearby birth dates — especially useful in connection with names transliterated from other alphabets.) If information is found, then a procedure specific to the reviewing agency is followed to decide whether it actually relates to the individual in question, and if so, whether the person should be refused admission as a result. The overwhelming majority of requests in refugee cases do not result in the discovery of information even potentially relating to the individual, and when information is discovered, further inquiry almost always results in clearing the case. A second CLASS check is done through WRAPS if a security advisory opinion is requested and comes back as cleared, in order to make sure that no new derogatory information has emerged in the meantime.

4. THE DHS INTERVIEW

Overview. In a few locations, such as Moscow and Bangkok, the DHS has virtually permanent refugee staffing, and cases can be presented on a regular basis to DHS officers for an interview and determination. But in most circumstances today, the DHS has no team of interviewers permanently posted to the location and so must schedule circuit rides. Certain difficulties with that process are described in Chapter IV. Genuine rough spots in the transition to the post–September 11 environment, including misunderstandings about the INS's newly strengthened site security requirements, have now largely been weathered, and it is widely hoped that the deployment of a full-time refugee corps will help smooth future deployments of the DHS teams.

The case file prepared by the OPE, after many hours of detailed interviewing, data entry, and form preparation, is presented to the DHS at the time the refugee applicant or family is scheduled for interview by the DHS officer. It becomes the basis for the officer to move through the interview, making the necessary determinations of identity, family composition, refugee status eligibility, and possible application of any grounds of inadmissibility. Obviously, the OPE system promotes efficient use of the time of DHS officers. Those officers need only verify, with possible handwritten amendments or refinements, the information set forth in the file, and need not take time to record all such information from scratch. The OPE-prepared statement of the applicant's persecution story (coupled in some instances with a UNHCR report on that subject) also enables the officer to concentrate promptly on the key elements of the refugee claim. Nonetheless, DHS officers must pause to write down a fair amount of information during the interview. Some people suggested that future refinements to WRAPS should be developed that would enable DHS officers to download information from WRAPS that could facilitate their quality-control efforts, data tracking, and generation of reports.

DHS interview work is also labor-intensive, and the demands have expanded after September 11, 2001, to make sure that the interview process pays full attention to security issues. The number of cases an officer can handle per day varies based on the features of the precise refugee population at issue, as well as with the size of the family included in a particular case or interviewing session. But understandably the pace has slowed with the post–September 11 measures. In one location, for example, the schedule dropped from an expected twelve interviews per day to six. The pacing of the interviews has been a sensitive issue on some occasions. The OPE strives to provide the number of cases requested by the DHS for a particular circuit ride. But it sometimes happens that upon arrival at the site, the DHS learns of features of the caseload that may call for a different pace. Speeding up, however, can present difficult issues of coordination with the OPE, which may have staffed up for, say, six cases per DHS officer per day, and cannot quickly shift to a pace of eight per day. If the applicants are also being bused in from remote sites

for the interviews, a changed pace will also complicate travel logistics. No system can completely obviate such difficulties, of course. But these kinds of coordination issues support the suggestion in Chapter II for involvement of an expert DHS officer as part of a scouting or preparation team that lays the groundwork weeks or months in advance of a circuit ride, and so facilitates more accurate planning and staffing for all parts of the process.

DHS officers usually do not announce final decisions on the spot. Under procedures fully implemented over the last year or so, their notes and summaries are now reviewed by the team leader before a final decision is transmitted to the individual, as part of a quality-control process. Some NGO personnel complained of additional delays resulting from this addition to the DHS procedures, but it has added an important guarantee of consistency and reliability to the process. As long as DHS staffs up adequately for these purposes, team-leader review is worthy of continuation.

Applying the statutory standards. Sometimes officers of PRM, the volags, or UNHCR misperceive certain key elements of the DHS role, leading to misunderstandings, recriminations, and operational snafus. The DHS is required by current US law to make a finding that each principal applicant has suffered persecution or has a well-founded fear of persecution, on account of one of the five grounds spelled out in the UN refugee treaties (race, religion, nationality, membership in a particular social group, or political opinion), before approving the case.[6] The officer cannot simply adopt a refugee status determination by UNHCR nor rely solely on general information regarding country conditions to make this finding — although, of course, such a determination or information may be quite relevant in the process, and sometimes can make the DHS decision process fairly swift. Normally the individual applicant must provide information in the interview that is at least helpful to the finding. If the person speaks only of leaving because of crop failures or because of rumors of generalized fighting in a nearby village, the DHS may not be able to approve the case. Similarly, the DHS cannot, without a statutory change, use broader refugee standards, like those set forth in the Organization of African Unity (OAU) refugee treaty, even if the UNHCR uses such a standard for its own purposes in a given region. (The OAU definition allows inclusion of persons fleeing armed conflict, without inquiry into a risk of persecution; see Chapter VII, Section F.)

I also heard occasional complaints that DHS officers were not devoting interview time to asking about the difficulties of life in the first-asylum country or about the individual's special vulnerabilities in the camp. These complaints are misplaced. Such factors may play an important role in designating a P-2 group or in choosing an individual for UNHCR referral to the USRP, but they do not cast light on the critical finding that the DHS must make before approving admission as part of the refugee program — the person's risk of persecution *in the country of origin*. Most DHS officers are willing to take as a given the person's or group's vulnerability in the asylum country; otherwise the referral or group designation probably would not have taken place. But they understandably reserve their interview time for the issues that have a real bearing on their statutorily required decisions.

For these reasons, an approval rate of 100 percent is an unrealistic expectation in any DHS interviewing process. In any event, predictions or implied promises — to UNHCR or others — of specific case approval rates are very likely to sow embarrassment or bitterness. The DHS needs to take a forthcoming and generous attitude toward applying the refugee standard in overseas refugee processing (as discussed in Chapter IV, Section B, it has incorporated steps to help assure a uniform and forthcoming approach to adjudication), but it cannot abandon its central focus on its statutory obligation.[7]

The DHS is also required to pay close attention to issues of identity and inadmissibility. For example, a person may be judged a refugee under the statutory definition, but denied approval for the USRP because of continued drug use or some other trait or past act that runs afoul of the applicable admissibility provisions in the Immigration and Nationality Act.[8] Refugees are exempted from a few of the inadmissibility grounds (such as likelihood of becoming a public charge), and many of the remaining grounds may be waived, in the discretion of the DHS, for humanitarian or family unity reasons, or when waiver is otherwise in the public interest.[9] The process changes implemented in late 2001 equip the system more effectively to deal with these issues, including the RAVU antifraud system, the CLASS check documentation requirement, and the expanded use of SAOs for selected categories of applicants. These aids are most efficient if the checks can be done in advance of the DHS interview, permitting the DHS officer to use in the course of the interview any potentially negative information received. As noted, the interview can also be used to clear up negative information that has been misattributed to the applicant. For all new cases, RAVU and CLASS checks must now be completed in advance of the interview. SAOs are also requested before the interview, if the triggering criteria are known in advance (as is usually the case — for example, when an SAO is required for all adult males from a certain country). But the SAO process often has not been completed by the time of the DHS circuit ride, and current policy permits the interviews to proceed in these circumstances. Final DHS approval cannot be granted until the SAO clearance is received, however. As the SAO process improves, the aim is to have the results of the SAO review in hand before the DHS interview, to obviate any need for a second interview.

Requests for reconsideration. A negative DHS decision may not be appealed as such. But it is now a fairly common practice for those applicants who are denied by DHS to file requests for reconsideration (RFRs, sometimes also referred to as motions to reopen) with the OPE or with the DHS Office of Refugee, Asylum, and International Operations in Washington, DC. Applicants may be assisted in this process by OPE staff, on limited occasions by UNHCR, or by other refugees in the camp or settlement. I heard accounts of some denied applicants who later set themselves up as a sort of "lawyer" or expert on the US process, who would, for a fee, draft RFRs for other individuals. Many such requests are highly generalized or cookie-cutter documents simply alleging a general failure to heed the evidence or an unexplained problem with translation. The most helpful requests provide details on the alleged defects in the initial interview or decision.

Views on RFRs varied greatly during project interviews. Some with whom I spoke were skeptical or hostile, viewing such requests as unnecessary steps that clog the system, at least when used indiscriminately. Some OPEs were regarded as overly aggressive in promoting RFRs or pressing them through multiple rounds of reconsideration. And it is true that RFRs, particularly if not dealt with promptly, can complicate other parts of the response to a refugee crisis. For example, UNHCR will usually withhold any effort to find another durable solution for the individual (such as placement with another resettlement country) while such a request is pending. Moreover, the request may delay any step by UNHCR to remove a denied refugee from a transit processing center back to the original refugee camp — thus hindering the smooth flow of new cases into the system in those locations where the host country places limits on the numbers of refugees at the processing site. On the other hand, most DHS personnel with whom I spoke (as well as several other people) were generally supportive of the RFR process. Mistakes can certainly be made in the initial decision, and the DHS is open to reconsideration when warranted — through either a paper review or, on infrequent occasions, a second interview. But they acknowledged that boilerplate filings serve little purpose except delay and can compound other processing complications. The DHS is now actively considering ways to standardize and improve the RFR process.[10]

5. MEDICAL SCREENING, SPONSOR ASSURANCES, AND CULTURAL ORIENTATION

After DHS approval, three further processes are set into motion, roughly simultaneously, all of which are to be completed before the refugee will be travel-ready. These are (1) medical screening; (2) the so-called assurance process by which the case is matched up with a US resettlement volag as a sponsor that will take charge of the person's reception and placement in the US destination community; and (3) cultural orientation — a training process meant to equip the refugees with certain basic knowledge and skills needed to function in the different culture to which they are moving.[11] Under ideal circumstances, these steps can be completed over the course of four to six weeks, but often they take longer.

If some other review or screening is required even after initial DHS approval, much longer postinterview delays can be introduced. Additional delays that exceed a year (as happened often in the immediate aftermath of September 11 but are now infrequent) compound other difficulties, because certain other clearances are valid only for a limited period of time. Most medical clearances are good for only one year, for example, and fingerprint clearances are valid for fifteen months. Travel delays beyond that period then require redoing the clearance.

WRAPS was designed and pilot-tested well before the added procedures introduced after the September 11 attacks. Hence, it was not initially well equipped to give precise information about the reason for postinterview holds — a frequent and frustrating occurrence for a great many refugee applicants through 2002 and part of 2003, because they were stalled awaiting SAO or RAVU clearance. This meant that early WRAPS reports could not adequately reveal the real-world status of a held case, which might appear to be generally travel-ready, having been DHS-approved (before implementation of the new clearance requirements), medically cleared, and assured of sponsorship. WRAPS has now developed ways to solve or work around such problems and generally to provide adequate information on holds. These problems have faded in significance anyway as screening systems have improved so that they can provide timely clearance in the vast majority of cases.

One other change in practices after September 11 often causes further delays. If the results of SAO or CLASS checks have not been received at the time of DHS adjudication, DHS officers no longer apply to the Form I-590 application the stamp showing approval of the case, despite a positive decision on the individual's refugee status. Thus the OPE has to resubmit to the DHS the physical Form I-590 and the case file once those results are received for the DHS to apply the stamp. Where there is a permanent DHS office, officers are reasonably accessible for this purpose. But because most refugee processing sites lack this advantage, OPEs must often send file and form via express courier to a distant DHS office — a cumbersome and costly process. Of course, it is essential that the individual not be allowed to travel until all those checks are complete, but several persons I interviewed thought that other procedures would be sufficient to guard against that result. After all, they pointed out, the DHS does stamp approval on the form well before completion of the (equally obligatory) medical screening or the sponsor assurance process. The OPE is then responsible to guarantee that the person does not travel until those steps are concluded.

Medical screening. All refugees must receive a medical clearance from a Public Health Service–approved physician before they may travel to the United States. In some locations these examinations are performed by "panel physicians," local doctors on the embassy-approved list. But when the numbers are substantial or the need urgent, PRM usually arranges with the International Organization for Migration to provide the medical screening. IOM has impressive capacities to deploy mobile labs and teams of health professionals to carry out the examinations efficiently and in full accordance with US requirements and protocols. Their doctors also help individuals deal with any medical problems that are identified, including treatment so that they can gain medical clearance.[12] Most medical clearances are good for one year. Thus, if other problems delay travel beyond that time frame (a common development over the last couple of years, but now diminishing), the medicals will need to be redone. Those refugees who are found to have certain medical conditions, such as tuberculosis, may receive only a limited form of medical clearance, good for six months or some shorter period. Cases with Class A excludable medical conditions, including HIV/AIDS, require a waiver of inadmissibility before movement to the United States. Cases with serious medical problems are specially flagged so that placement with a US resettlement volag can take account of this factor. Medical screening is paid for by the US government.

Sponsor assurances. Assurances from US resettlement volags are obtained through an intriguingly complex system whose centerpiece is a weekly meeting at the RPC in Arlington, Virginia. WRAPS generates a list of DHS-approved cases to be allocated among the ten volags whose representatives gather (in person or by video hookup to New York) for these meetings. The list, distributed in advance, indicates country of origin, family size, names and ages of the family members, religious preference, medical needs, and certain other characteristics that may be helpful in deciding on an appropriate placement. It also indicates if the members already have extended family or other connections in the United States, so that placement in a particular US location is desirable or requested. Separate family groups that must travel together are "hard cross-referenced"; other groups that are supposed to wind up in the same location but are not necessarily traveling together are "soft cross-referenced." At the meeting, cases with specific medical requirements but no specific geographical limits are first dealt with. After these cases are allocated, other "free cases" are distributed, largely according to an allocation formula meant to bring each volag as close as possible to its preset allocation percentage for the year. Finally,

"geo cases"(wherein the refugee has indicated a reason to go to a specific location) are allocated. Within that pool, those hoping to go to a city that has only one or two local volag affiliates are dealt with first.

This initial allocation is only the first step in the placement. After the meeting, the volag to which the case is assigned then contacts a local affiliate to make sure that it is prepared to handle the responsibilities of reception and placement. If it is not, or if the initial allocation was made on the basis of a relative in the stated city, but the relative cannot be found or expresses hostility or indifference to the arriving family, then the case may be returned to the pool at a future meeting for reallocation. On the other hand, if the placement suits the local office or affiliate — which is usually the case — the volag executes a written "assurance" that is transmitted to the RPC. WRAPS must show receipt of an assurance before the refugee can move forward to the next stage. The volags are expected to move from allocation to assurance within four weeks, and this guideline is usually met. More urgent cases can be expedited, either individually or by group designation.

Cultural orientation. Medical clearances and assurances are the major post-DHS obstacles to be cleared. Cultural orientation, usually provided under the auspices of the OPE, is sometimes delayed until those steps have been completed. The cultural orientation classes may all be held within the final week or two before actual travel. I heard many suggestions for changes in the length or emphasis of cultural orientation, especially the suggestion that classes held shortly before departure include several days of work on basic survival English. But I lacked the time to pursue these suggestions in detail.

6. TRAVEL, PORT-OF-ENTRY PROCEDURES, AND ARRIVAL AT THE DESTINATION

Once medical clearances and assurances have been received (as well as any security clearances not obtained before or during the DHS review), the refugees are "travel-ready." The OPE prepares, according to a specific ordering and protocol, a detailed travel packet that contains documentation of various kinds,[13] including the officially stamped and DHS-approved Form I-590. IOM, which has played a major refugee travel role since its founding in the 1950s, takes charge of booking the travel and making the final connections to get the refugees and their belongings on the airplane, along with all the documentation. The USRP for decades has treated the cost of the flights as a transportation loan to the refugee, eventually to be repaid.[14] The sponsoring volags in the United States are responsible for securing repayment, and they get to keep a portion (now 25 percent) of the proceeds as compensation for their collection efforts.

IOM typically meets any plane carrying refugees in any connecting foreign airport and assures that the refugees transfer without difficulty. Then IOM personnel meet the plane in the US port of entry, and escort the refugees through the inspection process there. IOM's highly professional staff performs this work with efficiency and care, including multiple steps to check and double-check lists and documentation, both before boarding and on arrival in the United States. Since September 11, as specified under expanded US government requirements, IOM is especially vigilant to verify the identity of the refugee prior to embarkation, to assure that the person who boards is the same as the one for whom the travel packet was prepared.

Upon arrival at the US port of entry, the refugees are usually kept together in a room separate from the main lines and booths of primary inspection. A designated DHS inspector meets them there, and with IOM's assistance, individually opens the travel packet and checks the documentation, then asks the necessary questions of each individual refugee before approving admission and entering that approval on the appropriate documents and records. Some of the documents will remain with the refugee to be used for onward travel or reception at the US destination.

New processing requirements imposed in the wake of the September 11 attacks have had a significant impact on travel arrangements. Among the security improvements adopted in November 2001 was a decision to do full fingerprinting of all refugees fourteen years old or older upon their arrival at the port of entry. Because of the cumbersomeness of that process, the INS imposed a thirty-person-per-flight limitation on refugee arrivals. Eventually, the government was able to transfer the fingerprinting work to a contractor at most ports of entry, using a specialized inkless process that immediately indicates whether valid prints were captured. As a result, the

per-plane quota was raised to thirty-five. In addition, the DHS now has sophisticated electronic fingerprint capacity deployed in four overseas locations. Refugees from those sites (Moscow, Vienna, Nairobi, and Kakuma Camp in Kenya) — nearly half of the refugees who moved in FY 2003 — do not need to be fingerprinted at the port-of-entry, save in a few cases where difficulty with the initial prints requires a new set. By most accounts the specialized contractor-operated fingerprinting process now moves quite swiftly at the ports, except for one contingency that has occasionally arisen. The contractor was not authorized (or at least not initially) to approve overtime pay for its employees. When a refugee flight was delayed or the work otherwise backed up, therefore, the prints often had to be taken by DHS inspectors, who usually were not as skilled at the process as the contract personnel, thus compounding delays.

These fingerprinting improvements might have enabled a significant increase in the per-plane refugee passenger limits, but for a legal change that took effect in November 2002. The Enhanced Border Security and Visa Entry Reform Act mandated, as of that date, that all refugees receive an employment authorization document (EAD) "immediately upon [their] arrival in the United States," and that the document contain a fingerprint and a photograph.[15] The INS initially implemented this requirement through the use of an older version of EAD-generating machinery, which is unfortunately quite labor-intensive. The INS and the DHS initially resisted suggestions that they contract out the physical preparation of the document. (Actual approval and issuance of the EAD would remain the responsibility of the inspector, of course.) As a result, a great deal of an inspector's time in dealing with the arrival of a refugee flight is currently consumed with the EAD process, and consequently the thirty-five-person-per-flight ceiling has remained in place. The ceiling had only a limited impact through FY 2002 and 2003, because admissions were generally running at a slower pace anyway. But with the pace of resettlement now rising, the per-plane ceiling risks becoming a major bottleneck, as well as a particular hindrance to the use of charter flights. The DHS and PRM have been working to overcome this problem, but a full resolution has taken an extraordinarily long time — to the frustration of NGOs and many governmental players.

Port-of-entry processing needs to move at a relatively predictable pace, because IOM books onward flights for the refugees after allowing a few hours for the inspection process. This practice avoids the added cost of obtaining lodging in the port city. If all goes well, IOM escorts refugees, after they clear inspection, onward to the flight that will take them to their destination. Refugees are not escorted on connecting flights within the United States. The sponsoring volag meets the arriving refugees at their final destination, takes them to their initial lodging, and is responsible for guiding them through the early steps of settling in to the new community, including obtaining social security cards, school registration, and a job search. The volag receives a per capita reception and placement grant from PRM to help support this initial work. Other federal programs are available to provide specific forms of assistance thereafter, mostly managed by the Office of Refugee Resettlement (ORR) in the Department of Health and Human Services.[16]

B. OVERALL OBSERVATIONS: THE NEED FOR A RESOLUTELY MANAGERIAL APPROACH

As is apparent from the previous section, our highly complex refugee admissions machinery requires the close meshing of many parts to operate effectively. Moreover, important responsibilities are divided among many players: international organizations, primarily the UNHCR and IOM; NGOs, chiefly in the roles of OPE and domestic resettlement sponsors; and several US government offices, principally USCIS in the Department of Homeland Security and PRM in the Department of State. When pieces fall out of alignment, restoring effective functioning can pose a major challenge. That overall monitoring and management task necessarily falls on the US government players. But on precisely whom? The division of crucial functions between USCIS (formerly the INS) and PRM means that no one entity is fully responsible and accountable for the operations of the refugee admissions program.

If each of these two offices were solely responsible for distinctly separate or sequential phases of the process, the division might be less problematic. The overlap of responsibilities, however, actually comes into play at many points. PRM plays the key role on access decisions, through its relationships with UNHCR (for referrals) and its centrality in

group designations. But group designation decisions must take account of where the refugees will be processed and interviewed, and the DHS's requirements for site security then become important. To assure safe sites requires close work with embassy security officers and often with UNHCR, which may be in charge of refugee camp facilities that need alteration to provide the needed security for interviewing. The more significant and potentially problematic division of responsibilities arises during the time the circuit ride team is on site. Much of the OPE's case preparation work is designed to fit effectively with the needs of the DHS officers during the interviews. If there are problems from DHS's point of view, however, with the pace of case presentation, case composition, interpreter quality, or other issues, the DHS cannot simply direct the OPE to function in a different fashion. The OPE has a cooperative agreement with PRM and looks primarily to the State Department refugee coordinator (Refcoord) for that country or region or to the PRM Admissions Office in Washington for direction and guidance. Similarly, an OPE that believes it has suggestions for improvements or changes in DHS operations on site, perhaps owing to its greater familiarity with the region or the caseload, often feels inhibited in raising such suggestions directly with the DHS. Instead it must go through the Refcoord, who may well be posted to a distant office and is on site only intermittently during the circuit ride, or to the clearly distant PRM headquarters.

Through much of the program's history, a sufficiently cooperative relationship between the INS and PRM has existed to permit joint action in solving problems despite the mix of responsibilities. But the division probably has always inhibited proactive measures to find efficiencies and to innovate. More pointedly, the strains imposed by the processing changes adopted in the wake of September 11 exposed the vulnerabilities of this dual system. Nimble response to new difficulties was hampered by the lack of clear lines of responsibility. Interviews for this project produced numerous accounts of drift and some of unseemly finger-pointing between government agencies, as officers felt the heat for the slowdown in admissions.

If it were only the September 11 changes that presented this sort of problem, then there would be less reason to worry about the implications of the divisions of responsibility, because the strains of a difficult transition are now diminishing. Obviously, September 11 brought a major shift in public and official attitudes, and also ushered in complex new changes to the overall US immigration systems. It is not at all surprising that such changes produced significant transition problems, problems that had an impact on the refugee program. Systems for security screening, to take but one example, had to be revised, not only substantively but also quantitatively, to handle a volume of work massively larger than before. The institutional transition from the INS to the DHS occurred in the middle of these changes, as did the changeover to the WRAPS computer system. To retool one of these systems would have been difficult; to redo many of them at once produced major challenges. That the overall admissions system lost productivity during the changeover is not surprising, nor that it would require a multiyear effort to restore functioning to a level that enables full use of the humanitarian resource that resettlement spaces and funding represent. Nonetheless, many of these changeovers are nearing a successful conclusion, and the new procedures or systems are now approaching routine functioning, on a reliable time frame. The key is to sustain efficient functioning now that heavy transition costs have been paid.

Here, then, is the reason for ongoing concern. The ability of this multiheaded system to adapt and find cooperative solutions before 2001 was greatly facilitated by the fact that admissions were dominated by a few major programs with relatively permanent operations and INS staffing. In an era where the program is dominated by a more diverse range of smaller admission initiatives, most of shorter duration, the program will not have the time or the infrastructure to enable a more leisurely discovery of ad hoc solutions.

The ideal organizational fix for such a situation would be to unify management responsibility and accountability in a single agency. Some interviews produced broad suggestions to this end, and in the abstract, they hold many attractions. Such a change, however, is simply not in the cards. It is essential that a major portion of refugee admissions decision making remain with the State Department. Such decisions must mesh with other elements of US foreign policy, particularly diplomatic initiatives, multilateral strategies, or military actions that might affect the range of possible refugee solutions — not to mention coordination with refugee assistance occurring entirely on other nations' territory.

Access decisions, especially group designations, must draw upon detailed country expertise that resides primarily in the State Department. And that department will also remain the key US point of contact with the UNHCR. It is equally unthinkable, under current conditions, that the DHS would be removed from a central role in overseas processing, given the substantial expertise it has developed in performing this function — with regard to both applying the refugee standard and screening for inadmissibility, fraud, and security risks. Congress and the public will continue to look to the DHS to perform close inquiry into these questions.

For these reasons, the United States is bound to continue with a system where two separate governmental agencies carry major responsibility for the program, and we need to design operations in a way that minimizes the disadvantages of such division. Better coordination, in this new era of refugee resettlement, thus becomes an imperative. Although some urged a greater role for the staff of the National Security Council (NSC) to accomplish such coordination, such a highly operational responsibility does not fit well with the basic responsibilities of the NSC.[17] Although the NSC staff can often be helpful, particularly in pressing hard to assure that key cross-departmental issues actually are resolved in timely fashion, the major remedy will have to derive from other changes.

The key offices therefore must take a resolutely managerial and systemic approach to resolving operational issues. In the past, operational issues have been resolved or worked around for a specific resettlement initiative. But on too few occasions did the experience become the basis for broader systemic modifications, to make sure that similar problems did not recur. This orientation needs to change. The imperative task is to learn from specific problems, find generalizable solutions, and, in a disciplined fashion, make them part of standard operating procedures to be implemented in both existing and future resettlement initiatives.

Some examples may be useful. DHS circuit ride teams, upon arriving in an interviewing location, have sometimes encountered misunderstandings over arrangements for vehicles or other elements of support the officers would need. Whether due to a UNHCR, an OPE, or a DHS mistake, the problem takes time away from primary tasks before a resolution can be reached. It should become part of a standard checklist to identify all specific issues of this sort that need to be resolved before the team arrives in the interviewing location — and it should be possible to provide a uniform resolution applicable in virtually all future initiatives. Each time some such issue arises, a standard solution should be incorporated into the checklist and the procedures meant to meet the items on the list. On other occasions, certain complicated legal issues surface on the earliest days of interviewing that prove to be common to a sizeable number of cases and that must be resolved in order to reach a final adjudication. For example, are former child soldiers excludable because of their past involvement in human rights abuses, or are there other considerations, linked to their youth, that might allow admission despite their actions? Do certain specific conditions in the country of asylum amount to firm resettlement of the refugees, so that they are disqualified from the US program?[18] Must the past payment of ransom to an insurgent group in order to free a kidnaped relative be treated as material support for terrorists, another disqualifying factor?[19]

Or take a final example of a somewhat different character. As indicated, the DHS now declines to stamp its approval on a Form I-590 for a person found to meet the refugee definition if security checks have not been concluded. That caution certainly is understandable in the post–September 11 climate. Without the stamp, the person is flatly unable to obtain either travel or admission to the United States, and the stamp will not be applied until final security clearances arrive. But as noted, in the absence of permanent DHS staff in a given location (today's norm), this change imposes inefficiencies and delays, which are borne primarily by the OPE and ultimately PRM. Alternative and less costly methods for assuring that the person is blocked from traveling are available and should be explored — with an eye to achieving both security and efficiency for the whole system, not just the DHS component. A more precisely defined DHS role in evaluating OPEs could provide both a greater incentive to think hard about such procedures and a greater willingness on the part of the DHS to entrust the OPE with a signed form that is not to be released until the security checks are concluded.[20]

Other such examples were recounted during interviews for this report. In each instance, the ostensibly disadvantaged agency may express chagrin at the

delays, but rarely has PRM or the DHS resolutely used such occasions to change overall preparations or arrangements for future circuit rides. Perhaps each thought this was primarily the other agency's problem or responsibility.

In short, past operations have too often been marked by ad hoc resolution of coordination issues. Perhaps the very nature of a refugee program fosters such an orientation. As noted by the late Arthur Helton, a leading scholar and activist on refugee issues:

> Humanitarian action after the cold war has become largely a management exercise founded on the unique characteristics of each situation, and informed, if at all, by broad principles relating to human rights, which for the most part have not been articulated in anything approaching operational guidelines. In part, this is due to the fact that humanitarian action is based on the notion of immediate reaction, perhaps seasoned with a pious hope that future disasters will not occur. This precludes investment in more systematic efforts to conceptualize new approaches. The last humanitarian response largely informs the next, and very little happens in terms of the accumulation of a body of doctrine to inform future action. But if this situation is not remedied by achieving more concerted proactive approaches, then the future of refugee policy is likely to remain largely a series of ad hoc responses characterized by situational frenzy.[21]

In true emergencies, creative ad hoc solutions may be all that can be expected. But most refugee resettlement does not take place under such urgent conditions, and it turns out that there are broad patterns and repeat issues in refugee processing, even for widely disparate groups. For the future, therefore, the ad hoc emergency response mode should be replaced by a managerial approach to the process of refugee admissions. Problems in processing, even large frustrations with the actions of another partner in the process, should not result in finger-pointing or temporary work-arounds, but should prompt efforts to derive longer-term lessons, and ideally to make changes, incorporated into standard operating procedures, that can avoid similar frustrations in the future.

Efforts to this effect have improved over the past year, as PRM has started several interagency working groups that might be the forum for this kind of approach. And the most recent attempts to revive working groups with the NGOs, if approached in the right spirit by both sides, could lead to similar gains. All players involved should strive to make sure that these processes take firm root and are regularly nurtured. The objective should be the development of standard operating procedures, including checklists of steps that should be taken at specific points ahead of, first, a group designation decision and, later, actual deployment of the DHS officers. Some flexibility will be required, of course, to take account of the unique characteristics of each refugee situation, but detailed advance guidance of this sort should help minimize ongoing frustrations and make for needed efficiencies. Each new operational problem should be considered not just for immediate solution but for further changes in the operating procedures, because such issues may well recur. In the long run, it might be worthwhile to charter a more thorough process-reengineering study by an outside entity expert in public administration to facilitate this process.

RECOMMENDATION V-1: PRM and the DHS need to move away from ad hoc responses to problems, adopting instead a managerial approach that resolutely seeks to adopt or modify standard operating procedures when problems recur, clarifying lines of authority and accountability. Current PRM-DHS working groups and PRM-NGO working groups should help in moving toward that approach. While that process matures, regular involvement of DHS officers and NGO representatives on investigatory teams considering candidate groups or doing other preparatory work in advance of a resettlement initiative, as recommended in Chapter II, should go far toward anticipating possible difficulties, taking steps to avoid them, and collecting a body of experience that will foster changes with wider application. Over the medium term, the working groups should strive to develop standard operating procedures governing all parts of the refugee admission process, with a checklist of cooperative steps needed at specific stages leading up to and through the deployment of DHS officers.

C. SPECIFIC OPERATIONAL RECOMMENDATIONS

1. OVERSEAS PROCESSING ENTITIES

In no area of inquiry for this project did I encounter more disparate views than I did with respect to the subject of the OPEs. And yet much of the sharp debate appears to derive from each person's exaggerated perceptions of the views or actions of other players involved in the OPE process. In practice, I detected a larger area of common ground than is generally appreciated. What is most needed with regard to OPEs is a concerted effort to discuss the details of operations and roles that have raised such sensitivities, and to reach a common set of understandings about the OPE role, whoever is performing it, embodied in concrete guidance and operating procedures. Recommendations in this section address these issues. But first a more complete exposition of the views I encountered is in order. The picture of the differing views set forth in this section is a composite, and may therefore distort somewhat or mask nuances of view held by particular individuals. But understanding the nature of the polarized views is an important starting point.

Contrasting perspectives. Many NGO representatives hold fond recollections of the early days of Joint Voluntary Agency operations, particularly in the Indochinese refugee program. JVAs then undertook a wide range of functions beyond simply the case file preparation tasks described in Section A of this chapter, although the latter certainly remained an important part of their responsibilities. In some circumstances they helped with registration of refugees in camps and with briefings on detailed country conditions that might be relevant in the adjudication of individual refugee claims. Under specific guidelines, they sometimes had a wider role in actually going out to find and identify refugees living in the host-country community, thus initiating processing for specific categories of persons who would fit US processing priorities — rather than simply waiting, for example, for UNHCR to refer cases or to present lists it had developed. Some suggest that JVAs should be restored to such a function.

Another frequent theme from NGO representatives was that OPEs (or JVAs) should serve as advocates for refugees.[22] When pressed about just what that meant, however, these interviewees offered a wide spectrum of views. Some suggested that OPEs really need to go to bat for the individuals in the caseload because, in their view, no one else will adequately look out for their interests. Most took a less ambitious view, not linking the idea of advocacy to specific cases, but instead likening the proper OPE advocacy role to that of an ombudsman. The OPE should be vigilant to spot broader problems in the functioning of the system, such as a particular DHS officer applying an unduly strict standard and thus rejecting meritorious refugee claims, or a broader flaw in the operations of a particular government office or team. In those circumstances, I was told, the OPE needs to be able to raise the issue of these problems at a sufficiently high level to assure prompt attention to a remedy. Sometimes such issues reflect a problem with systems or procedures, but other times they reflect a difference in policy — for example, whether a given set of risks for a particular subgroup of the refugee population is sufficient to meet the refugee definition.

Those who held these views suggested that PRM no longer wants OPEs to have such an active overall involvement in the program's functioning, but instead views the OPE role simply as paper pushing, preparing case files and moving product, without adequate attention to the quality of the end result.[23] Some read into PRM's change of terminology from JVA to OPE a deliberate effort to downplay the independence and expertise of these entities. The increasing role of IOM as the OPE in some locations was also seen as part of this trend. Many NGO representatives view IOM as more compliant and passive than a volag-related OPE — willing to do the processing role and make no waves, even if its officers spot problems in the DHS interviews or other parts of the process. Others expressed concern at IOM's growing role as an OPE, since IOM does not have refugee protection as a specific element of its mission statement.[24]

The view from the other side was often quite different. Some government officers (and a few other sources as well) offered accounts of JVA personnel who pushed for denied applicants beyond proper bounds, such as in submitting successive requests for reconsideration despite sound reasons for rejection — although they indicated that this was not common. Others held a view of NGOs as wishing to assume an inordinate amount of control over access to refugee admissions, without adequate

attention to the other constraints described in Chapter I, Section A, or to the need for refugee policy to fit with broader US government policies. They expressed the view that UNHCR is best situated to perform that sort of access role — even if it might not have been so equipped or inclined during the heights of the Indochina refugee program, when the JVA mechanism was developed. Some mentioned incidents where NGOs invoked congressional involvement — sometimes pressure, sometimes legislative amendments — in an effort to change US policy or activity in a certain situation.

Others saw advocacy by OPEs as inappropriate, perhaps inconsistent with the cooperative agreements entered into with PRM, but in any event distortive of the central case-processing role that the US government must count on OPEs to play impartially (although here too those voicing this objection often lacked a clear idea of precisely what the objectionable form of advocacy would be in this context). Adjudication of refugee cases by DHS officers does not and should not take place in an adversarial setting, they pointed out. The overseas processing interview cannot function as a version of an adversarial trial, with advocates for both sides battling out their positions before a neutral judge. In this designedly nonadversarial interview setting, DHS officers are supposed to take the initiative to pursue both the positive and negative elements of the case. They must be able to count on a balanced and complete presentation of the person's circumstances in the file prepared by the OPE, so that the officers can apply program standards accurately.[25] Some government officers spoke quite highly of the professionalism and thoroughness of IOM in those locations where it serves as the OPE (though other officers also voiced certain criticisms of IOM). They suggested that IOM would in fact raise issues with a DHS team leader or State Department Refcoord if they identified systemic or processing problems in the course of the interviews — and that they found such feedback useful. Some DHS personnel, however, voiced additional worries about OPE responsiveness to their precise concerns, given that OPEs have their contractual relationship with PRM, which is not the primary direct user of OPE services. One DHS officer pointed out that the DHS is dependent on the OPE for case scheduling, case preparation, file maintenance, data entry, statistical reporting, interpreters, and a variety of other services — yet the DHS often has limited leverage to assure that its concerns are promptly and thoroughly addressed if it believes that the OPE is not performing well. Some suggested that the contractual framework be changed, so that OPEs would enter into cooperative agreements with the DHS rather than PRM. Alternatively, it was suggested, the DHS could be given a more explicit role in setting OPE performance standards or in independently evaluating OPE performance. Under this suggestion, OPEs would have to achieve a minimum score with both PRM and DHS in order for performance to be considered satisfactory.

The site I visited where IOM serves as the OPE, in Cairo, bore out the view of its functioning as highly professional, well organized, and thorough. I asked several staff members there about how they viewed their role. None described it as an advocacy role, and several stated that they thought it would be improper for an OPE to serve as an advocate. Hence the language they used to describe their mission was quite different from the language used by many NGO representatives to describe their understanding of the proper OPE role. But when I went further to press IOM representatives (in Cairo and elsewhere) about how they interact with DHS teams and the Refcoord, and what they would do if they spotted certain regular flaws or mistakes in the process, they said they did not hesitate to raise such issues, quietly but directly, with the appropriate officer. What they described was not that different from the ombudsman vision mentioned by others — although never in that terminology.[26]

Preliminary evaluation. There certainly are differences in emphasis and style among OPEs, and different players have different images of the ideal functioning of the OPE in the process. But I came away from the interviews on this (clearly sensitive) issue convinced that the gulf is not nearly as wide as many participants, both government and NGO, believe. Neither PRM nor the DHS seeks docile paper pushers in the OPE role, but each generally respects the expertise of the OPE staff and usually welcomes initiatives from the OPE to help spot problems and seek correctives — at least if raised through proper channels. (Sometimes disputes or confusion have arisen over just what is the proper channel, however, requiring the OPE to go through the Refcoord even though the issue could be more efficiently dealt with by direct contact with the DHS team.) Moreover, whatever may be the preference of NGOs for a wider role, it will remain the case that the chief task of an OPE is to prepare

thorough, balanced, and complete case files. It is wholly proper for PRM and the DHS to focus on good performance in that role as perhaps the most important criterion in evaluating the OPE's work or in choosing among applicants to play the OPE role at a new site.

IOM performs some critical feedback functions in its existing OPE role, and would certainly be capable of doing more, if the role were better defined to include more of such activity (as recommended in this section). Furthermore, objections to IOM's involvement as an OPE that rest on the lack of an express protection mandate for that organization strike me as formalistic. The central question is what actually happens with the precise functions IOM or any other OPE is being asked to perform in the particular location, and these expectations should be clarified, as recommended in this section. In any event, UNHCR is present in the sites involved and is given a specific mission of refugee protection by treaty and UN resolutions. The quality of OPE performance has far more to do with the skills and outlook of the leadership and staff at a particular location than with the exact institutional identification of the OPE.

At the same time, PRM officers do sometimes read far more into suggestions by volag representatives than is really there. Although it is possible that some may desire a far wider or more free-wheeling NGO role in identifying or designating refugee groups for the admissions program, the representatives with whom I spoke had no intent to take over refugee priority setting and recognized the need for solid governmental guidelines and priorities. Though some NGO personnel are more careful and sophisticated on this point than others, PRM staff should not assume insensitivity, wide ambition, or empire building when NGOs suggest different approaches or new roles. In particular, when NGOs speak of an advocacy role for OPEs, they do not mean that OPEs should be designating groups for resettlement or otherwise controlling the broad contours of the program. A great many NGO representatives are fully aware of the risks and hazards that beset refugee resettlement, such as magnet effects and fraud, and affirmatively want to use their field experience to help PRM and the DHS administer a successful program that minimizes any such problems. PRM should make use of these offers of assistance from NGOs, including through a more careful definition of what is expected from NGO staff in OPEs (and that of IOM) in the way of observation and systematic feedback regarding the performance of government officers. Full and candid feedback from OPEs should be welcomed, as a way of monitoring and improving the program. At the same time, designation of refugee groups or the launching of major resettlement initiatives should definitely remain a governmental decision. NGOs properly provide a range of useful input into those decisions, as outlined in Chapter II, Section B, but that input properly comes through channels other than the OPEs.

Although the OPE role in preparing cases for DHS consideration is central, OPEs actually perform far wider functions as part of their ongoing relationship with PRM. It therefore makes sense, although the question is a close one, to retain the current framework whereby the cooperative agreement is negotiated and signed between PRM and the OPE, and PRM remains the primary supervisor. Nonetheless, it is vital to assure that the DHS's needs are met and that the DHS's experience is systematically taken into account. Late in my interviewing process, one DHS officer suggested a better and more systematic way to obtain DHS perspectives on OPE performance. After each circuit ride, it was suggested, the DHS team leader should complete a specific evaluation of the OPE's role. A form could be developed that would assure that the evaluation touches on all essential points, but much of the evaluation should probably be in narrative form. These evaluations would then be an ongoing part of OPE accountability and would be specifically employed in overall evaluation and supervision. This suggestion was well received by several key PRM staff as a way of giving clearer structure to an unsatisfying informal process at present. They felt that they often hear general "grumblings" from DHS about OPE performance, but they would much prefer to receive more precise information in a standardized fashion. Such a procedure deserves adoption.

Key to recommendations and the central points to address. Because the gulf between the various positions and views on OPEs is not nearly as wide in practical reality as many of the participants assume, I recommend that key players from the main entities with a stake in the process meet and discuss these questions in focused operational terms. The meetings should include current OPEs (both IOM- and NGO-based OPEs), resettlement volags, PRM, and the DHS. These would not be merely conversational sessions, but would have a

specific objective: to help develop a detailed set of guidelines and standard operating procedures specifying the OPE's role and that of other players in this segment of the process. In the course of these discussions, the current differences in language and terminology should narrow, and the output should focus on precise operations and operational outcomes.[27] Such sessions would also be important for a sharing of views among those in the nongovernmental community, because in my interviews those most critical of the current PRM-OPE arrangements tended to be representatives of domestic NGOs, not representatives of those organizations that actually perform OPE work.[28]

The central points to address should include the following:

1. Whatever other functions might be taken on by OPEs and their staffs, the central role of the OPE must be to prepare cases for efficient, comprehensive, fair, and accurate decisions by DHS interviewers. Guidelines need to set forth a full understanding about the OPE's role in this process, with clarity about the circumstances in which the OPE is to pursue negative information and include it in the file. The exact roles of OPEs in denying access to those applicants who plainly fall short of qualifications or present stories that lack all credibility should also be clarified, although these standards may vary from location to location depending on the ground rules for access in the particular refugee situation. That is, clear guidance should state whether such an applicant should be removed from the case or specifically flagged for the DHS officer to decide.

2. The discussions should address the question of OPE's advocacy role. OPEs do properly have a kind of advocacy role vis-a-vis individual cases, but in a limited sense. They are charged with developing a full and comprehensive picture of the applicant's best case for approval. Particularly with shy or inarticulate applicants or unaccompanied minors, OPEs must spend the necessary time and effort, applying their own expert knowledge of conditions in the country and region of origin, so that they can discover and record all elements supporting the person's refugee claim.

3. PRM and DHS managers will benefit greatly from a system that invites and encourages OPEs to play a feedback role, and to notify appropriate US

government officials of problems that they see developing in the program, including actions by US government players. Managing complex programs of this sort is a major challenge. Expanding the sources of information and feedback that government managers receive can contribute importantly to successful execution, and those managers should welcome such a channel of information. For this interaction to function best, the information or views must be both given and received in the proper spirit. The point is not to discipline or embarrass officials, but to enable measured and timely corrective action, for the health of the refugee program in that location. Therefore clear channels should be established for providing this sort of feedback, but in a confidential or discreet manner. Many locations already have such arrangements, for example through periodic meetings of the local OPE head with the DHS team leader, the Refcoord, or both. This system will not and should not guarantee that OPE suggestions will always be followed, and NGOs should not treat a good-faith rejection of a suggestion as a failure of the process. Government officials will retain responsibility for deciding on appropriate changes and initiating implementation, but their views and understanding will be enriched by this ongoing process.

4. Discussions should also cover the full range of other possible roles and functions that have been suggested for OPEs. Some may be judged useful, others applicable only in limited circumstances because of unique features of particular access criteria, for example, and others simply not practicable in the context of the different sorts of refugee resettlement programs likely to dominate during the coming decades. The discussions should help identify situations, however, in which OPE representatives can best play a role as part of targeted response teams investigating a possible new refugee initiative during the candidate-group stage.

5. The process should lead to the development of guidelines on a specific division of responsibilities among the various players — such details as the OPE's responsibilities to provide vehicles, interpreters who meet specific standards, or other forms of support for a DHS circuit ride team — and on performance standards that OPEs must meet. I do not recommend that OPE contracts be shifted from PRM to the DHS, but the standards and operating procedures must be designed so as to address the DHS's concerns fully and to maximize the OPE's

responsiveness to the DHS's needs in the interview process. Evaluations of OPE performance should give significant weight to the views of the DHS, given the primacy of DHS-OPE relationships, at least during circuit rides.

RECOMMENDATION V-2: Both NGOs and IOM can serve well as OPEs, and their roles are not as disparate as some of the usual discussion of this sensitive point suggests. To bridge the gap in perceptions, PRM should initiate a review process involving experienced representatives from PRM, the DHS, IOM, OPEs, and resettlement volags, designed to develop a shared understanding of the OPE role. This process should go beyond mere discussion sessions. It should be designed to result in a set of detailed guidelines and standard operating procedures applicable to all OPEs. Those guidelines and procedures should include explicit understandings about OPE "advocacy" (assuring the best possible presentation of all elements of the applicant's refugee claim and other qualifications) and OPE responsibility to develop and include in the file any negative information. PRM should set specific timetables for conclusion of the guidelines and standard operating procedures, preferably within one year after initiation of the process.

PRM and the DHS should develop a specific reporting format to be used by the DHS team immediately after each circuit ride to provide a detailed evaluation of the OPE's work and to replace the more ad hoc communications that now occur (or fail to occur). PRM should use these evaluations in its regular monitoring of OPE performance and to implement constructive changes. This system should be implemented promptly, without waiting for the conclusion of the broader guidelines and procedures for OPE operations, although the review process mentioned in the preceding paragraph could certainly provide additional suggestions for refinements. Government managers should also welcome a carefully channeled but vigorous system-feedback role for OPEs, whose personnel have a crucial perspective on the operations of these complex programs.

2. TRAINING AND PREPARATION OF INTERVIEWING OFFICERS

Circuit ride teams are often composed heavily of temporary-duty DHS officers drawn from other job functions, including asylum officers, examiners, and attorneys. Their training for this role could be improved, focusing on at least three key elements of the task they will undertake: legal framework, country conditions affecting the specific refugee population to be interviewed, and interview procedures and techniques.[29] Eventually, the development of a DHS refugee corps should mean that training on the first and third elements would become a standard part of the initial training of all corps officers, and it would not be necessary to repeat them before particular circuit rides. But even refugee corps officers would benefit from specific predeployment training on the second element, detailed country conditions.

Naturally, interviewers need to know well the contours of the legal standard to be applied, both the well-founded-fear-of-persecution concept that is the centerpiece and further grounds that might disqualify an individual, such as firm resettlement in a third country, material support for terrorism, or prior participation in persecution. The training on these points could be most effective if it were closely linked to the second element: country conditions. That is, not only should the training provide an opening survey of the recent history and government of the country of origin, but it would be most effective if it could help isolate patterns of persecution likely to be most relevant for the particular caseload, providing details about what the government (or nonstate persecutor) has done in specific types of situations in the past. Incorporating this background into concise written summaries that the interviewers could keep with them in the field would be useful. As much as possible, specific examples of the sorts of persecution practiced by the government, indicating the major targets for the persecution and the methods or techniques used, should be provided during the training. An officer who already is equipped with such details can ask better questions, both to understand the actual risk the applicant would face, and to expose falsehoods. For example, if the applicant claims to have been caught up in a roundup of individuals after a certain highly publicized demonstration in the capital, a well-briefed officer can ask focused questions (to which he or she already knows the answers) about the location of the demonstration, the direction from which the police came when they cracked down, and the detention centers where the demonstrators were incarcerated. Actual participants should be able to respond readily; those

falsely claiming involvement are likely to be spotted because they would not know such details. Information for such training should be drawn from a wide range of sources, including the DHS's Resource Information Center (which now plays a somewhat comparable role for asylum officers), the State Department's country desk and its Bureau of Democracy, Human Rights, and Labor (DRL), and the Commission on International Religious Freedom, as well as nongovernmental sources.

In this connection, many persons interviewed for this project suggested that DHS adjudication officers be provided with more detailed guidance, perhaps including formal presumptions that should lead to a finding of refugee status (or in some circumstances to a negative finding). Such presumptions would embody policy decisions that certain specific forms or levels of danger are sufficient to find that a member of the subject refugee population satisfies the refugee definition.[30] It will often be appropriate to centralize this kind of judgment call, rather than leaving it to each officer to decide when common forms of threat cross the line and make a fear of persecution well founded. For example, if the government suppressed an opposition movement by imprisoning or beating anyone identified as a leader of the movement, guidance could specify that those who held specified positions of responsibility with the movement (e.g., above the level of precinct captain) should be found to have a well-founded fear of persecution based on that fact alone, without having to recount personal encounters with the police, actual threats, incarceration, or beatings. Or the government of the home country may have forcibly evicted populations deemed sympathetic to the rebels from their home villages in a certain region. Depending on the nature of the government's action, it might be appropriate to decide centrally, as an overarching decision of policy and law, that all inhabitants of such villages have suffered past persecution on account of political opinion or perhaps ethnic background, including those who were not immediately present during the government's actions. Given such guidance, the officer's task would then be made more precise and focused, albeit still one that would require disciplined interviewing: namely, to decide simply whether the person actually held such a position in the movement or was from one of the specified villages. Such presumptions ordinarily would not provide fixed outer limits on the ranks of those who would qualify for resettlement, however. That is, persons who do not fit one of the guidance categories would still be allowed to show a well-founded fear of persecution based on other facts specific to themselves or persons similarly situated.

Developing such presumptions in a useful form poses significant challenges. It requires detailed knowledge about country conditions and about the specific caseload, and it calls for often difficult policy calls. But targeted response teams investigating candidate groups for a possible resettlement initiative could be asked to gather specific information about the caseload and conditions that would be useful in developing such guidance. The ultimate decision to establish such guidance or presumptions, however, must remain a centralized governmental responsibility. DHS team leaders during a circuit ride should also remain alert to common patterns that might lend themselves to this sort of treatment, and then seek central clearance to establish presumptive guidance that can facilitate later decisions. The DHS and PRM should also encourage the OPE to provide regular updates on any changes it is seeing in the caseload, such as a geographic shift, including OPE insights on the different patterns of action by the government or other persecuting entity that will be encountered during questioning of the new population.

The development of such presumptions would carry many advantages, but several officers to whom I mentioned this idea were deeply concerned about formalizing presumptions, even if placed only in internal guidance. They were concerned that such information frequently leaks, and if so, the presence of such a presumption might well result in hosts of applicants fraudulently tailoring their own stories to match. It could even happen that many applicants with a perfectly valid claim on other grounds not covered by a presumption would come to feel that they have to concoct such a story or else fail to qualify for the program.

These are wholly legitimate concerns, and they make the use of presumptions a close call. Such an approach is probably worth at least some pilot testing in the field, however. If disclosure of the guidance becomes a major problem, then the system could shift to primary reliance on training, rather than presumptions. That is, detailed country conditions training, as recommended above, can also include guidance and other signals, more discreet (and less readily discovered or manipulated) than express

presumptions, about policy-level decisions to treat certain patterns of harm as sufficient to call for favorable adjudication. In the end, it is imperative, of course, that all specific guidance, whether in the form of presumptions or simply suggested lines of questioning, be closely held, so that it can serve as a useful tool for the interviewers but cannot be used to develop or refine fraudulent applications.

The DHS will need to provide sufficient resources, in cooperation with the State Department, to assure the capacity to develop such presumptions or guidance and to design and implement the enhanced training curricula. The curriculum development process should assure inclusion of the training and guidance required under the International Religious Freedom Act of 1998.[31] Further, it would be advisable to develop multiple questioning patterns and varied tactics for obtaining reliable information or testing credibility, in order to limit the chances for successful fraud based on refugees sharing information in the camp or community about the nature of DHS inquiries.

The application of inadmissibility grounds and the statutory bars to refugee status could also benefit from similar approaches. As indicated in Section B of this chapter, sometimes there are common legal issues that should be settled by centralized legal guidance either before interviewing starts, if possible, or at least early in the process once the issue becomes apparent. These might relate, for example, to firm resettlement or exclusion as a persecutor or one who gave material support to a terrorist organization. Such decisions normally will provide specific benchmarks that the interviewers could look for in order to decide whether the factor applies.

Beyond legal guidance, for some populations additional background information or suggested lines of questioning can be especially useful in coming to grips with the elusive issue of past involvement in persecution. I was told that INS interviewers had highly useful sessions with representatives of the intelligence community before their deployment in one of the refugee initiatives dealing with the former Yugoslavia. The purpose was to help the officers know what to look for to decide whether applicants had earlier assisted or participated in persecution. These sessions provided specific lines of nonobvious questioning that could help reveal whether the individual was involved with specific violator groups or actions that amounted to persecution, and so should be excluded from the program. Preparation for all interviewing teams should include close attention to this objective — excluding past persecutors from the refugee admissions program — and the process should make regular use of help from intelligence agencies wherever possible.[32]

Finally, interviewing techniques and procedures should be addressed in the training. This should include the challenges of conducting interviews through an interpreter, as well as other specific difficulties the officers may face in the cultural and physical setting of the particular circuit ride. A kind of cultural orientation for DHS officers could be provided regarding the conditions of their existence during the circuit ride (particularly useful for any temporary-duty officers who have limited experience of living in developing countries). Guidance on safety and on how to minimize security risks during their stay in the refugee area should also be included. The need for such steps will decline with full deployment of the DHS refugee corps.

RECOMMENDATION V-3: The DHS, in cooperation with PRM and other State Department units, should arrange for improved training on country conditions and characteristics of the expected caseload before deployment of an interviewing team, including the provision of high-quality documentary material that the team can continue to use in the field. In preparing such training and materials, the DHS should draw on a variety of sources, including its own Resource Information Center, the State Department's regional bureaus and its Bureau of Democracy, Human Rights and Labor, the Commission on International Religious Freedom, and nongovernmental sources. Any targeted response team that investigated the particular candidate group now slated for interview should also participate, either in person or by providing specific information to be used in the training. The intelligence agencies often also have a role to play, particularly in helping to develop questioning strategies, tailored to the particular group and best designed to elicit information that might reveal terrorist connections, involvement in past human rights abuses, or other similar problems. PRM and the DHS should cooperate to assure that training is in compliance with the International Religious Freedom Act of 1998.

Finally, the DHS and PRM should give close consideration, in advance of interviews, to the development of detailed guidance, perhaps in the form of presumptions, that can facilitate the adjudication task — for example, identifying specific characteristics that should lead to a finding of a well-founded fear of persecution without requiring detailed questioning about further individual circumstances. Such guidance enables centralized policy-level decisions on how to view particular events or threats.

3. THE USE OF INTERPRETERS

Problems with interpreters were mentioned frequently during interviews for this project. Interpreters for the DHS interview are usually arranged for by the OPE and often are drawn from refugee populations. Several persons pointed out that it is often hard to find interpreters in the interviewing sites unless one draws upon the refugee population itself. Most of the time, the interpreters are competent and conscientious, and receive modest remuneration for their work. Nonetheless, this situation opens up opportunities for abuse, distortion, or corruption, owing to the interpreter's vulnerability to pressure within the refugee community or the temptation to misuse the role in order to extract payment. I heard allegations of coaching during interviews or direct mistranslation either to advance or destroy a case. Others expressed concern about occasional unfair favoritism by OPEs in the refugee admission process for the translators or their families. Some persons suggested that all interpreters should be direct US government hires, using embassy procedures. Such a change would add to the costs of the program, but in the view of these persons, the extra resources would be well spent.

RECOMMENDATION V-4: Integrity, competence, and completeness in interpretation services are highly important for the refugee program. PRM and the DHS should take proactive steps to assure high-quality interpretation, including increasing the resources devoted to this task. Measures could include adding specific requirements to the standard operating procedures for OPEs governing the selection, vetting, and supervision of interpreters, including provisions to minimize the use of interpreters drawn from the refugee community. Direct US government hire of interpreters should also be considered, and to the greatest extent possible, the DHS should seek to recruit adjudicators who themselves possess the relevant language skills.

4. REQUESTS FOR RECONSIDERATION

It would be useful for the DHS and other interested parties to develop standard procedures for dealing with requests for reconsideration (RFRs), as well as a consistent set of substantive standards against which to measure them. In some locations, OPEs have at times reviewed all denied cases, looking for those that appear unreasonable or mistaken. In those selected instances, the OPE would then help prepare a reconsideration request (or perhaps approach the DHS team more informally to suggest a second look). In other locations, OPEs have at times been less selective, pushing for reconsideration in virtually all rejected cases. In still other instances, OPEs apparently play a much reduced role, largely leaving RFRs to be prepared by the applicant himself or herself, perhaps assisted by self-styled experts within the refugee community. A more common set of standards and procedures would be appropriate. The DHS is reportedly working on just such a set of changes.

PRM and the DHS should also work with UNHCR to achieve shared understanding of how to treat such requests for UNHCR's purposes. For example, the mere filing of such a request should not necessarily result in blocking all UNHCR efforts to find alternative durable solutions or to move a person out of a limited-capacity transit center meant only to hold those whose cases are under active consideration. UNHCR should usually act on the assumption that RFRs will be unsuccessful in the vast majority of situations. Further, the DHS should arrange to review the written filings quickly and do a sort of triage, particularly if the requests have not already been through an OPE process that is itself selective. Those RFRs that contain only boilerplate assertions, without citing particulars, could perhaps be quickly and definitively rejected based just on the papers. Those that provide more detail and seem to raise legitimate issues might warrant a closer look at the material in the case file, ideally by the officer who made the initial decision. The decision could be reaffirmed or reversed based solely on the RFR and the file, or the case could be scheduled for a second interview.

RECOMMENDATION V-5: The DHS, in cooperation with PRM and OPEs, should develop standard procedures and consistent substantive standards for dealing with requests for reconsideration. These should guide both the OPE role in selecting those cases in which it will help prepare an RFR and the DHS process for dealing with RFRs. PRM should also work with UNHCR to clarify an appropriate stance for UNHCR's own further actions with regard to cases for which reconsideration has been requested.

5. SECURITY SCREENING

Well-designed security screening must remain a vital part of the refugee admissions process. Although the overwhelming majority of refugees pose no risk whatsoever, the chaos, confusion, incomplete record keeping, and consequent uncertainties about identity that mark many refugee situations do make the refugee admissions program a target of opportunity for terrorist or criminal organizations seeking to send operatives to the United States. This program vulnerability exists even though such operatives might have to live for lengthy periods in a refugee camp or settlement before inclusion in the program; a terrorist organization can be very patient. NGO representatives need to remain aware of this real and ongoing risk (most are clearly aware already) and should not disparage antiterrorism screening, even as they rightly press to make sure that such review is performed efficiently and fairly.

As indicated in Section A, a number of additional security screening measures were adopted in late 2001 but went through a very rocky period of initial implementation. One highly knowledgeable government interviewee described operations that related to the SAO process as "ugly" through much of 2002. The volume of new SAO requests overwhelmed some parts of the process, particularly because portions had not been automated or because different data systems used by requesting and requested agencies could not communicate efficiently. Also, some agencies were slow to provide adequate staffing. Refugees comprised only a small portion of the new demand, but the impact of these changes on the refugee program was particularly visible. All refugee movements had been suspended in the immediate aftermath of the September 11 attacks, a halt that lasted approximately two months. In the meantime, the new security and antifraud steps that were introduced beginning in November 2001 were applied not just to the consideration of new refugee applicants, but also to any refugees who had not yet traveled. Given the confusion and enormous backlogs resulting from problems at many steps of the process, many thousands of refugees who thought they had been approved and were ready to fly to the United States languished for months or years without a final decision on their cases. Most of those old cases have now been located and dealt with, but the image of thousands of refugees in limbo, awaiting such reviews, has lingered, to the detriment of the program.

The Bureau of Consular Affairs, which had previously handled all SAO-related functions for the Department of State, was also overwhelmed by early 2002, to the point that PRM officers volunteered to step in and take responsibility for certain stages of the SAO clearance process as it relates to refugee cases — primarily notification to posts of the results of the SAO review through time-consuming preparation of individual notification cables known as Visas 11. This initiative by the relatively small staff of the Admissions Office, which required the dedication of extra time on weekends and evenings, deserves high praise for overcoming crucial problems during a bleak time for the program. But in the end, their involvement amounts to a highly inefficient way to deal with this element of the system, diverting precious officer time that could be better used for caseload development and other monitoring.

Although the problems with security screening for refugees were once quite substantial, nearly everyone interviewed for this project indicated that most of the problems have been ironed out and that screening for new cases generally proceeds smoothly. In the overwhelming majority of SAO requests, for example, the process is completed within a reliable forty-five-day time frame, and the other parts of the refugee processing system have largely been adjusted to account for this new element of scheduling. Continued attention is required to assure that this time frame is maintained — and also to seek ways to shorten it whenever possible. Moreover, the Department of State, in cooperation with the Department of Homeland Security, should monitor the results closely, to adopt adjustments in the procedures and criteria as experience warrants. Changes and expansion of automated databases like CLASS and IBIS (the Integrated Border Information System, primarily in use by the DHS) may enable some reduction in the numbers of cases subjected to SAOs or other modifications in the screening. Expanded use of fingerprints in registra-

tion systems might someday also enable biometric-based security screening (which has the capacity to be more reliable and efficient than the current checks based on name and date of birth). And, of course, new intelligence will sometimes dictate the addition of targeted screening measures for selected populations.

Finally, PRM's direct role in the SAO process should be reduced, so long as that can be accomplished without sacrifice to the efficient clearance of refugee cases. The Department of State is developing a reformed and highly automated SAO process, under the authority of the Bureau of Consular Affairs, which is supposed to be largely paperless. It is essential that the final system take full account of the refugee portion of the SAO caseload and preserve the capacity to clear the vast majority of refugee cases within forty-five days. At least by the time that system is fully implemented, PRM officers should be relieved of their operational SAO role, freeing up their time for their other vital duties.

RECOMMENDATION V-6: Much progress has been made since the changed security screening procedures were introduced after September 11, 2001. After many months of confusion, inefficiency, and delays, security screening is now being worked into the normal routine of processing in most cases. The agencies involved need to assure continued full staffing of the security advisory opinion (SAO) process so that all initial review will be completed within the stated time frames (currently forty-five days), and so that hits may be resolved promptly. All agencies involved should set a deadline for closing old cases that became mired in the system in 2002 and early 2003, making a firm decision on clearance and promptly notifying those whose cases have been in suspense. Eventually SAO processing for refugees should return to the Bureau of Consular Affairs — certainly no later than completion of the larger SAO reform process — but with full provision for efficient completion of refugee cases.

6. THE WORLDWIDE REFUGEE ADMISSIONS PROCESSING SYSTEM

The Worldwide Refugee Admissions Processing System, described in Section A of this chapter, was designed as the central computer system for OPE data functions. Although some parts of the transition to WRAPS have been difficult, the idea to develop and use such a system is undeniably sound, and a great deal of thoughtful work has gone into its design and functioning. WRAPS has already been highly beneficial in helping to standardize and facilitate many parts of program operations. It could become the true centerpiece for wider development of standard operating procedures and better management and monitoring of the overall refugee admissions system. In order to accomplish these aims, certain key modifications and software updates are needed to WRAPS, both to facilitate individual case processing and to assure that WRAPS can generate all the kinds of detailed reports and data that managers need. Managers, both of OPEs and at headquarters of PRM and the DHS, should be able to use WRAPS to monitor, manage, and predict the flow of each part of the refugee pipeline. It is not surprising that a new system would need such changes as field experience is gained, and much ongoing work has been done to introduce such improvements in successive releases of the WRAPS software. But PRM and WRAPS leadership should make a major push to speed these modifications and develop the additional capacities. Devoting significant up-front resources to this process would be worthwhile, because such a tool would greatly facilitate the type of management needed for the diverse array of refugee initiatives that the United States will be pursuing in the current era of refugee resettlement.

With regard to using WRAPS in individual cases, interviews for this project produced several suggestions for changes, which have also been shared with WRAPS headquarters through its regular feedback mechanisms. The most pressing would appear to be changing the WRAPS screens for capturing family information, which both OPE and WRAPS personnel indicated are overly cumbersome and — some said — nearly unusable. Some OPEs apparently still use their own paper family tree forms, following earlier JVA models, because of the inutility of the WRAPS system for this purpose. As indicated elsewhere, precise family trees are a crucial tool in the refugee admissions process. A workable automated family tree format in WRAPS should be implemented as soon as possible.

I heard suggestions also for modifications so that WRAPS can generate the most useful types of comprehensive pipeline reports that would facili-

tate effective discharge of program managers' responsibilities. WRAPS is working on data cleanup deriving from the transition from former OPE systems to this central system, and on certain changes to the reporting format, but the effort needs to be pursued on a disciplined and comprehensive basis and with the highest priority. WRAPS should schedule thorough consultations with key headquarters managers and with highly experienced representatives of IOM and the NGOs, including both resettlement volags and OPEs, in order to generate a precise set of system requirements from the perspective of pipeline management and then modify the software to make sure it meets those needs.

The objective is to equip the system to provide specific reports to managers on both stock and flow at particular times, specific to each OPE and each refugee situation. Some data of this type are already available, of course, but only for certain specific parts or stages of the process — not sufficiently comprehensive, some told me, for management purposes. Also, WRAPS must be able to show more than a snapshot of the situation at the time of the query. Regular month-by-month data are needed, so that trends and changes can be analyzed and timely remedial action taken when necessary. Managers should be able to look at the reports and get an idea about precisely where bottlenecks have developed — both which refugee situation and exactly what part of the process — and what the average time frame will be for particular refugee groups to move from initial access through each part of the process.

Interviews for this project suggested several key elements that need to be accessible for managers, on a period-by-period basis and not simply as a current snapshot. The following list of needs is illustrative, not necessarily exhaustive. Also, in the time since some of my initial interviews, it is clear that WRAPS has made progress and has developed the capacity for additional types of reports. Therefore, some of the following needs may already be met. Nonetheless, I reprint a full range of suggestions so that they may be of use as refinements continue.

The system needs include the following: More comprehensive data would be helpful on how many cases each OPE has opened and is processing, not simply how many have reached the stage of being ready for DHS interview. To the extent possible, the system should show exactly what may be slowing the process before cases are "DHS-ready" — whether it be OPE delays, RAVU antifraud review, security screening, or other factors. In this way, managers will have a better idea of the potential pool of numbers for future admissions, and of the amount of time required for this part of the processing in each program site. With regard to the DHS interview stage, WRAPS should show both the number interviewed and the number approved, so that managers can spot any aberrant patterns in adjudications, inquire further, and take remedial action if called for. After the DHS interview, WRAPS now shows cases in an "approved, not departed" status. It can provide focused data on the numbers awaiting medical clearance or sponsorship assurances, but it is not well designed to show the nature of other sorts of delays or holds, particularly for security screening, including fingerprinting, or antifraud review. In part this state of affairs reflects the fact that WRAPS was designed before the additional screening measures were introduced after the September 11 attacks. The hold problem cropped up as a major issue for thousands of refugees approved before that date but then subjected retroactively to the new requirements — so that they were ostensibly approved for admission but then found their cases in suspense for reasons other than medical clearance or assurances. Although such postinterview holds have diminished as a problem (particularly now that RAVU review is completed before the DHS interview for incoming cases), the system still needs the capacity to identify such holds with precision. It may be advantageous to develop a separate set of generic hold categories that will reveal at a glance what is preventing the cases from being travel-ready.

Recommendation V-7: The deployment of the WRAPS data system has already provided major improvements and standardization for the admissions program, but more can be done, and resources should be provided to accomplish key changes as a matter of high priority. In particular, the family tree screens of WRAPS should be modified. Moreover, the management potential of WRAPS has not been fully tapped, because the system does not now generate reports with the sorts of detail that would be of greatest use to those engaged in pipeline management. Ongoing WRAPS revisions should assure that detailed stock and flow data are available on a month-by-month (or other periodic) basis for each refugee population.

7. PROCESSING AT THE PORT OF ENTRY

One element of current port-of-entry processing, the DHS ceiling of no more than thirty-five refugee passengers per plane, places serious constraints on refugee travel and the capacities of the admissions system. As indicated in Section A, the ceiling was originally imposed to accommodate new fingerprinting requirements adopted after the September 11 attacks. But it is now maintained primarily because of the cumbersomeness of the mandatory process for issuing employment authorization documents (EADs) at the port of entry, upon arrival of the refugees. Inspectors find it difficult, if they must handle more than thirty-five admissions per planeload, to complete all the needed card-creation steps within the two- to three-hour time frame usually allowed before the refugees' connecting flights.

This ceiling provides a paradigmatic example of a situation where a relatively small change in practices in one part of the process could bring major improvements and efficiencies — but efficiencies that would accrue to agencies other than the one primarily in control of the needed change. Consequently, the incentives have not been such as to promote a speedy interagency solution. Inspection and port-of-entry procedures are the province of the Bureau of Customs and Border Protection (CBP), in a separate division of DHS from the Citizenship and Immigration Services (USCIS) directorate, which carries nearly all other departmental responsibilities for the refugee program. A working group involving several components of the DHS as well as PRM has been at work for many months to find a solution that would permit more refugees to travel. The leadership of the Department of Homeland Security should signal its strong support for the reform process, insisting upon early solutions that would enable larger refugee flights. The thirty-five-person-per-plane limit is a significant impediment to a reliable pipeline, particularly in parts of the world (such as some current African processing sites) where only one or two international flights depart each day. (IOM can place more than thirty-five on departure flights that do not head directly to the United States, but must still break up the group at the connecting foreign airport — an unnecessarily cumbersome procedure.) When that limit is strictly enforced, charter flights also become impractical.

It should be possible to find short-term solutions that would increase per-plane refugee inspection capacity. A contractor could do the physical preparation of the current card, for example, perhaps using better equipment, thus freeing up officer time to handle core inspector functions for a far larger number of refugees. Actual issuance of the card would of course remain a duty of the inspector, to occur only after all other checks have been completed and the inspector has approved admission of the refugee.

But the process of reforming this rather simple procedure has been complicated because of other understandable and wholly praiseworthy objectives that the agencies wish to accomplish. For example, several officers involved in the reform process would like to use the occasion to change to a more secure document than the current laminated EAD, that is, to a document better linked to central databases and using more reliable technical means to capture the photo and fingerprint. The new document could then serve other vital purposes not provided for under the existing arrangements. Importantly, it could then be presented directly to the Social Security Administration and provide a sufficient basis by itself for the issuance of a social security card. Such a card is obviously needed by a refugee as soon as possible after arrival in the destination community in order to facilitate access to the job market, the opening of a bank account, and the like, but Social Security will not issue a card solely upon presentation of the current type of refugee EAD. Nonetheless, for the DHS to issue the more secure EAD under existing procedures from its central card-issuing facilities may require a period of several weeks after the refugee's arrival, thus both impeding the integration process and possibly transgressing the requirements of § 309 of the Enhanced Border Security Act, which calls for "immediate" issuance of an EAD upon arrival.[33] Alternatively, it may one day be possible to overcome these delays in issuance of the better EAD by capturing fingerprints and photos overseas before the refugee travels. Nonetheless, the needed equipment may not be usable in all refugee locations.[34]

Speeding issuance of social security cards and providing for a more secure EAD directly registered in central DHS databases are objectives that deserve priority attention. But their pursuit should not be permitted to delay a short-term increase in the per-plane limit, now that the program's capacity is otherwise growing and enhanced travel capacity is clearly needed. Despite promises of prompt resolu-

tion, this issue has somehow evaded resolution throughout the full twelve-month period of this study. Action needs to be taken promptly.

RECOMMENDATION V-8: In the short term, within a matter of months, the DHS should revise and streamline its procedures for issuing employment authorization documents, so that the per-plane limit of thirty-five refugees can be significantly increased and that IOM's use of charter aircraft for refugee transport again becomes practical. These changes would be without prejudice to more thorough reforms that would one day permit the prompt issuance of a more secure EAD or identity document that could better serve the needs of both immigration agencies and the Social Security Administration. As those longer-term reforms proceed, the agencies involved should make every effort to assure that refugees receive the document at the port of entry. If the more secure document can only be provided at some later point, then the procedures must be designed to assure receipt within about two weeks of arrival, because such documents are so important for the successful reception and integration of refugees in the destination city.

8. ADJUSTMENT OF STATUS

After one year in the United States, refugees are supposed to apply to the DHS for adjustment of status to that of a lawful permanent resident.[35] The standards are not highly demanding, but the forms and procedures can be somewhat daunting for the refugee, and even for many volag personnel who try to assist with the process. Chapter VII considers a possible statutory change that would admit refugees as permanent residents from the beginning of their time in the United States, thus obviating adjustment. In the absence of such an amendment, the adjustment procedure should be made as accessible and straightforward as possible.

One minor change that might be of real assistance toward that end would be to modify the generic adjustment form, the I-485, now used by refugees and by all other adjustment applicants — so as to provide specific guidance and instructions for refugee applicants. Such a change could be made fairly readily by the DHS, without the need for statutory amendment. Surprisingly, for over two decades, since the Refugee Act established the basic framework for refugee status adjustments, this form has contained no specific instructions for refugee cases, even though perhaps two million refugees have filed such forms. At the same time, the form does contain instructions and specific check-boxes for more obscure or less numerous adjustment categories, such as registry applicants, Cuban Adjustment Act cases, and asylees. The current instructions on Form I-485 list seven specific categories (not including refugees) that may use the form and then add, without elaboration, that others who believe they may be eligible for adjustment should "consult your local INS office." When I inquired as to why refugees have not been expressly included on the form, even though it is quite clear that this is the form the DHS expects refugees to use for the adjustment procedure, no one to whom I spoke had a satisfactory answer.[36] Refugees are supposed to check the box on the form marked "other," pencil in "refugee," and then go ahead and complete the form without any instructions that are specific to their situation.

RECOMMENDATION V-9: The DHS should revise the Form I-485 to include specific boxes and questions for use in connection with refugee adjustments and should revise the form's instructions to give specific guidance to refugees and those who assist them.

Chapter V. Endnotes

1 Detailed information on UNHCR's resettlement and referral procedures appears in the *UNHCR Resettlement Handbook*, particularly Chapter 5, Basic Procedures to be Followed in Field Office Resettlement Operations (July 2002), available at <www.unhcr.ch>.

2 See, e.g., GIL LOESCHER & JOHN A. SCANLAN, CALCULATED KINDNESS: REFUGEES AND AMERICA'S HALF-OPEN DOOR, 1945-PRESENT, 58-59 (1986).

3 Department of State, FY 2002 Refugee Admissions Processing Guidelines, State 43737, para. 24 (March 6, 2002), (unclassified cable).

4 For a general description of CLASS uses and procedures, see 9 FAM Part IV, Appendix D, § 200.

5 Senate hearings in October 2003 addressed these problems. *Hearings on the Post 9/11 Visa Reforms and New Technology: Achieving the Necessary Security Improvements in a Global Environment, Before the Subcomm. on International Operations and Terrorism, S. Comm. on Foreign Relations*, 108th Cong., 1st Sess. (2003). The testimony of an FBI official centrally involved in improving the systems used by that agency, David M. Hardy, Acting Assistant Director, Records Management Division, is particularly instructive on the precise procedures used, the increases in volume that the overall system faced after 2001, the resulting problems, and the changes made to address them. The FBI received 2.5 million namecheck requests in FY 2001. By FY 2003, the volume increased to over 6.3 million.

6 INA §§ 101(a)(42), 207(c)(1), 8 U.S.C. §§ 1101(a)(42), 1157(c)(1) (2000). The situation is different with cases covered by the special evidentiary standards of the Lautenberg Amendment, Pub. L. No. 101-167, Title V, § 599D, 103 Stat. 1195, 1261 (1989), as amended, 8 U.S.C.A. § 1157 Note (1999 & Supp. 2004).

7 Chapter VII includes a recommended statutory change that would permit broader group designations when the President finds that a genuine risk of serious harm affects the whole group and precludes return to the country of origin. If enacted, this procedure, in selected circumstances, would dispense with the requirement of individual proof of a risk of persecution, but the individual would of course still need to show membership in a designated group.

8 INA § 212(a), 8 U.S.C. § 1182(a) (2000).

9 INA § 207(c)(3), 8 U.S.C. § 1157(c)(3) (2000).

10 Reform may also change the name to "requests for review" (which would at least have the virtue of maintaining the same acronym in a field already cluttered with specialized terminology).

11 Sponsor assurance and medical screening are mandatory before the person is permitted to travel. Cultural orientation is not mandatory — in certain circumstances travel may be permitted even if the person has not had such a course — but PRM funds and encourages this process. It is clearly preferable for such orientation to be completed before the person leaves for the United States.

12 See MIGRATION HEALTH SERVICES, ANNUAL REPORT 2002 5-30 (IOM, 2003), available at <www.iom.int/iomwebsite/Publication/ServletSearchPublication?event'detail&id'3051>.

13 See 9 FAM Appendix O, Part 1500.

14 9 FAM Appendix O, § 1305.

15 Pub. L. No. 107-173, § 309, 116 Stat. 543 (2002).

16 See, e.g., DEPARTMENT OF HEALTH AND HUMAN SERVICES, REFUGEE RESETTLEMENT PROGRAM: MAKING A DIFFERENCE (Report to the Congress FY 2001).

17 This was one of the major conclusions of the Tower Commission's 1987 report. President's Special Review Board, Recommendations on Organizing for National Security V-3 (Feb. 26, 1987)

18 See INA § 207(c)(1), 8 U.S.C. § 1157(c)(1) (2000).

19 See INA §§ 207(c)(3), 212(a)(3)(B)(iv)(VI), 8 U.S.C. §§ 1157(c)(3), 1182(a)(3)(B)(iv)(VI) (2000).

20 The regulations decree a four-month limit on the validity of an approved Form I-590. 8 C.F.R. § 207.4 (2004). Most security screening is now completed (overwhelmingly resulting in clearance) within that time frame. Hence, retention by the OPE, with release only upon documented security clearance, would be feasible. If the case is sufficiently complicated that security clearance requires more time than that, it may be appropriate to require another DHS look. Alternatively, the time limit set forth in the regulation could be reconsidered.

21 Arthur C. Helton, The Price of Indifference: Refugees and Humanitarian Action in the New Century 270-71 (2002). Helton was writing about the full range of humanitarian responses to refugee crises, from refugee assistance in a country of haven to military intervention in the country of origin, but his words fit well the specific focus of this report: refugee resettlement.

22 See the comments from NGO representatives regarding OPEs during the debate on the FY 2004 appropriations legislation, summarized in FY 2004 Omnibus Bill Sets Funding for Refugee Protection and Assistance: Includes New Provision on Refugee Resettlement, Refugee Reports, Jan/Feb 2004, at 2-4.

23 A related but less common theme was this: Today there are inadequate linkages between OPEs and the volags that will ultimately receive the refugees. OPEs, they maintained, should provide more and better information that would promote successful placement and resettlement. (The standard OPE agreement, however, does specifically call upon OPEs to provide such information.)

24 See generally Human Rights Watch, The International Organization for Migration (IOM) and Human Rights Protection in the Field: Current Concerns (paper submitted to the IOM Governing Council Meeting, Geneva, Nov. 18-21, 2003), available at <www.hrw.org/backgrounder/migrants/iom-submission-1103.htm>. A portion of the controversy over which organizations should perform the OPE role was addressed in the FY 2004 omnibus appropriations legislation. Congress adopted a provision directing the Department of State to "utilize private voluntary organizations with expertise in the protection needs of refugees in the processing of refugees overseas." Pub. L. No. 108-199, Div. D, Title V, § 590, 118 Stat. 207 (2004). Although this provision probably should be read as a congressional provision that IOM not take over the OPE business entirely, the measure Congress finally enacted does not require that IOM be excluded from that function. NGO advocates for this legislative measure recognize that the adopted version permits an ongoing OPE role for IOM.

25 A 1996 State Department audit report on the refugee program found problems with some JVAs departing from the proper bounds of their processing role and suppressing negative information bearing on particular refugees. Department of State, Office of the Inspector General, Report of Audit: Refugee Admissions Program 32-38 (6-CI-008, January 1996).

26 Some persons affiliated with NGOs reported to me that they knew of officers at IOM-operated OPEs who had been told by their superiors not to raise such objections if they spotted problems, but I was not able to verify the claim. The IOM managers with whom I spoke manifested the opposite attitude and regarded such feedback as part of the OPE responsibility.

27 The standard operating procedures should also include the guidelines required by the International Religious Freedom Act of 1998, Pub. L. No.105-292, § 602(c)(2), 112 Stat. 2812 (1998), codified as amended in 22 U.S.C. § 6472(c)(2) (2000).

28 Governmental officers sometimes highlight this reality in questioning the salience of the NGO criticism of recent OPE developments, precisely because it comes from persons with a lesser involvement in the overseas portion of the process. This is a fair point, and it was notable that I heard little criticism of the broad arrangements for OPEs from those actually involved in that work. Nonetheless, in some contexts the distinction could cut in the other direction. That is, sometimes it requires a certain distance from daily operational decisions and crises to develop an adequate perspective to think about systemic problems and propose broader reforms. In any case, both parts of the NGO community, along with the governmental participants, could learn much from a process that requires close and sustained engagement with competing perspectives.

29 INA § 207(f), 8 U.S.C. § 1157(f) (2000), sets forth specific training requirements applicable to all officials who adjudicate refugee cases.

30 For reasons summarized in Chapter VII, Section F, any such presumptions should be considered a tool developed solely to facilitate the management of the overseas program, to facilitate the DHS officer's task for purposes of refugee admissions under INA § 207, and should have no bearing on asylum and related determinations inside the United States.

31 Pub. L. No.105-292, § 602, 112 Stat. 2812 (1998), codified as amended in INA § 207(f), 8 U.S.C. § 1157(f), and 22 U.S.C. § 6472 (2000).

32 Legislative proposals in recent years have sought to add highly specific provisions to bar human rights abusers from the refugee program (or other admission), but none have been enacted. See, e.g., House Immigration Subcommittee Hears Testimony on "Serious Human Rights Abusers" Bill, 77 Interpreter Releases 1404 (2000). Even without such measures, however, existing law provides solid grounds for excluding persons who have been engaged in such abuses. See INA § 101(a)(42), 8 U.S.C. § 101(a)(42) (2000) (second sentence). The DHS might want to consider adopting more specific regulations, as part of 8 C.F.R. Part 207, that would specify more precise grounds to bar human rights abusers from the admissions program. Still, the main issue will probably remain not legal authority but the development of usable information on individual applicants, so as to detect those with a history of such actions.

33 Enhanced Border Security and Visa Entry Reform Act of 2002, Pub. L. No. 107-173, § 309, 116 Stat. 543 (2002). I was informed that formal legal guidance within the DHS has interpreted "immediate" issuance to mean as soon as administratively practicable — a reading that would allow altered procedures that result in issuance of the better-quality EAD within a matter of a few weeks of arrival. Mindful of the need to promote a refugee's speedy integration into the job market, however, most DHS attorneys and USCIS officers with whom I spoke about this issue were keenly aware of the advantages of speedy issuance of these documents.

34 Stimulus for finding ways to assure wider deployment of such equipment may come, however, from § 303 of the Enhanced Border Security Act, id., which requires by October 26, 2004, the issuance to aliens of "only machine-readable tamper-resistant visas and other travel and entry documents that use biometric identifiers." Although use of such documentation is clearly a desirable goal, one which can perhaps be accommodated in many refugee processing locations, Congress should consider amending this provision to allow waivers for pressing refugee situations that do not lend themselves to these requirements.

35 INA § 209(a), 8 U.S.C. § 1159(a) (2000).

36 The closest to an understandable answer that I received was this: the process by which a refugee acquires permanent resident status is not technically an adjustment, and so the originators of the form may have been reluctant expressly to lump this procedure together with true adjustment-of-status categories. The foundation for this argument is found in the precise wording of the relevant statutory provision, which does not speak of adjustment per se (though the caption does). The operative language provides instead that the refugee shall "return . . . to the custody of the Service for inspection and examination for admission to the United States as an immigrant," INA § 209(a)(1), 8 U.S.C. § 1159(a)(1) (2000), and administrative practice has treated refugees denied this change of status as excludable or inadmissible aliens, rather than persons already admitted. See Matter of Garcia-Alzugaray, 19 I&N Dec. 407 (BIA 1986). Nonetheless, this legal technicality should make no difference whatsoever for purposes of providing a more easily usable form. The fact remains that refugees are told to use Form I-485, and hundreds of thousands have done so. I can think of no reasonable argument against providing more enlightening instructions and blanks on the form itself.

Chapter VI

The Role of the Office of the United Nations High Commissioner for Refugees

For over fifty years, the Office of the United Nations High Commissioner for Refugees (UNHCR) has played a central role in the world community's response to refugee needs. It also occupies a highly significant position in the functioning of the US resettlement program. Not only have US officers coordinated closely with UNHCR in many locations for operational purposes, to mutual advantage, but UNHCR also carries major responsibilities in the process that leads to actual selection of those refugees admitted to the United States. Two main areas of UNHCR functioning have drawn attention recently as fields where reforms could help secure major resettlement improvements: increasing use of group referrals and improved registration practices.

A. Background

1. The evolution of UNHCR's approach

UNHCR has consistently listed resettlement as one of the three classic durable solutions to refugee situations, along with voluntary repatriation and local integration. For a considerable period, however, resettlement was often referred to as something to be undertaken "only as a last resort," when the other two solutions had proven infeasible.[1] That relative ranking reflected a skepticism toward resettlement that had taken deep root in the organization, in part as a reaction to the lengthy and massive Indochinese resettlement program. As that program stretched into its second decade, many in UNHCR came to see it as a disguised immigration program rather than a refugee protection endeavor, or at least as a geopolitically driven effort that unfairly drew attention and resources from more pressing refugee needs.[2] Chapter I discussed the tension

within the US government between resettlement and assistance — because the funds used for resettlement of a relative few could serve many more persons if used to provide basic nutrition, shelter, or health care for assisted refugee populations. UNHCR has felt the same tensions, particularly in periods of serious funding shortfalls like those of the last few years, because its resettlement work has also been highly resource-intensive.

As a result of these factors, by the late 1980s UNHCR had come to describe resettlement in a fairly narrow way, primarily as a "tool of international protection." Correspondingly, headquarters responsibilities for resettlement were transferred to the Division of International Protection in 1990. This protection-oriented stance placed the focus on referring for resettlement individuals or families who had become highly vulnerable in the country of first asylum and who therefore needed protection beyond what could be expected in that location. In those circumstances, such a person might be individually referred to a resettlement country after fairly elaborate UNHCR procedures that could include a refugee status determination (RSD), a resettlement needs assessment, and the preparation of a resettlement registration form (RRF).[3] If all these steps are employed (one or more can sometimes be simplified), each case takes up many hours of officer time, including one or more extensive interviews.

In the last several years, however, the climate and orientation have changed so that resettlement is viewed in a more positive light, although one still finds the old skepticism in various quarters of UNHCR. (The United States played an important role in shifting the organization toward a more favorable attitude toward resettlement.) The

Agenda for Protection, adopted by UNHCR at the end of a process of Global Consultations on International Protection undertaken in connection with the Office's fifty-year anniversary in 2000, calls for the more efficient use of resettlement both as a protection tool and as a durable solution. This formulation widens the resettlement horizon to include refugees who might not be in immediate danger but for whom no other long-term solution is in sight.[4] Of major significance, the current High Commissioner, Ruud Lubbers, has made a broad effort to give resettlement a higher status and to encourage more states to participate in offering resettlement spaces — a theme he has emphasized since the early days of his tenure, which began in January 2001.[5] Official documents now refer routinely to resettlement as both a tool of protection and a durable solution (and often as a tangible indicator of international solidarity and burden-sharing as well). The "last resort" label has disappeared.[6] Voluntary return is still seen as the preferred solution, not surprisingly, but resettlement has clearly gained ground as a desirable outcome, when other difficulties, such as any pull factor, can be rendered manageable. UNHCR reports and agendas also have come to speak of the "strategic use of resettlement," an orientation that seeks to use resettlement in a way that will carry wider benefits than simply those that accrue to the resettled refugees themselves. For example, well-targeted resettlement offers can sometimes persuade first-asylum countries to maintain relative openness to new arrivals. Or longer-term offers of resettlement covering likely residual populations can enable the conclusion of a voluntary repatriation agreement that will enable the return home of the majority of refugees in a given camp or country.[7]

UNHCR has also made important changes over the last decade to improve the management of resettlement processing. A 1994 UNHCR evaluation report criticized the low priority then given to resettlement within the Office's operations and offered a host of suggestions for a change in approach and for specific management improvements.[8] Among the new initiatives undertaken thereafter was the adoption of the comprehensive UNHCR Resettlement Handbook, which includes useful guidance on practical issues that can arise in the course of dealing with resettlement, detailed procedures and standardized forms for each step, and a summary, in uniform format, of the resettlement standards and procedures of the major resettlement

countries.[9] At about this time, UNHCR also clarified and expanded its resettlement criteria to focus on eight elements that have now become a familiar part of its practice.[10] Some persons interviewed for this project urged a close review of these elements, to see if they could be refined and focused to address real needs more effectively and to minimize their susceptibility to manipulation. For example, the women-at-risk criterion is very broadly phrased,[11] and some worried that it could encourage the courting of harm as a way of qualifying for resettlement priority.

Another round of UNHCR reforms was triggered by a serious corruption scandal in Nairobi, discovered in 1999-2000, which resulted in criminal charges against some staff members and a criminal ring that helped to sell resettlement spaces.[12] UNHCR adopted systematic changes in response, including a new code of conduct, revisions to resettlement procedures and to the handbook, revised training, clearer lines of accountability for key resettlement decisions, better management controls, including requirements separating eligibility interviews from the decision-making process on resettlement cases, and a process for more systematic rotation of staff involved in resettlement, in order to provide additional safeguards against corruption.[13] Integrity is now a major theme of UNHCR's resettlement program. Nonetheless, I heard during the course of interviews ongoing concerns about the adequacy of UNHCR's efforts. Some urged that UNHCR rigorously avoid the use of locally hired staff to develop or process resettlement lists, instead using expatriate staff who should be less susceptible to pressure or threats. Several persons urged that UNHCR do more to share even preliminary information about corruption or fraud with the officials of host countries and other nations involved, early in the investigation process, so as to facilitate prosecution and to enable resettlement countries to adjust their own programs in light of developing information about such schemes.[14]

Other initiatives to strengthen the management of the program include the opening of regional resettlement hubs in Nairobi and Accra. The staff there perform regular training for field personnel, monitor resettlement activities, and help assure that UNHCR takes full advantage of resettlement possibilities. UNHCR has also worked to improve its annual projections of resettlement needs, which had been criticized for underestimating the real needs for such a durable solution.[15] It now makes a greater effort to make sure that its assessments are not artificially limited by a branch office's awareness of its own (very real) resource limits that would impede UNHCR's capacity to initiate or support resettlement.[16] Closer attention to resettlement needs has also contributed toward a push for better registration practices, to be described in Section C. As the new, more proactive approach to resettlement takes hold, the overall process is becoming more efficient, and the world community should find more opportunities to use resettlement as leverage for wider solutions to lingering refugee situations.[17]

The United States (along with its allies among other traditional resettlement countries) has been highly supportive of the High Commissioner's efforts to promote a more positive attitude toward resettlement. These initiatives are bearing fruit, although there is still work to be done to make sure that the attitudinal change takes deep root in the key operational offices of UNHCR, especially its regional bureaus.

2. THE UNHCR ROLE IN THE US PROGRAM

The current US system also reflects an important evolution in its own interaction with UNHCR in the resettlement program. The initial US process-ing priorities under the Refugee Act of 1980 did not make direct allowance for a significant UNHCR role (although there has always been a high degree of operational coordination). Building on the Indochinese experience, which of course then occupied center stage, the USRP established priority categories that mostly focused on the refugee's connections to the United States, either through family members already in this country or through earlier employment or other involvement with the US government or US-connected entities.[18] As that system matured, critics suggested that the priority system should be changed to place a greater emphasis on direct refugee needs and to make better use of UNHCR's expertise. In 1994, the State Department heeded these calls and adopted significant revisions to the priority sys-tem.[19] As more fully described in Chapter III, the first priority category, P-1, is now oriented toward individual cases of compelling need (with certain more detailed specifications). Procedurally, the priority is triggered by a referral from either UNHCR or a US embassy — and it was clear from the beginning that UNHCR referrals would carry

the bulk of the load for placing individuals into this priority.

Although this shift was generally welcomed by the NGO community, because it gave prominence to cases of compelling need, interviews for this project encountered a regular complaint about the revision of the priorities. Many NGO representatives pointed out that UNHCR was given a major gate-keeper role in connection with the US admissions program in the 1994 changes, but that the US pro-vided no significant infusion of resources that would enable UNHCR to refer cases at a level commensurate with our system's needs and capaci-ties.[20] Several attributed the decline in admission numbers through the late 1990s to precisely this overreliance on UNHCR, and some even suggested that such a reduction was a US objective in giving UNHCR that role. I found no evidence of such alleged motivation. After all, the 1994 priority sys-tem retains other major categories that are not nec-essarily tied to UNHCR referrals and which have historically accounted for the largest components of US admissions. But it is true that the new priority system in 1994 was not accompanied by a compre-hensive vision of the likely practical impact of the changes on overall admissions, nor with carefully designed operational changes to cushion or shape that impact.

Developments of the last several years, including the sharp post-2001 decline in US admission num-bers, have caused the US government to focus more intently on the role of UNHCR in identifying refugees who might be included in the USRP. Funding to UNHCR for resettlement-related activ-ities was raised. When this produced only limited increases in P-1 referrals, PRM pressed for more precise output standards for FY 2003 to assure that the funds were used efficiently and with a focus on the objectives the United States was seeking. This US push coincided with several internal initiatives at UNHCR to make such referrals more efficient, in part as an outgrowth of the new High Commissioner's interest in resettlement, and these have borne some fruit. But at the same time, UNHCR was also investigating certain past referrals and working to add safeguards to the process, as a response to the serious integrity problems that had been discovered in Nairobi. Greater safeguards, at least initially, required additional paperwork and some added monitoring — working at cross-purposes (albeit understandably) to the push for added efficiency and large increases in output. Nonetheless, efforts continue to find ways to streamline UNHCR's procedures, and they should gain some momentum now that many of the integrity-focused reforms are being worked into the routine operation of the system.

RECOMMENDATION VI-1: PRM, while remaining fully supportive of the UNHCR integrity initiatives, should continue to press UNHCR to make its individual referral process more efficient, disciplined, and productive. UNHCR should consider closely whether some parts of its process, including the lengthy Resettlement Registration Form, could be streamlined, especially for those cases that are likely to be referred to countries, like the United States, which perform their own detailed processing and interviewing. UNHCR should also be encouraged to take a close look at its current resettlement categories, in light of a decade's worth of experience operating under this framework, in order to refine and improve the criteria so that they better meet real needs and minimize any incentive to manipulate either the system or the refugee's own personal situation in order to qualify.

B. UNHCR's DEVELOPMENT OF A GROUP REFERRAL CAPACITY

The *UNHCR Resettlement Handbook* recognizes that its eighth resettlement criterion, refugees without local integration prospects, differs in quality from the other seven, which tend to focus on individual characteristics and on immediate dangers or acute vulnerabilities.[21] That is, if refugees in a particular first asylum country lack the prospect of a satisfactory durable solution there, that characteristic will generally affect whole groups, not simply a handful of individuals. This insight, coupled to some extent with a realization of the challenges UNHCR faces to meet resettlement countries' expectations through the cumbersome individual referral process, has moved the organization toward a new approach.

As a result, UNHCR has been working systematically to develop a new group methodology that can implement the proactive stance toward resettlement called for by the High Commissioner.[22] It is not intended as a replacement for but as a supplement to UNHCR's historic individual referral

process, which of course will continue to address the cases of vulnerable individuals. Although still in an early phase, this initiative appears to hold considerable promise to revitalize resettlement as a durable solution and to make more efficient use of UNHCR resources. It also dovetails nicely with recent trends in the USRP and with the approach recommended in this report — to expand systematically the program's capacity to find and process a series of new groups for resettlement. The Resettlement Management Working Group within UNHCR played a key role in developing the new group methodology, with the ultimate goal of incorporating proactive resettlement planning into country operations plans. The new methodology was officially adopted in October 2003, although ongoing testing and refinement are expected.

In general outlines, the new approach asks UNHCR branch offices to analyze the local situation by breaking down refugee populations into appropriate groups and subgroups and then to consider carefully the durable solution prospects for each. For those that lack a realistic chance for local integration (thereby fitting the eighth resettlement category in UNHCR's traditional list), the plan provides a detailed and well-thought-out questionnaire that will generate a group profile. That document is meant to serve as the basis for UNHCR decisions on whether to propose resettlement of the group to other willing countries. Step-by-step, the questionnaire asks about such things as details of the protection context affecting the group, the group's composition, and the effectiveness and reliability of registration or other measures that would enable clear identification of members. The objective is to identify finite groups that can become the focus of resettlement efforts. Such clarity about the group's dimensions is important, both to guard against fraud and to minimize any magnet effect generated by the resettlement activity. This theme was repeated to me many times during my interviews, along with an emphasis on the need for confidentiality of resettlement plans until preparatory work has been fully completed — because the prospect of resettlement can distort camp dynamics and particularly hinder the acquisition of accurate information needed to make sound resettlement decisions.[23] One UNHCR officer commented, "Even a hint of resettlement distorts; it can take all of your energy just to deal with the crowd that gathers [after word of resettlement begins to circulate]."

The new methodology reflects careful thinking about how to overcome the sometimes reflexive opposition to resettlement that can be encountered within UNHCR ranks or among the leadership of the host government. Such opposition often rests on concerns about a new pull factor or on a reluctance to disturb a delicately balanced status quo — even though life for the refugees themselves in the host country may be quite stagnant and difficult. (In these respects, UNHCR debates mirror some characteristics of internal US debates that can accentuate the negative case against resettlement, as discussed in Chapter I.) In order to get beyond hasty resistance to the very idea of resettlement, the questionnaire calls for systematic analysis of the conventional obstacles and concerns. It poses questions, for example, meant to evaluate the precise nature of any anticipated pull factor and to draw forth information on techniques or resources that might be available to diminish the concerns, such as the possibility of a new verification exercise (undertaken before the prospect of resettlement is publicized) or targeted communications strategies to be directed toward populations remaining in the country of origin after resettlement commences. The point is to force deeper analysis of the actual risk of a magnet effect, or of concerns about fraud, and not to let the mere mention of those possibilities become a conversation-stopper. Obviously, after the more thorough evaluation, some initiatives may still be rejected because such risks remain too high or because other problems intrude. But the UNHCR team developing the methodology believes that this patient approach can help planners and country officers see beyond immediate reactions and often find their way to viable strategies that result in well-focused resettlement initiatives.

Once such a group profile has been prepared by the branch office, it is to be sent to Geneva for further evaluation and an eventual decision on whether or not to proceed. If the answer is yes, a group submission document will be prepared for use in seeking resettlement opportunities, to be followed thereafter by detailed group resettlement plans, designed to fit with the selection and processing procedures used by the countries that agree to provide resettlement spaces.

Although this approach obviously could mesh well with US interests in expanding group resettlement, it is not being developed solely for US processing. Other resettlement countries, particularly Canada, have provided strong backing for this more proactive approach, and the working group also hopes that this methodology will help increase interest in resettlement from an expanded range of countries. NGOs have also generally voiced support, although they have expressed concerns that the daunting length of the questionnaire may deter branch offices from using it. They have suggested enhancing some of the integrity safeguards and also making regular use of NGO partnerships, perhaps through standby deployment schemes, in implementing the methodology.

The top leadership of the Division of International Protection has been highly supportive of this approach and agrees that it holds real promise. It remains to be seen whether the regional bureaus of UNHCR, which have historically manifested skepticism of large-scale resettlement, will fully accept this approach. But a few successful early programs based on this model could do much to win over the skeptics. For those who share the objective of expanding the provision of durable solutions for refugees, a lot is riding on early successes in using the group methodology. If early initiatives succeed in helping to find workable solutions for significant numbers of refugees, without greatly complicating other problems in refugee camps or for the host government, then one can expect to see a greater buy-in to this methodology by governments and by the operational components of UNHCR.

RECOMMENDATION VI-2: The US government should do all it can to support the further refinement and early successful deployment of UNHCR's group referral mechanism. It should give such referrals quick and favorable consideration for inclusion in the US Refugee Program, and it should encourage other nations to join in the resettlement effort.

C. Improving Refugee Registration

There was wide agreement among virtually everyone interviewed for this project that improvements in UNHCR (and national) registration practices deserve high priority. Such steps would not only facilitate resettlement, but they would also enhance the ability to discharge other functions, including well-targeted refugee assistance. A variety of official and nongovernmental reports also echo this theme.[24] Specifically, a thorough registration system can help identify those persons or groups most in need of resettlement. It can provide useful tools to deter or detect fraud and to minimize any pull factor. Reliable registration information gives decision makers contemplating a resettlement initiative solid assurance about the dimensions of the group under consideration, and so should make it easier to say yes.

In order for registration to serve these purposes, it must be undertaken at a time well before the valued prize of resettlement is in the picture. Early in the unfolding of the refugee situation, the registering officer is far more likely to get a full and honest picture about identity, family structure, and dates of arrival, before the individuals being registered have any incentives to distort the information in ways believed (rightly or wrongly) to enhance resettlement chances. Family tree information, for example, then becomes a baseline against which to measure later claims of relationship that might support a "new" relative's inclusion in the resettlement program. As to the pull factor, reliable registration enables the crafting of resettlement initiatives that cover only persons who arrived in the asylum country, or in a specific camp, before a certain date, without much concern that later arrivals can successfully pose as members of the group. This effect can be enhanced by well-targeted communications efforts directed toward populations still in the home country, to make sure that it is understood that no new arrivals will be eligible for resettlement.

Such a heavy reliance on registration must take account of other difficulties, however. Much of the early registration in refugee camps has historically been associated with food rationing or the distribution of other benefits or entitlements. For many, registration is manifested in the possession of a World Food Program ration card, which usually does not even contain a photograph. Furthermore, food is often distributed by household, which creates incentives to split the actual family into multiple households in order to claim extra cooking oil or other necessities. These distortions, once recorded, can then greatly complicate the task of keeping families together if resettlement later becomes a possibility. Further, distribution practices have often resulted in giving a key and controlling role to the person designated as the head of household, who very often is a male (unless the family group consists only of women and children). This form of household registration can therefore contribute

toward perpetuating the second-class status of women.

UNHCR has been working on improved registration for some time through an initiative called Project Profile — motivated both by the desire to improve assistance practices and by the recognition of benefits to resettlement that would flow from more reliable registration systems.[25] That project resulted in a detailed *UNHCR Handbook for Registration*, published in provisional form in September 2003.[26] A great deal of careful thought has gone into the proposed changes, which are meant to provide a common process and common standards for future registration and data management. The handbook recognizes the need to register individuals and households, but also families (which may or may not coincide with the household), including information about family members not then present in the asylum country or the specific camp. It calls for separating identity registration from immediate connection to benefit registration so as to minimize temptations to distort family information in order to claim benefits. It directs individual documentation of all refugee men and women and recognition of multiple adult representatives for households, in order to counteract any dependency of women on male relatives for access to food or essential services. It sensibly divides the registration process into what will normally be three phases — capturing minimum essential information shortly after arrival in the camp and then recording progressively more extensive individual biodata and other information, including photographs, at approximately the three-month and twelve-month milestones. The handbook specifically recognizes that "[w]henever resettlement is expected to be one of the likely durable solutions, as much information as possible should be collected at an early stage."[27]

Some persons interviewed for this project were skeptical of deploying overly elaborate registration early in the process, in part because of concerns about how to provide for secure but accessible record keeping, as well as for updating to take reliable account, for example, of births, deaths, and marriages. They suggested instead a modest initial registration, followed later by a more detailed verification when the officers have a clearer idea of just what additional information might be most useful — ideally still gathered before the possibility of resettlement becomes known in the refugee community. But these suggestions really are but variations on a theme that remains strongly supportive of more thorough and well-designed registration or verification. Moreover, the registration handbook (which was published after these particular interviews) addressed many of these concerns, and makes specific and detailed provision for using improving technology to allow for the right kind of data management, including a capacity to record changes in the circumstances of individuals, families, and households.

Many logistical challenges still must be resolved in order to assure widespread use of the new approach. Furthermore, registration improvements of this sort cannot be expected to bear fruit for resettlement purposes for many years. Nonetheless, the focus on improved registration is thoroughly justified. The sooner that standard registration practices (taking adequate account of the data that will become useful if resettlement becomes a possibility) become routine, the sooner we will have the benefit of this potentially vital tool to facilitate resettlement access decisions.

The United States government should continue to support this valuable UNHCR registration initiative at every step. It should also use its influence to assure that the standard procedures, as they are refined, capture data elements needed for effective resettlement programs. Moreover, although the handbook is careful to require photographs at all stages beyond the initial registration, it does not currently mandate biometric identifiers, such as fingerprints or iris scans. The current issue of the handbook goes only so far as to recognize that a biometric identifier might be appropriate, if needed, in connection with Level 2 registration. Because such identifiers remain a sensitive subject for many people around the world (living in cultures that do not readily accept fingerprinting in the way that is common in the United States), this acknowledgment and acceptance represent a significant forward step. But UNHCR should be urged to go further and do all it can to require the routine inclusion of biometric identifiers at the appropriate stage of registration,

probably in the form of fingerprints, given the widespread use of fingerprints in existing national systems.[28] There remain significant barriers to the use of sophisticated biometrics, to be sure, particularly given the wide variety of settings in which UNHCR must operate, including many without reliable electric power. Nonetheless, assurance of positive identification via biometrics throughout the refugee assistance process and especially the resettlement process would carry enormous advantages in the post–September 11 climate.

The United States should also share with UNHCR its successful experience in using inkless fingerprinting technology in remote locations. The DHS office that deals with these issues has worked to develop truly mobile systems that are capable of collecting fingerprints, photos, and biographic information. These units are reasonably priced and use technology that is compatible with UNHCR's Microsoft systems. US funding should be provided to help UNHCR acquire such equipment for use in connection with its pilot implementation of the new registration.

RECOMMENDATION VI-3: Standardized registration practices, using carefully designed data elements, can have enormous long-run advantages in enabling and improving resettlement. Their potential is so great that registration advances deserve the highest priority. Enhanced registration can provide a payoff for assistance purposes immediately. Its benefits to resettlement will appear only in the long run, but the advances in avoiding fraud, minimizing magnet effects, and improving initial decisions about access will be substantial. The US government should therefore continue to support the development and early deployment of improvements in UNHCR registration practices. It should also encourage UNHCR to work toward inclusion of biometric identifiers in registration documents and records wherever possible and should provide US funding for early UNHCR use of mobile fingerprint technology developed by the DHS.

Chapter VI. Endnotes

1 See, e.g., *Executive Committee of the High Commissioner's Programme, Conclusion No. 67*, para. (g) (1991). The conclusions are available on the UNHCR website, <www.unhcr.ch>, and are formally published each year as part of the report of the Executive Committee, which itself is an addendum to the High Commissioner's report to the General Assembly. Conclusion No. 67, for example, appears at *Addendum to the Report of the United Nations High Commissioner for Refugees*, at 10, para. 23(g), UN Doc. A/46/12/Add.1 (1992).

2 See, e.g., John Frederiksson & Christine Mougne, Resettlement in the 1990s: A Review of Policy and Practice 20-21 (UNHCR Evaluation Report, Dec. 1994); Joanne van Selm, Tamara Woroby, Erin Patrick, & Monica Matts, Feasibility of Resettlement in the European Union 7-10 (Migration Policy Institute, 2003); Gary Troeller, *UNHCR Resettlement: Evolution and Future Direction*, 14 Int'l J. Refugee L. 85, 94-95 (2002).

3 See UNHCR Division of International Protection, Resettlement Handbook, Section 5.4 (July 2002 version), available at the UNHCR website, <www.unhcr.ch>.

4 See *Agenda for Protection*, particularly Goals 3(6), 5(5), and 5(6), *Executive Committee of the High Commissioner's Programme*, 53d Sess., UN Doc. A/AC.96/973 (2002), *reprinted in* 21/4 Refugee Survey Quarterly 35 (2002). The chief papers from the consultations are reprinted in Refugee Protection in International Law: UNHCR's Global Consultations on International Protection (Erika Feller, Volker Türk & Frances Nicholson eds., 2003).

5 See, e.g., Ruud Lubbers, United Nations High Commissioner for Refugees, Opening Statement at the Fifty-third Session of the Executive Committee of the High Commissioner's Programme (Sept 30, 2002), *reprinted in Report of the Executive Committee of the Programme of the United Nations High Commissioner for Refugees*, at 19, UN Doc. A/57/12/Add.1 (2002).

6 See, e.g., *Executive Committee of the High Commissioner's Programme, Conclusion No. 79*, paras. (q), (r), (s) (1996); *Conclusion No. 95*, para. (q) (2003).

7 See, e.g., Executive Committee of the High Commissioner's Programme, The Strategic Use of Resettlement, U.N. Doc. EC/53/SC/CRP.10/Add.1 (June 3, 2003) (a discussion paper prepared by the Working Group on Resettlement), *reprinted in* 23/1 Refugee Survey Quarterly 150 (2004).

8 Frederiksson & Mougne, *supra* note 2, at 20-21.

9 Resettlement Handbook, *supra* note 3. The handbook is available on the UNHCR website, <www.unhcr.ch>, and has undergone periodic updating.

10 They are: legal and physical protection needs, medical needs, survivors of violence and torture, women at risk, family reunification, children and adolescents, elderly refugees, and refugees without local integration prospects. Resettlement Handbook, *supra* note 3, Chapter 4.

11 See generally Kathleen Newland, US Refugee Policy: Dilemmas and Directions 22 (1995) ("Priority for resettlement should be set according to not only the degree of suffering but also the kind of remedy available to the individual. . . . [C]are should be taken not to define the 'women at risk' category too widely.").

12 See *Report of the Office of Internal Oversight Services on the investigations into allegations of refugee smuggling at the Nairobi Branch Office of the United Nations High Commissioner for Refugees*, UN Doc. A/56/733 (Annex) (Dec. 21, 2001). Another incident involved the former UNHCR representative based in Accra — leading to a reorganization of that office and a thorough revision of its procedures. van Selm et al., *supra* note 2, at 12.

13 See Strengthening and Expanding Resettlement Today: Dilemmas, Challenges and Opportunities, UN Doc. EC/GC/02/7, para. 17 (April 25, 2002) (prepared for 4th Meeting of the Global Consultations on International Protection), *reprinted in* 22/2-3 Refugee Survey Quarterly 249, 254 (2003); UNHCR Resettlement Handbook, *supra* note 3, especially the revised Chapters 5 and 7 (July 2002). Other reforms implemented at that time are listed in UNHCR Receives Report on Nairobi Investigation (UNHCR press release, Jan. 25, 2002), available at <www.unhcr.ch>.

14 Others reported that the resettlement system is sometimes subject to other forms of distortion, such as the use of resettlement spaces simply to move out persons who are persistent or annoying in demanding that UNHCR officers find them a durable solution. The Office's oversight procedures need to promote vigilance in guarding against simply giving resettlement to those who are the pushiest, rather than those most in need according to established criteria.

15 See, e.g., Commission on Immigration Reform, Legal Immigration: Setting Priorities 134-35 (1995).

16 See, e.g., UNHCR, Introduction, UNHCR's Projections of Resettlement Needs 2003, at 3 (March 2003); UNHCR Introduction, UNHCR Projected Resettlement Needs 2004, at 3-4 (June 2003).

17 See generally John Frederiksson, *Reinvigorating Resettlement: Changing Realities Demand Changed Approaches*, 13 Forced Migration Rev. 28 (June 2002) (Special Issue on "September 11th: Has Anything Changed?").

18 See, e.g., Proposed Refugee Admissions and Allocations for Fiscal Year 1982: Report to the Congress II-1 - II-2 (Sept. 1981); US Coordinator for Refugee Affairs, Proposed Refugee Admissions and Allocations for Fiscal Year 1987: Report to the Congress for Fiscal Year 1987, at 18 (Sept. 1986).

19 Department of State, Proposed Refugee Admissions for Fiscal Year 1995: Report to the Congress 19-21 (Sept. 1994).

20 See Newland, *supra* note 11, at 15-16.

21 See Resettlement Handbook, *supra* note 3, at Section 4.9 (July 2002).

22 The INS and later its organizational successor, the DHS, offered important support for the initiative, through the secondment of a highly experienced US officer, a former director of International Affairs for INS, to help develop the group referral capacity.

23 See REPORT ON THE UNHCR P-2 SOMALI BANTU VERIFICATION EXERCISE IN DADAAB (18 Feb. 2002). In commenting on the future of UNHCR group processing, this very thorough report commented that operational success will be "primarily dependent on the quality of registration information and the timeliness and the *confidentiality* of the execution of a particular resettlement activity." (Emphasis in original.)

24 See, e.g., *Executive Committee of the High Commissioner's Programme, Conclusion No. 95, paras. (q)-(s) (2003)*; NGO *Statement on Resettlement* (May 22-24, 2002), Recommendation 4 (submitted in connection with the Global Consultations on International Protection), *reprinted in* 22/2-3 REFUGEE SURVEY QUARTERLY 433, 440 (2003). An important US working group on fraud, involving participation by DHS, PRM and NGO representatives highlighted the importance of registration, stating in its first recommendation: "*UNHCR should be encouraged to move quickly to improve refugee registration procedures.* . . . The working group believes that this recommendation is the most important of all." Memorandum from Joseph D. Cuddihy to Kelly Ryan, et al., Recommendations Paper from Fraud Working Group (Aug. 11, 2003) (transmitting report of working group) (emphasis in original).

25 The Executive Committee adopted a comprehensive Conclusion on the subject of registration, which set forth key standards and led to Project Profile. *Executive Committee of the High Commissioner's Programme, Conclusion No. 91* (2001). See also PRACTICAL ASPECTS OF PHYSICAL AND LEGAL PROTECTION WITH REGARD TO REGISTRATION, UN Doc EC/GC/01/6* (Feb. 19, 2001) (document submitted in connection with the Global Consultations on International Protection), *reprinted in* 22/2-3 REFUGEE SURVEY QUARTERLY 70 (2003).

26 UNHCR, UNHCR HANDBOOK FOR REGISTRATION: PROCEDURES AND STANDARDS FOR REGISTRATION, POPULATION DATA MANAGEMENT AND DOCUMENTATION (provisional release, Sept. 2003), available on the UNHCR website <www.unhcr.ch>.

27 *Id.* at 44.

28 *Executive Committee Conclusion No. 91, supra* note 25, para (d), is supportive of such a step. It "encourages States and UNHCR to introduce new techniques and tools to enhance the identification and documentation of refugees and asylum seekers, including biometrics features, and to share these with a view towards developing a more standardized worldwide registration system."

Chapter VII

Statutory Amendments

A great deal can be done administratively to improve and invigorate the US Refugee Program. All the suggestions in the preceding chapters could be implemented without altering the governing statutory framework, and there is no reason whatever to postpone those initiatives while awaiting statutory changes. Further, proposing statutory changes always runs some risk, because a well-crafted bill may be radically changed in the course of congressional consideration or, even if unchanged, become the vehicle for ill-considered additions. Nonetheless, twenty-four years of experience under the Refugee Act reveal some portions of the statute that have not worked out as intended or have had unforeseen negative effects. A few carefully targeted statutory changes could facilitate improvements. The following amendments, particularly the last one listed, should be given serious consideration.

A. Provide for Continued Refugee Movements at the Beginning of the Fiscal Year, Even if the Presidential Determination is Delayed

Official issuance of the annual Presidential Determination (PD), which sets refugee admissions levels, has frequently been delayed past the beginning of the fiscal year. This timing causes serious operational disruptions that have not been given sufficient attention. Even wholly travel-ready refugees must wait until the PD issues, because under current law they cannot be admitted at the port of entry in the absence of official approval of admissions spaces, which occurs only by means of the PD. Forward planning for refugee flights must be placed on hold at some point each September as the end of the fiscal year approaches, and new bookings cannot comfortably resume until the PD actually issues — often several weeks into October. IOM, in coordination with PRM, sometimes acts in October to venture future bookings before actual issuance, based on best guesses or promises about the date of the presidential action. But if these guesses prove wrong, the program incurs charges for the unused airline seats.

To be sure, regular issuance of the PD in August or early September would avoid these problems (and would carry other advantages, as suggested in Chapter II). But even with process changes designed to achieve that end, there will remain enough hurdles to clear, involving both executive branch clearances and the scheduling of consultations with Congress, that a further statutory change would be worthwhile. It would also bolster a general reorientation of the program toward assuring a more even flow throughout the year, through better management and more successful allowances for contingencies, as this report recommends.

An amendment should authorize the continuing admission of refugees at the beginning of the fiscal year whenever the PD is delayed. It could set forth a specified rate of allowed admissions — probably best pegged at a rate equivalent to the monthly rate permitted under the previous year's PD — and could, if Congress felt it necessary, be limited to a certain period, in order to assure that there is still an incentive for reasonably timely consultations and issuance of the new PD. It is hard to imagine a substantive argument against a statutory change of this type. There will be ample time to adjust later refugee movements to assure that refugee admissions for the full fiscal year conform to the new PD level, whether that is higher or lower.

B. Allow congressional consultation by both Cabinet secretaries and Deputy secretaries

Section 207(e) of the Immigration and Nationality Act (INA) requires that the annual refugee consultations with the congressional committees be carried out by "designated Cabinet-level representatives of the President." In practice, consultation is carried out by the Secretary of State, typically accompanied by the Assistant Secretary for Population, Refugees and Migration and a representative from the department with immigration responsibilities. Congressional consultation is often delayed, sometimes past the beginning of the fiscal year, because of complications in meshing the Secretary's schedule with that of the chairpersons and ranking minority members of the House and Senate Committees on the Judiciary — all of them important officials with a great many demands on their time.

Interviews for this project produced several suggestions for changes to permit a wider range of executive branch officials to conduct the consultation. Many suggested that the Assistant Secretary should be the one to conduct the consultations, because, on substantive grounds, he or she will be the most knowledgeable about the program and the details of the proposed admissions. Others supported some change, but believed that the Congress would continue to insist on engaging higher-level officials in the process, at least at the Under Secretary level. Some also suggested that the Cabinet-level requirement helps assure that the Secretary retains a personal engagement in the refugee program.

The rank of the executive branch official carrying out the consultation was a point of some sensitivity in the initial negotiations over the Refugee Act of 1980. The key members of Congress viewed Cabinet-level consultation as the price for the wide flexibility being given to the executive branch to set annual refugee admissions levels.[1] Nonetheless, in recognition of the vast scope of demands on the Secretary's time in the twenty-first century, a modest change to permit consultations by either the Secretary or the Deputy Secretary would be warranted and may be acceptable to Congress. Such a procedure would of course still assure engagement by the highest levels of the executive branch — an important consideration — both in the dialogue with Congress and in ongoing monitoring of refugee developments.

C. Repeal the ceiling on asylee adjustments

Although not strictly involving the refugee admissions program, the backlog in asylee adjustments has become a sufficiently compelling problem that any amendment package for the Refugee Act must address the issue. INA § 209(b) allows the President to make available in the annual PD up to 10,000 admissions to be used to adjust the status of persons granted asylum under INA § 208, to the status of a lawful permanent resident (LPR), after a minimum of one year's residence in the United States as an asylee.[2] For many years now, asylum grants — which are not capped (with the minor exception addressed in the next section) and which could not reasonably be subjected to a ceiling — have exceeded 30,000 annually, leading to the creation of a massive backlog in adjustments. It is growing rapidly; over 45,000 asylees applied for adjustment in FY 2002.[3] Persons granted asylum today face a wait of well over ten years before obtaining permanent resident status. The problem has also resulted in class-action litigation, and a district court recently ordered the immigration authorities to make up for the failure to use all 10,000 adjustments in recent years.[4] That order, if not overturned on appeal, will provide some amelioration of the backlog problem, but its effects will be temporary. The backlog will continue to grow.

There are solid reasons supporting a modest delay before asylees can obtain LPR status and justifying a backup authority in the President to restrict asylee adjustments in extraordinary circumstances. But there is no defensible reason for an implacable and expanding ten-year delay, which hinders full integration and certainly postpones the ultimate US citizenship of asylees. We should instead be helping asylees to rebuild their lives in their new homeland. A simple statutory amendment could promote that important goal, without sacrificing the policies that led Congress to require delayed adjustment in the first place.

The provision setting a ceiling on asylee adjustments received scant attention in the committee reports and recorded debates over the Refugee Act of 1980. The addition of a permanent asylee adjustment provision was welcomed at that time, because earlier law had not provided any clear avenue for persons granted the equivalent of asylum to obtain lawful permanent resident status.

Congress clearly wanted to make sure that LPR status became routinely available after a delay — pegged at one year under what were expected to be the normal circumstances. As long as asylum grants remain below the adjustment ceiling, the basic procedure makes a fair amount of sense. The asylee must apply to the government for adjustment after a minimum of one year's presence and provide certain pertinent information. If there was anything questionable about the initial grant (which would happen infrequently), or if another disqualification, such as a criminal conviction, has developed during this period, the examiner has a chance to identify the problem and take appropriate action. Of greater substantive importance, the examiner is specifically directed by INA § 209(b)(3) to consider whether the asylee remains a refugee — i.e., to apply once more the substantive protection standard and determine whether the individual still has a well-founded fear of persecution in the home country. The provision reflects a congressional judgment that asylees should not automatically graduate to permanent status here if the home-country situation has greatly changed within a year or so after the asylum grant. If the threat of persecution has clearly ended in the home country, then asylum could in principle be terminated and adjustment denied — precisely because the person can safely return home.

Moreover, the discretion given to the executive branch to decide how many asylee adjustments will be provided each year is best understood as an exceptional safeguard to be used in case of a massive influx or other extraordinary event.[5] If the government decides that it must depart from the norm of eventual permanent residence for the asylees, owing to the magnitude of a particular crisis or a belief that international diplomacy or military intervention will enable legitimate repatriation (or some other solution such as resettlement in a third country), then declining to adjust status facilitates that course of action. But it bears noting that, without fail, Presidents have made available the maximum number of annual adjustments in every PD issued since the provision was enacted in 1980.

In contrast to asylees, persons admitted in the overseas refugee program (under INA § 207) are not subjected to any equivalent limitations. Although such refugees are also called upon to apply for adjustment of status after one year, the overall standards for refugee adjustment are far less demanding — essentially only a renewed test against the inadmissibility grounds, which were already considered at the time of initial admission.[6] Adjustment cannot be denied to a § 207 refugee — in sharp contrast to the situation of an asylee — even if the political situation in the country of origin has changed completely and there is no basis for a continued fear of persecution. No fixed ceiling exists on the number of refugee adjustments, and Presidents have no discretion to limit the total. Such a differential in treatment is defensible: overseas refugees were carefully screened and selected before they set foot on US soil, and their numbers were already subject to deliberate decisions by the US government, made before they arrived. Asylees, in contrast, made their way to US shores on their own, in a process that is an important part of America's humanitarian commitment, but which is inherently unruly and sometimes provokes concern over unmanageable numbers. Congress has manifested greater wariness toward the asylee category, and so has applied a different set of adjustment measures in response.

But the key point is this. Nothing in these rationales that make for greater care in adjusting asylees — a second look at whether the persecution threat continues in the homeland and explicit discretion to withhold adjustments if judged appropriate (for example, in the face of an extraordinary influx) — remotely justifies a ten-year delay for the ordinary asylee in normal times. And no one, to my knowledge, has affirmatively argued for delay on that scale. Instead a consensus exists that, after some modest initial period (one year is a good benchmark), asylees do and should sink roots in the United States and that their status should both reflect and promote that process.

Congressional changes to the asylee adjustment provisions in 1990, although mostly temporary in impact, reflected a judgment that uprooting asylees after several years of presence would be bad policy. It also manifested a judgment that lengthy backlogs preventing timely acquisition of LPR status are undesirable. At that time the adjustment ceiling was 5,000 annually, and a backlog had developed during the 1980s, delaying adjustment by as much as thirty-one months.[7] But by 1990 the world had experienced historic geopolitical changes that might have permitted fairly extensive repatriation of asylees among those in the backlog. The Cold War had largely ended, and many asylees from eastern and central Europe probably would not have been able to show that they still had a well-founded fear of persecution in their countries of origin, now ruled by democratically elected regimes. (At about the same time, many of the conflicts in Central America were nearing negotiated settlements, with a potentially similar impact on the refugee qualifications of at least a substantial number of applicants for asylee adjustment.) But instead of firmly insisting on the close review of such qualifications and the repatriation of persons who no longer faced a threat, Congress chose precisely the opposite course. In the Immigration Act of 1990, it permanently exempted from the asylee adjustment ceiling all persons who had applied for adjustment before June 1, 1990. Moreover, it expressly allowed such persons to qualify for adjustment without regard to any change in circumstances in the country of origin. And finally, it permanently raised the annual ceiling to 10,000, in the apparent hope that the doubled quota would avoid future backlogs.[8]

That hope was not realized, and any statutorily fixed ceiling is subject to being overtaken by the caseload. We need a new statutory amendment congruent with the 1990 change, but of a more enduring character. It would be best to amend INA § 209(b) to eliminate the 10,000 ceiling and leave the total of available adjustments to be set by the President each year in the PD, after full consultation with Congress. Because the President would still retain ultimate authority over adjustments, if there were a massive influx or any other undue problems in the management of the asylum system, numerical ceilings could be activated. But in ordinary circumstances, they would not exist, and asylees would then be able to adjust to lawful permanent residence within a reasonable time after the first anniversary of the grant of asylum. That change would greatly facilitate a successful transition to a productive and secure new life in this country.

If the statute is changed to eliminate the ceiling on asylee adjustments, it may also be appropriate to advance the citizenship timetable for those asylees who have already spent many years in the asylum adjustment backlog. The current section of the law already provides for recording the asylee's admission as a lawful permanent resident as of a date one year in advance of the date of the adjustment.[9] The assumption behind this provision was that retroactive recording would promote citizenship by starting the citizenship clock running at a date not far removed from the time of the initial asylum grant. That objective would be more fully accomplished, however, if the statute specifically provided that the LPR status, once adjustment takes place, would be recorded as of the date of the initial grant of asylum — which would exactly parallel the treatment of refugees admitted under § 207.[10] If that step proves unacceptable to Congress, however, it would still be worth considering a temporary measure focused on long-pending applications. Congress could retain the current recording provision (one year retroactivity) for future cases, when no ceiling will apply, but provide a more generous allowance (perhaps three or four years' retroactivity) for cases that have languished for a lengthy period in the backlogs.

D. RECONSIDER THE CEILING ON REFUGEE AND ASYLEE STATUS GRANTS BASED ON COERCIVE POPULATION CONTROL MEASURES

In 1996 Congress amended the statutory definition of "refugee" to add a special provision that assures inclusion of persons who face specified harms as a result of coercive population control programs.[11] Congress's principal concern was with asylum for persons harmed in connection with the family planning practices in the People's Republic of China. But in an apparent effort to assuage opposition based on concerns about numbers, the measure's drafters placed an annual ceiling of 1,000 on the number of persons who may receive refugee or asylum status under that special provision.[12] As a result, the DHS and the Executive Office for Immigration Review (EOIR) in the Department of Justice now must observe cumbersome procedures in the asylum cases that fall within this provision. Those judged to qualify must initially receive only a conditional grant of asylum, in order to make sure that the combined totals of persons given refugee protections by the EOIR and the DHS (including any such admissions in the overseas refugee program) do not exceed the ceiling. Although the numerical caution may have been politically understandable in 1996, postponing asylum (or simply denying it once an arbitrary ceiling has been reached) is out of keeping with the basic protection decision Congress made that year.

In recent years conditional grants of asylum in these cases have exceeded the ceiling.[13] Moreover, the numbers found eligible for asylum on these grounds are quite likely to continue growing, perhaps at an accelerated pace, because recent case law has significantly expanded the eligibility standards that apply to coercive family planning cases.[14] What the 1996 Congress intended the agencies to do in this situation is not clear, but it is not conceivable that the government will simply return persons found to have conditional eligibility for asylum on these grounds. In practice, those beyond the ceiling generally remain in the United States pending the full grant of asylum, usually with protection in the form of withholding of removal,[15] and they then wind up waiting in a growing backlog. All the objections to backlogs set forth in the preceding section apply here. Hence, Congress should make a serious and candid decision, one that its 1996 amendments evaded. Either it should decide to provide full asylum protection in these circumstances, or it should admit that the concern about excessive numbers requires narrowing the eligibility standards that apply to such cases. Whichever the choice, it makes no policy sense to cap the asylum grants. Repealing this ceiling would both avoid backlogs and enable such cases to be handled within the normal asylum grant procedures, eliminating unnecessary administrative complications.

E. CONSIDER ADMITTING OVERSEAS REFUGEES AS LAWFUL PERMANENT RESIDENTS

The requirement that § 207 refugees apply for adjustment of status after one year in the United States, INA § 209(a), creates an additional burden for them and requires that the DHS process tens of thousands of lengthy applications each year. The original rationale for this procedure was to assure a second look at an admitted refugee and to allow enforcement action if new derogatory information came to light. But there was also substantial support during the congressional consideration of the Refugee Act for admitting refugees as LPRs from the beginning. The Senate Committee on the Judiciary reported its version of the Refugee Act with such a provision.[16] With the overall changes in the refugee admissions process and in removal grounds and proceedings in the decades since 1980, this procedure should be given another close look.[17]

As indicated in Section C of this chapter, the substantive standards for judging refugee adjustment applications are not highly rigorous, especially when compared with the more demanding criteria for review of asylee adjustment applications. The standards essentially demand only another application of the inadmissibility grounds — a second application of standards that the person has already been judged to satisfy after close DHS questioning. To be sure, the government may enjoy some modest advantages under this procedure, in those infrequent cases where derogatory information, such as a criminal conviction or falsehood on an application, comes to light at the one-year mark, deriving from the fact that the individual bears the burden of proof when requesting adjustment. But even if adjustment is denied, the DHS must still initiate a removal proceeding to secure the actual deportation of the individual, and in many such cases the derogatory information would provide a straightforward basis for removing the person even if he or she held LPR status. Whatever advantages may have existed along these lines in 1980, when the Refugee Act was passed, have surely diminished (though they have not disappeared) in the wake of the 1996 immigration amendments. The previous differences between an exclusion proceeding, to which refugees denied adjustment were formerly subjected, and a deportation proceeding (applicable to LPRs) have lessened. Both kinds of cases are now handled under a single procedure known as a removal hearing.[18] Moreover, although inadmissibility grounds still cover a wider range of crimes than do deportability grounds, that gap was considerably narrowed in 1996 when Congress expanded the reach of the criminal removal grounds that apply to LPRs. A refugee who commits a crime of virtually any degree of seriousness within the first few years after admission would be fully subject to removal, even if initially admitted as an LPR.

Although I was told during interviews that the DHS sometimes has found it useful to require a refugee to take the initiative and provide the stated information by means of the adjustment procedure, no one disputes that the overwhelming majority of refugee adjustment cases are wholly routine. The real question is whether the process is cost-effective — whether the nature or quantity of the information gained in a handful of cases is worth this large volume of additional and largely duplicative work. Particularly now that the screening of refugees before admission, for both fraud and security concerns, has been significantly improved, the question is worth pursuing closely. I had hoped to make a closer judgment in this report of the relative costs and benefits, but I was unable to obtain data on the exact numbers of refugees denied adjustment, the reasons therefor, and the ultimate disposition of the cases. I recommend that USCIS compile such data in a systematic fashion, to provide a solid basis for a considered judgment of the cost-effectiveness of the refugee adjustment procedure, as compared with the lead-driven enforcement actions that would of course remain applicable if these persons were admitted as LPRs from the beginning. Restoring timely processing of all immigration benefit applications has been set forth as a high priority for this Administration, reiterated by USCIS since its creation in March 2003. Eliminating the refugee adjustment process would potentially eliminate tens of thousands of filings each year, thus freeing up substantial resources for that broader effort, without significant harm to the long-term quality of refugee admissions. It would also alleviate a burden for the refugees themselves.

F. ALLOW THE PRESIDENT TO DESIGNATE SPECIFIC CLASSES OF PERSONS TO BE ADMITTED AS §207 REFUGEES WITHOUT INDIVIDUALLY APPLYING THE CONVENTION REFUGEE DEFINITION

When Congress changed the statutory provisions governing refugee admissions in 1980 to tie eligibility to the UN Convention definition, its main purpose was to expand potential eligibility for the program, by removing the previous "geographical and ideological restrictions" on refugee admissions.[19] Congress did not fully consider then the fact that the UN definition itself has limits that fit unevenly with genuine humanitarian needs — as a matter of both substance and efficient processing — or that the treaty was never intended to limit discretionary refugee admission programs. Some further expansion in statutory eligibility, if provided in a carefully structured fashion, would be consistent with America's humanitarian tradition and could carry other useful benefits for the USRP. Such an amendment would contribute more than any other legislative change toward enabling the program to respond efficiently to genuine refugee needs under the conditions of the twenty-first century. Some persons interviewed regarded such a change as indispensable if the program is to return to the admission levels of the 1990s.

Background. The 1951 Convention relating to the Status of Refugees[20] was adopted primarily to deal with lingering issues generated by the continued presence in European countries of persons displaced during World War II and unable to return safely to their homes in countries that had come under Soviet domination. The treaty's focus was on matters suggested by its title — issues of status, including employment rights, public education, and access to public assistance.[21] As described by Guy Goodwin-Gill, a leading scholar of refugee law:

> The 1951 Convention was originally intended to establish, confirm, or clarify the legal status of a known population of the displaced. This met the needs of the time, and most provisions focus on assimilation, or are premised on lawful residence or tolerated presence. There is nothing on asylum, on admission, or on resettlement.[22]

The definition of "refugee" contained in Article I, with its core criterion of "a well-founded fear of being persecuted for reasons of race, religion, nationality, membership of a particular social group, or political opinion" was thought to cover the European populations at issue. But over time the Convention definition turned out to provide the centerpiece for the development of extensive systems for deciding whether to grant political asylum to individuals who make their way to the territory of states that have accepted the treaty, primarily because of its linkage to Article 33 of the Convention. That article forbids return (refoulement) of a refugee to a country where his or her life or freedom would be threatened on account of one of the same five grounds, even if the refugee is present in the country illegally. In this respect, the definition helps to mark the boundaries of firm *legal* obligations that states must honor before deciding to remove anyone from national territory. Because the definition essentially trumps normal immigration controls in this setting — political asylum claims filed by persons already on national territory — and because the treaty basically precludes the application of numerical limits or additional selection criteria, states understandably and justifiably apply the definition with rigor in their political asylum systems.[23]

Obligation versus authorization. Those same dynamics do not apply to the quota resettlement system. By linking discretionary refugee admissions so tightly (for most purposes) to the Convention refugee definition, the current statute takes insufficient account of the original intent and practical operations of that treaty provision. That definition, coupled with the nonrefoulement requirement of Article 33, marks out a legal obligation that applies to persons already on the territory of a state that is party to the treaty — the domain of the asylum system. But the treaty does not purport to speak to discretionary resettlement. In asylum, the Convention definition is virtually the only permissible screening criterion. In quota resettlement, the receiving state is free to adopt any further limiting criteria that it wishes, or indeed to go beyond the confines of the Convention definition in setting its acceptance standards. Under existing US law, then, a concept meant to set a minimum obligation in one setting, asylum, has thus been transposed to set a maximum outside boundary in a highly different setting, resettlement. In asylum, the definition is part of a law that *obligates*. In the overseas program, it is now being used as part of a law that merely *authorizes*, but does not and could not obligate this nation to accept any particular population. It would make sense to provide a wider range of carefully structured discretion in the latter setting.

US law has already recognized the value of going beyond the Convention refugee definition for some purposes related to the overseas refugee program. The original Refugee Act includes a provision permitting the President to authorize resettlement of persons still within their countries of nationality, if they have the requisite risk of persecution on account of a Convention ground.[24] Such persons do not fit the Convention refugee definition at the time of selection, because the Convention requires that refugees be outside their country of origin. Later, in the 1989 Lautenberg amendment, Congress decided to assure that certain categories of individuals, from Southeast Asia or the Soviet Union, could qualify for resettlement based on less demanding standards than the Convention definition.[25] A further category, members of Iranian religious minorities, was added to the Lautenberg amendment in January 2004, based on Congress's judgment of the degree of risk faced by all such minorities in Iran.[26] Thus they can qualify for admission even if they cannot provide a detailed account in the DHS interview of targeted threats or individual past persecution. Hence, some authority to admit wider categories of persons as refugees is not a stranger to US law.[27]

Functional differences between asylum and overseas resettlement programs. Further functional differences support a careful modification of the current statute. Most importantly, there is no chance that quota resettlement numbers will rise uncontrollably, even if INA § 207 is expanded. The possibility of large-scale influxes has often been a point of particular concern with respect to the asylum system, for legislatures and often for the public. The very nature of the quota resettlement process, in contrast, with its elaborate procedures governing access and screening well before anyone boards an airplane to come to the United States, assures firm control over qualifications and volume, no matter how narrow or expansive the underlying criteria.

Furthermore, other features of the overseas resettlement program provide, in many circumstances, objective indicators of the genuineness of the dangers in the home country — indicators that are manifest without the need for a probing interview to dissect the person's history and motivations. People who fled their country of origin and went, not to a wealthy country, but to a cross-border refugee camp, and who have remained there for many years of enforced idleness, with meager rations and perhaps ongoing threats from armed bands, have demonstrated by that very endurance the reality of the risks they face at home. The same objective indicators of genuine dangers simply do not exist for those who travel directly to a stable and developed country on their own and then claim asylum. To apply the Convention refugee definition carefully, through a labor-intensive interview, makes sense in the asylum setting. Only such a procedure is reasonably available to distinguish those with real risks of persecution from persons with other motivations that do not justify trumping immigration controls. But with the overseas program, we should make it possible to respond selectively to a wider range of dangers, such as the risk of violence from a prolonged civil war, than what is captured in the Convention definition, precisely because of the other tools available to assure a controlled admission system. For many purposes the international community has recognized this reality, and has adopted wider definitions of "refugee" to be used in specific settings.[28]

These observations do not mean that the Convention definition should be left aside in the overseas refugee program. Not all refugee camps or settlements match the description of the previous paragraph. Moreover, even when they do, resettlement states may often choose to limit their programs to those who have the specific risks of persecution highlighted by the UN treaties. That definition can also help steer the overall program toward focusing on displaced persons with the most acute need. In short, the Convention refugee definition will and should continue to play a major role in the overseas refugee program. But it need not mark absolute outer boundaries for that program, limiting even the President's discretion to respond to a wider range of endangered individuals.[29]

Processing advantages. Such a statutory change would also bring additional processing advantages. Under current law, even with regard to persons who have spent many years in a bleak refugee camp and have been given access to the application process because of a P-2 group designation, DHS officers are now obligated to spend interview time exploring the individualized risk of persecution that the applicant would face. Some officers with whom I spoke expressed a concern that applicants in this setting often have difficulty articulating an individualized basis for a fear of persecution, precisely because it has been so many years since they lived in the country of origin. In the interview, they tend to want to speak of the miseries of life in the refugee camp, not realizing that US law makes risks in the home country the crucial factor. Much interview time is then diverted to drawing out the details of their distant experience in the home country, slowing overall processing and taking time away from questions addressed to identity and possible grounds of inadmissibility. As Chapter V, Section C2 discussed, certain changes in training and briefing of DHS refugee officers could alleviate this problem, even without statutory change. But it would be more straightforward to recognize directly that the United States has made a policy decision at the highest levels to respond to the needs of this camp population through resettlement, based on a broader judgment that the risks in the home country preclude any reasonable prospect of safe return. If the law were changed to empower the President to designate groups for admission in the refugee program, he could, for example, designate all individuals on a verified UNHCR registration list in camp X who arrived there before date Y (say, five years before the designation). The DHS officer could then swiftly decide whether the person meets these objective qualifications and could

devote the balance of the interview to a closer inquiry into identity and any inadmissibility grounds (such as possible drug use or security risks).

Some persons interviewed for this project, both within and outside the government, felt strongly that a statutory change of this type is indispensable for the program to succeed in sustaining a significantly higher level of admissions, such as the level at which the program operated in the 1990s. Particularly if the program is to respond more readily to persons in protracted refugee situations, they stated, it must be possible to provide an additional "humanitarian track" toward admissions, as a supplement to the Convention refugee definition track. Others disagreed, arguing that administrative changes of the type discussed in previous chapters could succeed in expanding the program adequately. But few of the latter actively opposed a statutory expansion. Instead, many expressed broader worries about what might result if the possibility of statutory amendment is affirmatively pressed in an unpredictable congressional climate. (Some of these concerns are considered in the next subsection.)

Countervailing concerns. Interviews for this project unearthed two important concerns about proposing a statutory change of the kind advocated here. First, going beyond the Convention refugee definition might expose the program too much to distortions based on domestic political or foreign policy pressures, divorced from any notion of genuine needs for refugee protection. If so, the change might only exacerbate complaints voiced by program skeptics, to the effect that it has gotten away from resettling "real refugees." Second, I heard concerns that designations of groups for admission without regard to the Convention criteria, once made, would be very hard to terminate, even if the objective need declined or disappeared. Pointing to experiences with the Lautenberg amendment, several people worried that categories, once designated, tend to "calcify."[30] Though subject to a sunset provision, the Lautenberg amendment has been routinely extended in one- or two-year increments since its enactment, without careful congressional assessment of whether the need really continues and despite the significant changes in conditions that have occurred, particularly in the Soviet Union, since 1989. These commenters were not necessarily asserting that conditions were so safe in the covered countries as to end all resettlement. But many thought that any ongoing need could be adequately addressed through a program that went back to applying the Convention refugee definition directly.

The proposed amendment. Both of these are valid concerns, and any statutory amendment should be shaped so as to minimize the risks they identify. The statutory proposal set forth in the annex to this chapter is crafted for precisely those ends. First, any designation process that goes beyond the Convention refugee definition should be available only in circumstances where real dangers preclude return to the home country. Such persons should then be considered "real refugees" in the most important sense: their access to the program is based on demonstrable need and not simply domestic lobbying. Accordingly, the proposed amendment authorizes admissions beyond the Convention definition only when the President determines that the designated group is unable or unwilling to return "owing to a genuine risk of serious harm" in the country of origin.

The risk of calcification may be harder to counter. Any admissions program, once initiated, generates a kind of momentum and a set of expectations that make the program hard to terminate. This momentum appears to be at its strongest with regard to group designations specifically enshrined in statutory language. Even with a sunset provision, Congress is unlikely to have the inclination or the specific procedures that will result in a disciplined look at whether the need really continues. The path of least resistance becomes a simple extension without hearings. Therefore the amendment proposed here would authorize such group designations only in a Presidential Determination, issued after the currently prescribed form of congressional consultation. Any designation is therefore valid for a maximum of one year. Renewal is possible, but would occur only after the normal process for full interagency review and congressional consultation, including the provision of detailed information already called for by INA § 207(e). Though they admittedly provide no guarantee, these processes improve the odds for an executive branch decision to allow the designation to lapse when the need no longer exists.

Calcification could also be minimized if the groups are designated in a fashion that more readily lends itself to a fixed endpoint. That is, I strongly recommend that group designations under the proposed amendment, as incorporated in the PD, be highly detailed and focused. Instead of designating, say, all persons of ethnic group W, or from country X, it will work far better to designate, for example, only all such persons who were in camp Y as of date Z, on the basis of a reliable camp registration system. As discussed in Chapters I and II, in the current era we will generally find it advisable to focus our resettlement program on finite groups whose boundaries are marked as much as possible by other objective criteria such as a prior verified registration — in order to minimize magnet effects and also to help counter fraud. The presidential designations of groups should usually reinforce and build upon that approach. If they are done in this fashion, then it is clear that resettlement under the designation will end once all members of the finite group have been processed. I do not recommend that the statute absolutely require such an approach, however. There may be extraordinary situations justifying a wider or more open-ended designation, such as a sudden mass influx affecting an important ally, or a situation like the border camps in Macedonia at the beginning of the Kosovo crisis, requiring speedy resettlement in order to avoid border pushbacks. Such use of the group designation process should be rare, however. Most of the time, the power ought to be used for highly specific group designations.

Equal status for persons admitted as part of a designated group or category. Some who supported a new capacity to go beyond the Convention refugee definition for purposes of the resettlement program suggested that persons brought in as part of such a "humanitarian track" receive only a more limited form of entitlements or status, perhaps time-limited. Some analogized that approach to temporary protected status (TPS), which provides a more restricted range of protections and entitlements to persons already in the United States, when their return is judged unsafe owing to civil war, natural disaster, or other similar conditions.[31]

I strongly recommend against any such measure. Decisions to designate a class for admission as part of the overseas refugee program should occur only when voluntary repatriation is highly unlikely on any reasonable time frame. When that is the case, we should not presume that the admission, rescuing persons from indefinite stay in a bleak refugee camp, will be temporary. In those circumstances, the United States has every reason to promote a full, speedy, and successful transition to a flourishing new life in the United States. A temporary status would impede that process of integration. Again, the functional differences between the asylum and overseas resettlement setting are important. The temporariness of TPS is best understood as an expression of congressional concern about potential loss of control in a program that covers persons who establish presence on US territory on their own. Those same concerns do not apply to choices to resettle others as part of carefully designated classes in the overseas resettlement program. We have a well-established and generally well-functioning system for moving refugees to this country and helping them make a successful transition to life in this country. We should employ that system fully to achieve the same ends for persons selected under the amendment proposed here. The designation of the group under this new statutory authority would make a difference for DHS processing and interviewing, but thereafter it should have no bearing. Persons thus selected would thereafter be treated as full-fledged refugees under § 207 for all other purposes.

Summary. A proposed amendment to achieve the objectives described above is attached in the annex to this chapter. The change is placed in INA § 207(c) in order to make it abundantly clear that the designations apply only to admission as part of the overseas refugee admissions program, and have no application whatever to asylum or to related domestic decisions, whether applying INA § 208, § 241(b)(3), or the Convention Against Torture. Persons admitted under this new authority would be admitted as full § 207 refugees, under the same procedures and with the same entitlements as all other persons included in the overseas refugee admissions programs. Upon enactment of such a provision, it would make sense to repeal the Lautenberg Amendment, effective at the end of the fiscal year, but with committee language indicating that the President should use the new designation power to provide for the ongoing admission of current Lautenberg categories for as long as the need for such special treatment continues.

Annex to Chapter VII

Statutory Amendment Governing Refugee Admissions under INA § 207

Amend § 207(c) of the Immigration and Nationality Act [8 U.S.C. § 1157(c) (2000)] to read:

(1) (A) Subject to the numerical limitations established pursuant to subsections (a) and (b), the Secretary of Homeland Security may, in the Secretary's discretion and pursuant to such regulations as the Secretary may prescribe, admit

(i) any refugee, or

(ii) any person who is a member of a group or category designated under subparagraph (B), who is not firmly resettled in any foreign country, is determined to be of special humanitarian concern to the United States, and is admissible (except as otherwise provided under paragraph (3)) as an immigrant under this Act.

(B) The President may, in such special circumstances as the President after appropriate consultation (as defined in subsection (e)) may specify, designate specific groups or categories of persons who may be admitted as refugees under this section, without regard to the definition appearing in section 101(a)(42). Such designation shall apply only to a group or category that the

President determines is unable or unwilling to return to the country of nationality or, in the case of groups or categories composed in whole or in part of persons having no nationality, to the country of last habitual residence, owing to a genuine risk of serious harm in that country, and whose resettlement in the United States is justified by humanitarian concerns or is otherwise in the national interest. Any such designation shall take effect only with respect to admission under this section and shall have no bearing on decisions to grant asylum under section 208 or protection under section 241(b)(3) or under the regulations implementing the United Nations Convention against Torture and other Cruel, Inhuman or Degrading Treatment or Punishment.

(2) (A) A spouse or child (as defined in section 101(b)(1)(A), (B), (C), (D), or (E)) of any principal alien who qualifies for admission under this subsection shall, if not otherwise entitled to admission under paragraph (1), be entitled to the same admission status as such principal alien if accompanying, or following to join, the principal alien and if the spouse or child is admissible (except as otherwise provided under paragraph (3)) as an immigrant under this Act. Upon the spouse's or child's admission to the United States, such admission shall be charged against the numerical limitation established in accordance with the appropriate subsection under which the principal alien's admission is charged.

(B) An unmarried alien who seeks to accompany, or follow to join, a parent granted admission under this subsection, and who was under 21 years of age on the date on which such parent applied for status under this section, shall continue to be classified as a child for purposes of this paragraph, if the alien attained 21 years of age after such application was filed but while it was pending.

(3) The provisions of paragraphs (4), (5), and (7)(A) of section 212(a) shall not be applicable to any alien seeking admission to the United States under this subsection, and the Secretary may waive any other provision of such section (other than paragraph (2)(C) or subparagraph (A), (B), (C), or (E) of paragraph (3)) with respect to such an alien for humanitarian purposes, to assure family unity, or when it is otherwise in the public interest. Any such waiver by the Secretary shall be in writing and shall be granted only on an individual basis following an investigation. The Secretary shall provide for the annual reporting to Congress of the number of waivers granted under this paragraph in the previous fiscal year and a summary of the reasons for granting such waivers.

(4) No person shall be admitted under this subsection who ordered, incited, assisted, or otherwise participated in the persecution of any person on account of race, religion, nationality, membership in a particular social group, or political opinion.

(5) The status of any alien (and of the spouse or child of the alien) admitted under this subsection may be terminated by the Secretary pursuant to such regulations as the Secretary may prescribe if the Secretary determines that the alien was not in fact qualified for admission under this subsection at the time of the alien's admission.

[Technical corrections to other provisions, such as INA § 412, may be necessary to conform to the change in paragraph (1). The intent is that all persons admitted under the revised paragraph (1) shall be treated as section 207 refugees, on equal terms with all other such refugees, including with regard to processing, assistance, family unification, and public support during the process of travel to and resettlement in the United States.]

CHAPTER VII. ENDNOTES

1 See HOUSE COMM. ON THE JUDICIARY, THE REFUGEE ACT OF 1979, H.REP. NO. 96-608, at 14 (Nov. 9, 1979).

2 8 U.S.C. § 1159(b) (2000). (Before a 1990 amendment, the maximum number of adjustments was 5,000.) Technically, the statute places the discretion in the Attorney General to use up to 10,000 admissions for adjusting the status of asylees, taken from the total set forth in the annual Presidential Determination. But in practice, PDs since the beginning have specifically provided separately for additional numbers to be used for asylee adjustments, and the immigration agencies have considered those numbers available only for those purposes. Special legislation has also exempted a few nationalities from being counted against the adjustment cap. See Ngwanyia v. Ashcroft, 302 F.Supp.2d 1076, 1081 n.9 (D.Minn. 2004).

3 Id. at 1080 n.7.

4 Id. at 1083, 1088.

5 See David A. Martin, *The Refugee Act of 1980: Its Past and Future*, 1982 MICH. Y.B. INT'L L. STUD. 91, 110 & n.87.

6 INA§ 209(a), 8 U.S.C. § 1159(a) (2000).

7 See T. ALEXANDER ALEINIKOFF, DAVID A. MARTIN, & HIROSHI MOTOMURA, IMMIGRATION AND CITIZENSHIP: PROCESS AND POLICY 763 (3d ed. 1995).

8 Pub. L. No. 101-649, Title I, § 104, 104 Stat. 4978, 4985-86 (1990).

9 INA § 209(b), 8 U.S.C. § 1159(b) (2000) (final sentence).

10 INA § 209(a)(2), 8 U.S.C. § 1159(a)(2) (2000).

11 INA § 101(a)(42), 8 U.S.C. § 1101(a)(42) (2000) (third sentence).

12 INA § 207(a)(5), 8 U.S.C. § 1157(a)(5) (2000).

13 In FY 2002, there were 2,392 conditional grants of asylum under these provisions. DEPARTMENT OF HOMELAND SECURITY, 2002 YEARBOOK OF IMMIGRATION STATISTICS 57.

14 See, e.g., Matter of Y-T-L-, 23 I & N Dec. 601 (BIA 2003); Ma v. Ashcroft, 361 F.3d 553 (9th Cir. 2004); Li v. Ashcroft, 356 F.3d 1153 (9th Cir. 2004) (en banc).

15 Matter of X-P-T-, 21 I & N Dec. 634 (BIA 1996) established that the statutory change in INA § 101(a)(42), treating harms under coercive family planning programs as persecution on account of political opinion, also applies to determinations under the withholding of removal section.

16 SENATE COMM. ON THE JUDICIARY, THE REFUGEE ACT OF 1979, (S.REP. NO. 96-256, at 7 (June 21, 1979).

17 The Commission on Immigration Reform also recommended in 1997 that refugees be admitted as LPRs, with a possible exception for those infrequent occasions involving a hasty evacuation. COMMISSION ON IMMIGRATION REFORM, US REFUGEE POLICY: TAKING LEADERSHIP 53 (1997).

18 INA § 240, 8 U.S.C. § 1229a (2000).

19 S.REP. NO. 96-256, at 4. See also H.REP. NO. 96-608, at 9. Earlier refugee admissions provisions were limited to persons who fled Communist countries or the Middle East.

20 *Done* July 28, 1951, 189 U.N.T.S. 137. Although the United States is not a party to the Convention directly, it became derivatively bound to the treaty's requirements in 1968 when it adhered to the Protocol relating to the Status of Refugees, *done* Jan. 31, 1967, 19 U.S.T. 6223, T.I.A.S. No. 6577, 606 U.N.T.S. 267.

21 See David A. Martin, *Refugees and Migration*, in THE UNITED NATIONS AND INTERNATIONAL LAW 155, 166-68 (C. Joyner ed., 1997).

22 Guy Goodwin-Gill, *The Future of International Refugee Law*, in REFUGEES, Oct. 1988, at 28.

23 This discussion glosses over some technical shadings that do not detract from the main points. For example, no state is required to grant asylum to a refugee illegally present, nor to provide such an individual most of the status protections in the treaty — because most of those protections depend not only on meeting the refugee definition but also on a further exercise of state discretion to give the person a lawful immigration status. The state is therefore bound only to honor the nonrefoulement obligation — i.e., to avoid sending the refugee to the country of persecution — not to grant asylum. Most states with developed asylum systems, however, including the United States, have wisely decided to go ahead and provide full legal status once the individual is found to meet the Convention refugee definition, with only limited exceptions.

United States doctrine also draws a distinction between the threshold standard for nonrefoulement and the well-founded fear standard, treating the former as more rigorous. INS v. Cardoza-Fonseca, 480 US 421 (1987). This doctrine differs from the approach taken in virtually all other states, which consider the threshold requirements for both the definition and nonrefoulement identical. See, e.g., Regina v. Sec'y of State for the Home Dept., ex parte Sivakumaran, [1988] AC 958, at para. 5 (House of Lords 1987). But in practice the most important standard for protection in the United States remains the Convention refugee definition, because discretionary denials of asylum to persons who meet that definition are strongly disfavored. Matter of Pula, 19 I&N Dec. 467 (1987); Matter of Kasinga, 21 I&N Dec. 357, 367 (1996). For these reasons, the discussion here will speak of US obligations that attach to asylum and the refugee definition, even though technically the absolute minimum obligation is the province of the withholding of removal (or nonrefoulement) provision and its somewhat more narrow governing standard.

It might be further noted that many states, particularly in Europe, have gradually added further and more expansive legal criteria that require protection against return — often called "subsidiary protection." See Kay Hailbronner, *Principles of International Law Regarding the Concept of Subsidiary Protection*, in SUBSIDIARY PROTECTION OF REFUGEES IN THE EUROPEAN UNION: COMPLEMENTING THE GENEVA CONVENTION? 1-18 (Daphné Bouteillet-Paquet ed., 2002). The United States generally has not taken this further step, with the exception of its 1994 acceptance of the Torture

Convention's obligation against return to face torture (whatever the grounds for its infliction). Convention Against Torture and other Cruel, Inhuman, or Degrading Treatment or Punishment, art. 3, *done* Dec. 10, 1984, G.A. Res. 39/46, U.N. GAOR, 39th Sess., Supp. No. 51, U.N. Doc. A/39/51. But even when additional criteria have been adopted, governments have still tended to apply them with strictness, including close attention to the credibility of the applicant's story, in the adjudicative systems that deal with protection claims filed by persons who make it on their own to the national territory.

24 INA § 101(a)(42)(B), 8 U.S.C. § 1101(a)(42)(B) (2000).

25 Pub. L. No. 101-167, Title V, § 599D, 103 Stat. 1261 (1989). This statute has been amended since 1989; the most recently compiled version appears at 8 U.S.C.A. § 1157 Note (1999 & Supp. 2004). Persons covered by the amendment can establish their eligibility for admission as a refugee under § 207 (but not for asylum) by asserting a fear of persecution and "asserting a credible basis for concern about the possibility of such persecution."

26 Pub. L. No. 108-199, Div. E., Tit. II, § 213, 118 Stat. 253 (2004).

27 It also bears noting that US law authorizes, but does not obligate, response to a wider range of risks even for those who make their way to US soil on their own — through the provision allowing for temporary protected status (TPS). INA § 244, 8 U.S.C. § 1254a (2000). This section authorizes the discretionary designation of specific categories of persons who will be temporarily protected against removal from the United States, based on a finding of ongoing armed conflict, natural disaster, or other "extraordinary and temporary conditions" that preclude return in safety. Further, even with regard to asylum itself, US statutes contain certain special allowances that expand eligibility beyond the strict confines of the Convention refugee definition. See Section D of this chapter (discussing the special provisions for persons at risk under coercive population measures), and Matter of H-, 21 I & N Dec. 337 (BIA 1996) (discussing the significance of past persecution, which may be the basis for an asylum grant under US law even in the absence of a future threat).

28 A leading example of this appears in the definition of refugee used in the Organization of African Unity Convention Governing the Specific Aspects of Refugee Problems in Africa, art. 1, *entered into force*, June 20, 1974, 1001 U.N.T.S. 45. That treaty employs the UN definition plus the following:

The term "refugee" shall also apply to every person who, owing to external aggression, occupation, foreign domination or events seriously disturbing public order in either part or the whole of his country of origin or nationality, is compelled to leave his place of habitual residence in order to seek refuge in another place outside his country of origin or nationality.

The General Assembly has also used expanded concepts of refugee in authorizing action by the UNHCR to assist or protect persons who do not fit the standard definition. See Martin, *supra* note 21, at 159-62.

29 It is worth noting that the other leading refugee resettlement countries, Canada and Australia, both anchor their programs in the Convention refugee definition but go on to allow admission, under specified conditions, of persons who face other kinds of threats. See JOANNE VAN SELM, TAMARA WOROBY, ERIN PATRICK, & MONICA MATTS, FEASIBILITY OF RESETTLEMENT IN THE EUROPEAN UNION 77-83 (Migration Policy Institute, 2003) (Part I, Section 4 of that study usefully summarizes the resettlement laws and practices of over a dozen resettlement countries). Canada's system specifically allows for admission, in addition to Convention refugees, of a "source country class," in many ways similar to US provisions for the admission of "in-country refugees" under INA § 101(a)(42)(B), 8 U.S.C. § 1101(a)(42)(B) (2000), and of a further "country of asylum class," which includes persons "seriously and personally affected by civil war or armed conflict." REFUGEE RESETTLEMENT DIVISION, REFUGEE BRANCH, CITIZENSHIP AND IMMIGRATION CANADA, CANADA'S REFUGEE AND HUMANITARIAN RESETTLEMENT PROGRAM 5 (Nov. 8, 2002) (paper prepared for IGC Workshop on Resettlement, Geneva), available on the department's website, <www.cic.gc.ca>. Over the last five years preceding the cited 2002 report, Canada admitted 40,662 Convention refugees and 10,196 members of the latter two classes. Id. Canadian officials with whom I spoke warmly supported the extra flexibility made available by the statutory provisions permitting resettlement beyond the confines of the Convention definition.

30 This apt verb was applied to the Lautenberg categories by Bill Frelick in Senate hearings held in 2002. See *Empty Seats in a Lifeboat: Are There Problems with the US Refugee Program?: Hearing Before the Subcomm. on Immigration, S. Comm. on the Judiciary*, 107th Cong. 21-22 (2002) (statement of Bill Frelick, Director of Policy, US Committee for Refugees).

31 INA § 244, 8 U.S.C. § 1254a (2000). See *supra* note 27.

CONSOLIDATED RECOMMENDATIONS

CHAPTER I. THE CONTEXT

Recommendation I-1: The US Refugee Program should be explicitly based on a broad perspective about the use of resettlement. The President, the Secretary of State, the Secretary of Homeland Security, the Assistant Secretary for PRM, and the Director of the Bureau of Citizenship and Immigration Services (USCIS) should make it abundantly clear that the USRP is not limited to rescue from grave life-threatening dangers, but will work actively to rescue displaced individuals and groups who face a wider range of harms, including the wastage of human potential that can result from protracted stay in a refugee camp. These latter needs are real and compelling, and there are large populations meeting these wider criteria. Therefore, the program can still be prudent and selective in choosing among them, with full attention to countervailing factors such as possible magnet effects, other political impacts, and near-term prospects for voluntary repatriation. This approach should be accompanied by a determination to sustain fully viable budgets for refugee assistance, minimizing as much as possible any direct financial competition between assistance and resettlement.

On the other hand, if the Administration and the State Department are unprepared to make a firm declaration of this sort, including adequate funding for both admissions and assistance, they should then be fully candid and consistent about the likely outcomes in the current era, which lacks large-scale programs like those formerly in place for Indochina and the Soviet Union. That is, without new initiatives premised on this broader perspective, admission totals will almost surely remain low and admissions will fluctuate widely, whatever other operational improvements are introduced for pro-

cessing those given access to the program. Without top-level candor on these points, officials responsible for the system are placed in an extremely difficult and unfair position. They will be judged by most outside observers against a high admissions total placed in the annual Presidential Determination, but not given the more specific policy directives and resources that are indispensable to meet that benchmark.

Recommendation I-2: The number of admissions set in the annual Presidential Determination should be treated as a goal, not a ceiling. It should therefore provide a firm benchmark (following a reasonable transition process) for accountability of the offices that have a role in access decisions and management of the system, including not only PRM and USCIS but also the regional bureaus of the Department of State and the enforcement bureaus of the Department of Homeland Security. Because of the potential volatility of refugee flows, and the program's vulnerability to unforeseen problems, the benchmark should apply with reasonable tolerances, which can probably diminish once a system built on this new approach has matured. To perform this function, the PD admissions number must be set at reasonable, though challenging, levels congruent with the resources being made available through the budget process.

Access decisions should still pay attention to countervailing factors, both logistical and political, that might appropriately weigh against a resettlement initiative. Such decisions must still be done case-by-case, with full attention to the context. But treating the PD as a firm goal by which performance will be measured will help counter a long-standing tendency to give undue weight to the disadvantages of a proposed initiative.

CHAPTER II. REFORMING THE SYSTEM FOR DECIDING ON RESETTLEMENT INITIATIVES

Recommendation II-1: PRM, as the lead office in the process of group designation, must develop a sense of mission about adding one or two new groups to the pipeline development process each month. PRM must impart energy and vision to this mission, in a way that will promote added efforts on the part of the other players in the process, both governmental and nongovernmental. It must seek innovative ways to accomplish the various functions involved. The Admissions Office staff should also expand in view of the very different requirements in this new era of refugee resettlement. Without abandoning its own critical perspective on admissions proposals, the Admissions Office must come to think of itself as the component in the decision making system that gives the benefit of the doubt to resettlement, so as to serve as a counterweight to negative arguments that will readily appear from other governmental or international quarters.

Recommendation II-2: The Department of State should establish a Refugee Admissions Committee, to meet no less often than bimonthly. In a multi-level decision process, the committee should consider lists of potential groups and select candidate groups for more thorough investigation. After the investigation, which could involve field visits by targeted response teams that include representatives of NGOs, the DHS, and perhaps UNHCR and IOM, the committee will ultimately designate groups for priority resettlement, at a rate needed to meet the PD target and to sustain a reasonably steady flow of admissions. The committee should also play a central role in the adoption of the annual congressional consultation document. It should schedule its deliberations so as to assure that the document is prepared in a timely and complete fashion that will enable consultation with Congress before its August recess and signing of the Presidential Determination by early September.

CHAPTER III. THE PRIORITY SYSTEM FOR ACCESS TO THE ADMISSIONS PROGRAM AND ARRANGEMENTS FOR URGENT CASES

Recommendation III-1: The priority system should be revised modestly, so that P-1 becomes the priority for individual referrals from UNHCR, US embassies, or, in some circumstances, other referring entities; P-2 covers all decisions for designated groups; and P-3 remains the category for close family members of US residents. P-4 and P-5, now covering more distant family relationships, should be removed as priorities, although those same family connections might sometimes be characteristics used in specific P-2 designations. UNHCR group referrals should be worked into the group designation process under P-2, and should cease being thought of as P-1 groups. Such UNHCR referrals should generally enjoy additional momentum for approval as an access category. PRM should consider refining the list of factors for P-1 referrals accordingly, as well as adding a factor for persons facing persecution that is based on their real or imputed ties to the US government or US entities. PRM should also regularly post on its website a list of P-2 groups currently being given access to the US system.

Recommendation III-2: PRM should press UNHCR to continue expanding its individual referral capacity, possibly streamlining the referral process for US-destined cases, and enhancing its mechanisms for quality control and consistency. Procedures for embassy referrals of P-1 cases should be simplified, and State Department training should better equip embassy personnel for this role. PRM should systematically evaluate the past experiences with NGO individual referral schemes, so that the process can be refined and made available elsewhere. Such referrals will ordinarily be done quietly by NGO personnel present in the camp or settlement for other reasons, and can be expected to produce only modest numbers, because they will focus on urgent, compelling cases.

Recommendation III-3: The Department of State should give close attention to NGO suggestions, including the annual RCUSA recommendations report, when developing the potential group list. Concomitantly, NGOs should work to address more concretely the trade-offs, barriers, and obstacles that would affect any resettlement initiative — and that sometimes counsel against undertaking it. No legislative sanction is needed or desirable with regard to that sort of input. Once a group has been chosen as a candidate group, further investigation of group needs and characteristics should take place. It will often prove advantageous to proceed through a field mission by a targeted response team, which should ordinarily include NGO representation and one or more participants from the Department of Homeland Security.

Recommendation III-4: The Visas 93 process needs to work reliably and efficiently, because it serves a vital function: reuniting a resettled refugee with his or her spouse and minor children. At the least, Visas 93 training should be a regular part of consular training, and the State Department should adopt additional procedures (possibly including a greater monitoring role for WRAPS) to assure that such cases do not languish. The DHS should also either revise the Form I-730 or develop two separate forms for Visas 92 and Visas 93 cases, so that the form will better guide the consular officer through all the distinctive steps needed for Visas 93 cases, owing to their inclusion in the special benefits of the overseas refugee program. The DHS and PRM should also consider arrangements that could take most Visas 93 work from consular officers and have it handled through standard OPE procedures, with ultimate adjudication by the DHS.

Recommendation III-5: Review of family cases by DHS's Refugee Access Verification Unit (RAVU), which includes checking asserted family relationships against earlier family information in the anchor relative's A-file, has been a highly worthwhile development. RAVU also provides an institutional location for ongoing innovations to respond to what will inevitably be new schemes and patterns of fraud. The DHS should continue to work cooperatively with PRM and the NGOs in developing such refinements, and PRM should make the affidavit of relationship, with revisions, into an official government form. The DHS and PRM should also pilot-test wider use of DNA testing and should closely consider the costs and benefits of routine DNA testing as part of the medical examination all refugees must pass, particularly as testing costs decline. Ongoing improvements in the safeguards against fraud should permit an expansion in the availability of P-3 admissions.

Recommendation III-6: Now that antifraud capacity has significantly improved, PRM should continue expanding the list of nationalities for whom P-3 access is available. It should also give serious consideration to implementing a carefully designed universal P-3 category for a few years on a trial basis, at least until the other priorities come closer to using all available admission spaces. This universal program, however, should use the AOR filing restrictions implemented in FY 2004 (permitting filings only by those persons admitted to the United States as refugees or asylees). Additionally, it should allow filings only within a stated number of years after the principal relative's admission, and should warn explicitly that cases in low-volume locations may not be processed, or may have to wait many months or years for processing. Such a pilot test should be carefully monitored for problems with either processing or fraud.

Recommendation III-7: PRM and the DHS should work together to restore the capacity to act in a matter of days or weeks to approve and resettle as § 207 refugees persons who are in grave and immediate danger and whose cases are referred by UNHCR or a US embassy. This procedure for urgent action cases should replace the use of parole to the greatest extent possible. Such cases will be exceptional and the volume of such cases can be expected to be quite low, thus making such special arrangements feasible.

Recommendation III-8: The President has the legal authority to designate all countries for in-country processing, provided that other precise limitations confine its effect, thus honoring the "special circumstances" requirement of the statute. Such a designation would hold advantages for a handful of urgent cases each year, involving the rescue of individuals from immediately dangerous circumstances in their country of nationality. But a full exploration of possible drawbacks should be undertaken before deciding on such a step.

CHAPTER IV. THE ROLE OF THE DEPARTMENT OF HOMELAND SECURITY

Recommendation IV-1: The DHS should place a high priority on developing a system for prompt resolution of internal disputes over immigration- and refugee-related guidance and policy, a problem that arises when a given issue holds implications for both enforcement and services. The system must assure that services-related perspectives are given a full airing and are not drowned out by concerns emanating from DHS enforcement offices. Such a system will likely require a far more active policy and coordination role in this realm for the office of the Secretary or Deputy Secretary, the only officials who have direct authority over both the enforcement and services units of the DHS. The Department should also move promptly to resolve currently pending matters for which a decision or clearance has been requested by other departments.

Recommendation IV-2: The DHS should continue to use and refine existing quality-control measures to assure consistency in refugee adjudications, properly applying a generous interpretation of the refugee definition in overseas processing. It should also give ongoing consideration to other measures, such as detailed training on conditions in the country of origin, as well as guidance on specific situations that should be presumptively regarded as justifying a finding of a well-founded fear of persecution. Such steps would both advance quality control and consistency and also free up interview time to address questions of identity and inadmissibility, including security concerns.

Recommendation IV-3: The DHS should continue its cooperative work with PRM and embassy security officers to bring about the timely creation of secure sites for interviewing refugees designated for access to the program. It should also place a priority on developing new techniques that can expand the range of possible deployments, because a large number of circuit rides to potentially hazardous locations will be needed in the current era of refugee admissions. Better security training of deployed officers and more use of experienced officers permanently assigned to refugee responsibilities, for example, will help lower the deployment threshold. The DHS should also continue and enhance its active exploration of video hookup possibilities that could enable effective interviewing, when necessary, from a remote location, taking full account of confidentiality and other concerns.

Recommendation IV-4: The DHS should move ahead as soon as possible with deployment of an expert refugee corps. This is exactly the kind of creative institutional change needed to handle the demands of admission processing when most future admissions are likely to derive from a multitude of disparate groups located in far-flung and often dangerous sites, to be handled by circuit rides rather than permanently stationed staff. Having a corps of full-time and experienced refugee officers should alleviate a great many of the problems that other players have raised in the past with DHS performance, and the concept has wide support throughout the government and among NGOs. The DHS should resolve the remaining design questions promptly and begin deployment as soon as possible.

CHAPTER V. OPERATIONAL ISSUES AND AN OVERVIEW OF THE RESETTLEMENT PROCESS

Recommendation V-1: PRM and the DHS need to move away from ad hoc responses to problems, adopting instead a managerial approach that resolutely seeks to adopt or modify standard operating procedures when problems recur, clarifying lines of authority and accountability. Current PRM-DHS working groups and PRM-NGO working groups should help in moving toward that approach. While that process matures, regular involvement of DHS officers and NGO representatives on investigatory teams considering candidate groups or doing other preparatory work in advance of a resettlement initiative, as recommended in Chapter II, should go far toward anticipating possible difficulties, taking steps to avoid them, and collecting a body of experience that will foster changes with wider application. Over the medium term, the working groups should strive to develop standard operating procedures governing all parts of the refugee admission process, with a checklist of cooperative steps needed at specific stages leading up to and through the deployment of DHS officers.

Recommendation V-2: Both NGOs and IOM can serve well as OPEs, and their roles are not as disparate as some of the usual discussion of this sensitive point suggests. To bridge the gap in perceptions, PRM should initiate a review process involving experienced representatives from PRM, the DHS, IOM, OPEs, and resettlement volags, designed to develop a shared understanding of the OPE role. This process should go beyond mere discussion sessions. It should be designed to result in a set of detailed guidelines and standard operating procedures applicable to all OPEs. Those guidelines and procedures should include explicit understandings about OPE "advocacy" (assuring the best possible presentation of all elements of the applicant's refugee claim and other qualifications) and OPE responsibility to develop and include in the file any negative information. PRM should set specific timetables for conclusion of the guidelines and standard operating procedures, preferably within one year after initiation of the process.

PRM and the DHS should develop a specific reporting format to be used by the DHS team immediately after each circuit ride to provide a detailed evaluation of the OPE's work and to replace the more ad hoc communications that now occur (or fail to occur). PRM should use these evaluations in its regular monitoring of OPE performance and to implement constructive changes. This system should be implemented promptly, without waiting for the conclusion of the broader guidelines and procedures for OPE operations, although the review process mentioned in the preceding paragraph could certainly provide additional suggestions for refinements. Government managers should also welcome a carefully channeled but vigorous system-feedback role for OPEs, whose personnel have a crucial perspective on the operations of these complex programs.

Recommendation V-3: The DHS, in cooperation with PRM and other State Department units, should arrange for improved training on country conditions and characteristics of the expected caseload before deployment of an interviewing team, including the provision of high-quality documentary material that the team can continue to use in the field. In preparing such training and materials, the DHS should draw on a variety of sources, including its own Resource Information Center, the State Department's regional bureaus and its Bureau of Democracy, Human Rights and Labor, the Commission on International Religious Freedom, and nongovernmental sources. Any targeted response team that investigated the particular candidate group now slated for interview should also participate, either in person or by providing specific information to be used in the training. The intelligence agencies often also have a role to play, particularly in helping to develop questioning strategies, tailored to the particular group and best designed to elicit information that might reveal terrorist connections, involvement in past human rights abuses, or other similar problems. PRM and the DHS should cooperate to assure that training is in compliance with the International Religious Freedom Act of 1998.

Finally, the DHS and PRM should give close consideration, in advance of interviews, to the development of detailed guidance, perhaps in the form of presumptions, that can facilitate the adjudication task — for example, identifying specific characteristics that should lead to a finding of a well-founded fear of persecution without requiring detailed questioning about further individual circumstances. Such guidance enables centralized policy-level decisions on how to view particular events or threats.

Recommendation V-4: Integrity, competence, and completeness in interpretation services are highly important for the refugee program. PRM and the DHS should take proactive steps to assure high-quality interpretation, including increasing the resources devoted to this task. Measures could include adding specific requirements to the standard operating procedures for OPEs governing the selection, vetting, and supervision of interpreters, including provisions to minimize the use of interpreters drawn from the refugee community. Direct US government hire of interpreters should also be considered, and to the greatest extent possible, the DHS should seek to recruit adjudicators who themselves possess the relevant language skills.

Recommendation V-5: The DHS, in cooperation with PRM and OPEs, should develop standard procedures and consistent substantive standards for dealing with requests for reconsideration. These should guide both the OPE role in selecting those cases in which it will help prepare an RFR and the DHS process for dealing with RFRs. PRM should also work with UNHCR to clarify an appropriate stance for UNHCR's own further actions with regard to cases for which reconsideration has been requested.

Recommendation V-6: Much progress has been made since the changed security screening procedures were introduced after September 11, 2001. After many months of confusion, inefficiency, and delays, security screening is now being worked into the normal routine of processing in most cases. The agencies involved need to assure continued full staffing of the security advisory opinion (SAO) process so that all initial review will be completed within the stated time frames (currently forty-five days), and so that hits may be resolved promptly. All agencies involved should set a deadline for closing old cases that became mired in the system in 2002 and early 2003, making a firm decision on clearance and promptly notifying those whose cases have been in suspense. Eventually SAO processing for refugees should return to the Bureau of Consular Affairs — certainly no later than completion of the larger SAO reform process — but with full provision for efficient completion of refugee cases.

Recommendation V-7: The deployment of the WRAPS data system has already provided major improvements and standardization for the admissions program, but more can be done, and resources should be provided to accomplish key changes as a matter of high priority. In particular, the family tree screens of WRAPS should be modified. Moreover, the management potential of WRAPS has not been fully tapped, because the system does not now generate reports with the sorts of detail that would be of greatest use to those engaged in pipeline management. Ongoing WRAPS revisions should assure that detailed stock and flow data are available on a month-by-month (or other periodic) basis for each refugee population.

Recommendation V-8: In the short term, within a matter of months, the DHS should revise and streamline its procedures for issuing employment authorization documents, so that the per-plane limit of thirty-five refugees can be significantly increased and that IOM's use of charter aircraft for refugee transport again becomes practical. These changes would be without prejudice to more thorough reforms that would one day permit the prompt issuance of a more secure EAD or identity document that could better serve the needs of both immigration agencies and the Social Security Administration. As those longer-term reforms proceed, the agencies involved should make every effort to assure that refugees receive the document at the port of entry. If the more secure document can only be provided at some later point, then the procedures must be designed to assure receipt within about two weeks of arrival, because such documents are so important for the successful reception and integration of refugees in the destination city.

Recommendation V-9: The DHS should revise the Form I-485 to include specific boxes and questions for use in connection with refugee adjustments and should revise the form's instructions to give specific guidance to refugees and those who assist them.

Chapter VI. The Role of the Office of the United Nations High Commissioner for Refugees

Recommendation VI-1: PRM, while remaining fully supportive of the UNHCR integrity initiatives, should continue to press UNHCR to make its individual referral process more efficient, disciplined, and productive. UNHCR should consider closely whether some parts of its process, including the lengthy Resettlement Registration Form, could be streamlined, especially for those cases that are likely to be referred to countries, like the United States, which perform their own detailed processing and interviewing. UNHCR should also be encouraged to take a close look at its current resettlement categories, in light of a decade's worth of experience operating under this framework, in order to refine and improve the criteria so that they better meet real needs and minimize any incentive to manipulate either the system or the refugee's own personal situation in order to qualify.

Recommendation VI-2: The US government should do all it can to support the further refinement and early successful deployment of UNHCR's group referral mechanism. It should give such referrals quick and favorable consideration for inclusion in the US Refugee Program, and it should encourage other nations to join in the resettlement effort.

Recommendation VI-3: Standardized registration practices, using carefully designed data elements, can have enormous long-run advantages in enabling and improving resettlement. Their potential is so great that registration advances deserve the highest priority. Enhanced registration can provide a payoff for assistance purposes immediately. Its benefits to resettlement will appear only in the long run, but the advances in avoiding fraud, minimizing magnet effects, and improving initial decisions about access will be substantial. The US government should therefore continue to support the development and early deployment of improvements in UNHCR registration practices. It should also encourage UNHCR to work toward inclusion of biometric identifiers in registration documents and records wherever possible and should provide US funding for early UNHCR use of mobile fingerprint technology developed by the DHS.

Chapter VII. Statutory Amendments

A. Provide for continued refugee movements at the beginning of the fiscal year, even if the Presidential Determination is delayed.

B. Allow congressional consultation by both Cabinet secretaries and deputy secretaries.

C. Repeal the ceiling on asylee adjustments.

D. Reconsider the ceiling on refugee and asylee status grants based on coercive population control measures.

E. Consider admitting overseas refugees as lawful permanent residents.

F. Allow the President to designate specific classes of persons to be admitted as § 207 refugees without individually applying the Convention refugee definition.

Afterword

I n the eight months since I completed the report that appears in the preceding sections of this volume, several promising developments have taken place in the US admissions program. The resettlement system is definitely changing, generating a better capacity to handle the challenges that this new era of refugee resettlement presents. Many of the changes are consistent with the recommendations my report contains. Nonetheless, progress remains measured, and a few dark clouds linger, particularly with respect to government funding.

I. Positive developments

Most importantly, resettlement to the United States in FY 2004 took a major quantitative step in the right direction. The United States admitted 52,875 refugees, an 86 percent increase over the 2003 total of 28,422.[1] Some NGO representatives have eagerly noted that the same percentage growth in FY 2005 would take us over 90,000 admissions (a total that the Administration had targeted back in August 2001).[2] But clearly this growth rate cannot be sustained, even though the system now appears capable of steady, solid increases. The 2004 performance reflected the maturation of several new processes and structures put into place in the wake of the September 11 attacks — the end of a difficult shake-down period that had taken two full years. For example, as the book discusses, security checks now work much more smoothly, and proper allowances for efficient screening of this sort have now been built into the normal processing schedule. Further improvements in that realm are nearing deployment — for example, a highly auto-mated system for notifying posts of the results of the security advisory opinion (SAO) checks, with-out the need for time-consuming individual cables.

Changes like this are certainly welcome, but they will not bring quantum leaps in processing capacity.

In another sign that the program is regaining its footing, a State Department review found that 78 percent of those approved for resettlement in FY 2004 actually arrived in the United States within 180 days of their DHS interview.[3] This represents a major improvement over the repeated delays that had so hobbled the system in the preceding two years, often requiring that medical and security clearances be redone from scratch, because of the time limits on their validity.

Exceeding 50,000 admissions for FY 2004 boosted the morale of beleaguered participants in the process — both governmental and nongovernmental — and contributed to a constructive change of tone in much of the debate. The totals made clear that we are no longer mired in the stagnation brought on by September 11, but can now begin to think of targeted refinements focused more clearly on refugee needs, while still working steadily to expand capacity. The gains afford no reason to relax — the system needs to raise that 180-day arrival percentage, for example — but they provide some space for patient work to build thoughtful long-term improvements, rather than simply scram-bling to add numbers.

The document prepared by the key executive departments for congressional consultation in advance of the FY 2005 PD depicts increased activity to identify good candidates for group initiatives and for expanded individual access. It describes eight new P-2 groups, plus four more "under active consideration for group designation."[4] As of March 2005, the groups among the former who are already arriving in the United States or undergoing DHS interviews include Meskhetian Turks from Russia, a group of about 15,000 Hmong Lao from Wat Tham Krabok in Thailand, Somali Benadir, principally from Dadaab Camp in Kenya (a location that had been too dangerous for circuit rides in earlier years), and specific Liberian groups from Ghana and Guinea. In addition, DHS will begin interviews in June 2005 for approximately 2,000 Vietnamese who have resided for decades in the Philippines.

The Wat Tham Krabok resettlement initiative was well-received by the Thai government and may have contributed to its greater willingness to consider other steps toward resolving long-term refugee situations. There is new momentum, for example, in the resettlement of urban Burmese from Thailand, based on individual UNHCR referrals. And UNHCR is undertaking a detailed refugee registration in the border regions that have housed tens of thousands of Burmese displaced for many years, in order to lay the groundwork for developing durable solutions. Perhaps resettlement could be among those solutions, at least for select subgroups.[5]

Other salutary PRM initiatives are also in evidence. WRAPS will soon deploy revised family tree screens, meeting an insistent request I often heard from OPE personnel. The Bureau has made regular use of targeted response teams, which include NGO representatives, to examine possibilities for resettlement in various refugee camps and settlements, and remains committed to this technique for identifying appropriate initiatives. The consultation document reports that teams were sent to Uganda, Guinea, Ghana, and Mozambique during 2004 to examine possibilities for resettlement. The first three have led or will lead to group referrals from UNHCR, and the fourth to an increase in individual referrals.[6] This process must continue and expand, so that a steady flow of new candidate groups can be given careful consideration for P-2 designation. Individual referral activity has also increased, notably including in Malaysia, where UNHCR is expected to refer about 2,000 Burmese Chin for resettlement, perhaps half of them to the United States.[7] UNHCR seems to have met its US referral targets for FY 2004, exceeding 20,000 (targets set as part of the negotiations over PRM's multiyear enhanced funding for this activity).[8] Group referrals are part of the picture, even if the more systematic group referral process described in Chapter VI has not fully gotten off the ground.

And State Department security officers, working with the DHS, have had real success in arranging secure sites for DHS interviewing.[9] As a result, the pace of circuit rides has picked up, and schedules have encountered fewer disruptions. PRM has also added its voice to the worldwide campaign against refugee warehousing, an issue that provided the focus for the US Committee for Refugees' *World Refugee Survey 2004*, although with somewhat different emphasis than that favored by the NGOs.[10]

The Department of Homeland Security is also making strides in addressing the demands of this new resettlement era. The proposed FY 2006 budget contains funds for a centralized policy planning office for the Department under a new Assistant Secretary, reporting directly to the Secretary.[11] Much depends on as-yet unresolved details, but the DHS should use this opportunity to develop a sorely needed mechanism to ensure immigration policy coordination among the three bureaus of the DHS that inherited pieces of the former INS, as Chapter IV recommends. At the very least, the new policy office should help the Department avoid situations where decisions that affect the refugee program remain stalemated because the three bureaus disagree. In the meantime, some DHS policy decisions that had been long awaited by other players in the process have finally been resolved. DHS policy on the processing of various Middle Eastern refugees has now been issued, for example, meaning that cases that had waited in limbo since September 11, 2001, are now being adjudicated or readjudicated and will receive a definitive decision, up or down. Final decisions on a permanent, speedy, and secure EAD issuance process for refugees have not been achieved, but a new procedure was pilot-tested in late FY 2004 with charter flights of Hmong refugees. Despite several glitches, the experience may point the way toward a better system that can deliver to refugees the most secure version of the work authorization card no later than two weeks after arrival — a timeline that remains important in order to facilitate the refugees' integration into the destination community.

Above all, the DHS is moving ahead smartly with the Refugee Corps, a key process change that should pay considerable dividends for decades to come. (See Chapter IV.) It recently created a new high-level position in the Senior Executive Service, the Director of the Office of Refugee Affairs, who will oversee the Refugee Corps and international operations. The position should be filled by late summer 2005. The Refugee Corps itself has gone from the drawing board to implementation. After a thorough design process that included extensive studies and recommendations by Booz Allen Hamilton, a high-powered management consulting firm, the DHS is now beginning to fill positions in the corps, and expects to achieve full staffing by the end of FY 2006. The corps, which will have approximately 90 positions, will include a policy direction group, an antifraud unit, a training and program integrity unit, and enhanced administrative support, in addition to the officers deployed to the field. When the corps is complete, circuit rides will be largely staffed by expert corps members, but the Department expects to continue using asylum officers on temporary assignment for perhaps 20 percent of a circuit ride team.

II. NEGATIVE SIGNS

Many NGO representatives were disappointed that the PD ceiling for FY 2005 remained at 70,000, the same stated level as the past three years, and particularly that the PD again includes 20,000 spaces parked in an unallocated reserve.[12] (They were quite pleased, however, that this year the PD was signed on September 30, thereby avoiding the processing lapses that PD delays had caused in earlier years.) Some see retention of the unallocated reserve as a sign of incomplete commitment to use the full resource of resettlement spaces. But this year there may have been a new reason for keeping that category: a shortage of funding. In part, the funding shortfall reflects the higher costs entailed in resettling refugees in this more security-conscious era: roughly $3,500 per capita as compared to $2,200 in FY 2001 (counting only the State Department's component of the cost).[13] PRM officials have expressed some confidence that the system's processing infrastructure — from identification of groups and individuals for resettlement, through OPE processing and DHS interviews, on to travel and port-of-entry inspection — could readily handle over 60,000 refugees this fiscal year. But the funding available for resettlement is sufficient to handle only about 42,000. Although support exists for a supplemental appropriation, the longer it takes to secure additional funding, the more difficult it will become to crank up the machinery and assure a higher level of admissions for FY 2005.

It would be deeply ironic if the enormous efforts of the last two years to restore the system's capacity were to be thwarted by a lack of funds, just at the point where the system could begin treating the PD number as a genuine target, not a remote and unattainable ceiling.

In the medium term, there are reasons for somewhat greater optimism about funding. The President's budget for FY 2006, otherwise austere, calls for spending an additional $154 million on the admission of refugees and their resettlement in the United States, permitting about 20,000 more refugees to arrive that year. Press reports say that this against-the-tide increase in discretionary spending derives from the President's personal interest in refugee resettlement and that leading immigration restrictionists in Congress do not intend to fight this funding.[14] Even if it passes, however, it will still yield a capacity for FY 2006 no higher than the 70,000 admissions that have marked the last several PDs. This is certainly not the admissions figure the program's most faithful supporters would wish for. But in the long run, it unfortunately may have to count as a real achievement if they can attain and then hold even that level in the chilly budgetary winds that are likely to blow for many years, given our massive annual deficits.

III. THE FUTURE

One hopes the President will join the battle for supplemental funding of refugee admissions in FY 2005 and for a more ambitious, if measured, expansion thereafter. If so, it may be a good idea to couple that push with an effort to enact some of the statutory changes suggested in Chapter VII. PRM's anti-warehousing gestures could find practical and concrete expression in a campaign to amend INA § 207 so as to make it easier to admit long-stayers on the basis of a special Presidential designation made in the annual PD. (See Section F of that chapter.) The DHS's protracted drive to reduce its adjudications backlog could receive a big boost if overseas refugees were admitted as lawful permanent residents from the beginning, thereby eliminating tens of thousands of adjustment applications (Section E). And more and more asylees are stacking up against the annual ceiling on asylee adjustments; the backlog has reached a wholly indefensible 17 years.[15] (See Section C.)

Whether now is an auspicious moment to seek substantive statutory changes is a much harder call. Today's Congress does not seem awash in humanitarian goodwill. It included provisions in the intelligence reform bill enacted in December 2004 that bespeak a mood of hostility and deep skepticism toward asylees, which could easily spill over onto those admitted through the USRP, if amendments to that program are offered.[16] The Real ID Act, which passed the House in February 2005 and awaits action in the Senate, carried a slightly more mixed message, however. Though it contains some ill-advised tightening of standards imposed on asylum applicants, it sweetens the package by eliminating the asylee adjustment cap.[17] Perhaps the Senate could soften the restrictions while keeping the repeal of the cap — and even find ways to add other changes that might benefit overseas refugee admissions. That seems unlikely, but Presidential leadership to attain these ends could have an enormous impact.

New faces are taking up the top positions in the Department of State and the Department of Homeland Security at the time of this writing. Refugee admissions, of course, will form only a small part of the daunting agendas awaiting those new secretaries, deputy secretaries, and under secretaries. But their attitudes toward this vital part of America's historic mission remain critical. They can do much to boost the USRP simply by signaling their own commitment to it, even if most of the time they must focus their attention on other issues. It remains to be seen whether they will exert sufficient leadership to realize the full promise of the hard-won progress made over the past year.

AFTERWORD. ENDNOTES

1 Department of State, Refugee Admissions for Fiscal Year 2004 (press release, Oct. 4, 2004).

2 See REFUGEES: SEEKING SOLUTIONS TO A GLOBAL CONCERN: HEARING BEFORE THE SUBCOMM. ON IMMIGRATION, BORDER SECURITY, AND CITIZENSHIP, S. COMM. ON THE JUDICIARY, 108th Cong. (Sept. 21, 2004) (hereafter SEPT. 2004 HEARINGS) (statement of Mark Franken, Chair, Refugee Council USA, at 2-3, available at http://www.rcusa.org/library.html).

3 Information provided by PRM, Feb. 2005.

4 DEPARTMENT OF STATE, DEPARTMENT OF HOMELAND SECURITY & DEPARTMENT OF HEALTH AND HUMAN SERVICES, PROPOSED REFUGEE ADMISSIONS FOR FISCAL YEAR 2005: REPORT TO THE CONGRESS 8-9 (2004).

5 See id. at 8-9, 21-23.

6 Id. at iii, v, 4.

7 Id. at 22.

8 See id. at ii-iii; information provided by PRM, Feb. 2005.

9 See Achievements and Prospects for the US Refugee Admissions Program, SEPT. 2004 HEARINGS, supra note 2 (statement of Arthur E. Dewey, Assistant Secretary for Population, Refugees, and Migration, available at http://www.state.gov/g/prm/rls/36394.htm).

10 See id.; Arthur E. Dewey, Unwarehousing Refugees, WASH. TIMES, SEPT. 10, 2004; US COMMITTEE FOR REFUGEES, WORLD REFUGEE SURVEY 2004 — WAREHOUSING ISSUE.

11 See Transcript of Press Conference with Acting Secretary of Homeland Security Admiral James Loy on the FY 2006 Budget, Feb. 7, 2005, available on the DHS website, http://www.dhs.gov/dhspublic/display?content=4338.

12 Presidential Determination No. 2004-53, 69 Fed.Reg. 60943 (2004).

13 Dewey statement, supra note 9.

14 Tom Hamburger & Peter Wallsten, Refugees' Tales Heard by Powerful Audience of One, L.A. TIMES, Feb. 14, 2005, at 1.

15 PROPOSED REFUGEE ADMISSIONS FOR 2005, supra note 4, at 6.

16 See Intelligence Reform and Terrorism Prevention Act of 2004, Pub. L. No. 108-458, § 5403, 118 Stat. 3638 (2004).

17 H.R. 418, § 101(a), (b), (f), 109th Congress, 1st Sess. (2005) (as passed by the House, Feb. 10, 2005). The bill eliminates the asylee adjustment cap altogether, rather than retaining uncapped authority in the President to decide on the number of admissions to be made available each year. For reasons discussed in Chapter VII, Section C, retaining that Presidential authority might provide a reassuring bit of potential control in the unlikely event of a mass influx — although Presidents normally would have every reason to enable all asylees to adjust after a year.

INDEX

A

Adjustment of status, 93-94, 96n.36
  of asylees, 107-09, 129
  of refugees, 108, 110-11
Affidavit of relationship (AOR), 39, 48-49, 52, 69
Agenda for Protection (UNHCR), 98
al Rehaief, Mohammed, 54
Asylum, resettlement vs., 112-13
  adjustment of status ceiling, 107-09

B

Best interests determination (BID), 42, 71
BID. See Best interests determination (BID)
Border and Transportation Security (BTS), 59
BTS. See Border and Transportation Security (BTS)

C

Carter, Jimmy, 32
CBP. See Customs and Border Protection,
    Bureau of (CBP)
Central Intelligence Agency (CIA), SAO
    process and, 72
Christopher, Warren, 32
Christopher Committee, 32
CIA. See Central Intelligence Agency (CIA)
Circuit rides, 63-64, 79-80, 85-88
Citizenship and Immigration Services, Bureau of
    (USCIS), 59, 92
  coordination with PRM by, 78-79, 81
  refugee corps in, 64-65
CLASS. See Consular Lookout and Support System
    (CLASS)
Coercive population control, refugee status based on,
    109-10
Comprehensive Plan of Action, 4
Congressional consultations, 15, 16, 23-24n.45, 34,
    35, 38, 55, 60, 106, 107
Consular Lookout and Support System (CLASS),
    71-72, 90

Convention relating to the Status of Refugees, United
    Nations, 6-7
  definition of refugees in, 111-15, 117-18n.23
  use of by Canada and Australia, 118n.29
Corruption, 6, 98
Cuban Adjustment Act, 94
Cuban Freedom Flights, 38
Cultural orientation, 76
Customs and Border Protection, Bureau of (CBP),
    59, 92

D

Department of Homeland Security (DHS)
  adjustment of status and, 93-94, 96n.36
  consistency in interviewing by, 61-62, 122
  deployment of circuit ride teams by, 63-64,
    79-80, 85-88
  group designation process and, 31-32, 45-46
  immigration policy development and, 59-60
  improvements to, 66n.1, 127
  interviews by, 72-75, 86, 87, 88, 123
  managerial approach to, 81, 122
  refugee corps for, 64-65, 66n.9, 122, 127-28
  requests for reconsideration and, 74-75, 89, 123
  role of, in USRP, 31-32, 59-66, 79-81, 121-22
  security of interviewing sites and, 63-64, 122
  Visas 93 process and, 47-48
Department of Justice (DOJ), as example for DHS,
    60-61
Department of State (DOS), 31
  Refugee Admissions Committee and, 32-33,
    34, 120
  and revision of USRP priority system, 37
DHS. See Department of Homeland Security (DHS)
DNA testing, in family verification, 50-51, 121
DOJ. See Department of Justice (DOJ)
DOS. See Department of State (DOS)

E

EAD. *See* Employment authorization document (EAD)
Employment authorization document (EAD), 77, 92, 93, 124
Enhanced Border Security and Visa Entry Reform Act of 2002, 93, 96n.33
European Council on Refugees and Exiles, on resettlement, 14
Executive Office for Immigration Review (DOJ), 109

F

FAM. *See* Foreign Affairs Manual (FAM)
Family-based access, 25-26, 27, 39-40, 46-54, 69, 116
  fraud concerns and, 49-51
  functional family relationships and, 53-54
  Visas 92 process in, 48
  Visas 93 process in, 47-48
  See also P-3 category
FBI. *See* Federal Bureau of Investigation (FBI)
Federal Bureau of Investigation (FBI), SAO process and, 72
Fingerprinting, 103
  and port-of-entry processing, 77
Foreign Affairs Manual (FAM), 47
Form I-485 (DHS), 93-94, 124
Form I-590 (DHS), 75, 76-77, 80, 95n.20
Form I-730 (DHS), 47-48
Fraud, 5-6, 49-51, 121. *See also* Refugee Access Verification Unit (RAVU)
Frelick, Bill, 11
  USRP priority system restructuring proposal by, 40-41

G

Goodwin-Gill, Guy, 111
Group-based access, 38-39, 44-46, 67-68, 94n.7.
  See also P-2 category
Group designation process, 8, 26, 67-68, 100-01, 124
  challenges in, 35n.2
  DHS and, 31-32
  equal status for admissions, 114-15
  new groups in, 113-14, 126-27
  NGOs and, 30, 44-46, 83
  P-2 category and, 38-39
  PRM and, 28-29
  proposal for Refugee Admissions Committee and, 32-34
  of UNHCR, 100-101, 124, 127

H

Hebrew Immigrant Aid Society (HIAS), 43
Helton, Arthur, 80

HIAS. *See* Hebrew Immigrant Aid Society (HIAS)
Host countries, resettlement issues for, 3-4

I

ICE. *See* Immigration and Customs Enforcement, Bureau of (ICE)
ICMC. *See* International Catholic Migration Commission (ICMC)
IDP. *See* Internally displaced persons (IDP)
Immigration Act of 1990, 108-09
Immigration and Customs Enforcement, Bureau of (ICE), 59
Immigration and Nationality Act of 1952 (INA)
  recommended statutory amendments to, 106-18
  section 207, 47-48, 57n.24-25, 107, 111, 114-16
  section 209, 108, 109
  and universal in-country designation of refugee status, 55-56, 121
Immigration and Naturalization Service (INS), former role of, 59. *See also* Department of Homeland Security (DHS)
In-country processing, 55-56, 121
INA. *See* Immigration and Nationality Act of 1952 (INA)
Individual referrals, for access to USRP, 25, 42-44, 67
  by NGOs, 43-44
  by UNHCR, 42-43, 55, 99-100
  by United States embassies, 43, 55
  See also P-1 category
Interest groups, resettlement policies and, 11-13
Internally displaced persons (IDP), 3
International Catholic Migration Commission (ICMC), 42
International Organization for Migration (IOM), 48, 70
  medical screening by, 76
  as OPE, 85, 122
  preliminary evaluations by, 83
  as refugee advocate, 83
International Rescue Committee (IRC), 43
Interviews (DHS), 61-62, 72-75, 86, 113, 122
  application of statutory standards in, 73-74, 87
  use of interpreters in, 88, 123
IOM. *See* International Organization for Migration (IOM)
IRC. *See* International Rescue Committee (IRC)

J

Joint voluntary agency (JVA), 81-82
  case preparation by, 69
  See also Overseas Processing Entity (OPE)
JVA. *See* Joint voluntary agency (JVA)

L

Lautenberg Amendment, 4, 11-12, 27, 112, 113, 115, 118n.30
Lawful permanent resident (LPR), adjustment to, 107-09, 110-11
LPR. See Lawful permanent resident (LPR)
Lubbers, Ruud, 98
Lynch, Jessica, 55

M

Magnet effect. See Pull factor
Medical screening, 75-76
Migration and Refugee Assistance (MRA), 14

N

National Security Council (NSC), coordination with USRP and, 79
NGO. See Nongovernmental organization (NGO)
Nongovernmental organization (NGO)
    group designation role, 28-29, 30, 44-46, 83, 120-21
    individual referrals by, 43-44
    and interest group politics in USRP, 12-13
    as OPE, 85, 95n.28
    role of, 35-36n.5
    See also Voluntary agency (Volag)
NSC. See National Security Council (NSC)

O

Office of Refugee, Asylum, and International Operations, 59
Office of Refugee Resettlement (ORR), 78
OPE. See Overseas Processing Entity (OPE)
Operation Fair Refuge, 50
Organization of African Unity (OAU), refugee definition of, 7, 73-74
ORR. See Office of Refugee Resettlement (ORR)
Overseas Processing Entity (OPE), 67
    case preparation by, 69-71
    JVAs and, 81-82
    NGOs and, 83-85, 95n.23, 122-23
    preliminary evaluations by, 83-84
    as refugee advocate, 82-83
    requests for reconsideration and, 89
    staffing of, 69

P

P-1 category, 33
    definition of, 37-38
    parole mechanism in, 55
    UNHCR referrals in, 99

See also Individual referrals
P-2 category
    definition of, 26, 38-39, 56n.3
    new designations for, 31, 126-27
    See also Group-based access
P-3 category, 46-47
    anti-fraud considerations, 49, 50, 52-53, 56n.12
    changes to category, 51-53
    definition of, 39
    DNA testing of, 50-51
    exceptions to, 57n.28
    nationality list for, 26, 51-52, 53, 121
    processing, 48-51
    RAVU verification of, 49, 57-58n.30
    See also Family-based access
P-4 category, definition of, 39
P-5 category, definition of, 39
Parole, in urgent cases, 55
PD. See Presidential Determination (PD)
Population, Refugees, and Migration, Bureau of (PRM), 7
    coordination with USCIS by, 78-79
    group designation by, 28-29
    managerial approach to, 81, 122
    NGOs and, 28
    OPEs and, 83-84
    requests for reconsideration and, 89
    role of, 28-31
    staffing needs of, 30-31, 120
    Visas 93 process and, 47
Port-of-entry processing, 76-78, 92-93
Presidential Determination (PD), 15-19
    asylee adjustments and, 107-08
    broader use of, 18-19, 119
    ceilings in, 16, 17, 23n.32, 128
    changes to, 18, 30, 109, 114
    delay of, and continued refugee movements, 106
    developments in, 16-17
    and passage of Refugee Act, 23-24n.45
    proposal for Refugee Admissions Committee and, 34
    and restructuring of priority system, 41
Priority system, for access to USRP, 67-69
    family-based access in, 25-26, 27, 46-54
    Frelick proposal and, 40-41
    functional family relationships and, 53-54
    group-based access in, 26, 44-46
    in-country designation in, 55-56, 121
    individual referrals in, 25, 42-44
    P-1 category in, 37-38, 42-43
    P-2 category in, 38-39
    P-3 category in, 39-40, 48-51
    P-4 category in, 39
    P-5 category in, 39
    restructuring of, 40-42, 120

universalization of P-3 category in, 51-53

urgent cases in, 54-56

See also Family-based access; Group-based access; Individual referrals; *specific priority categories*

PRM. *See* Population, Refugees, and Migration, Bureau of (PRM)

Project Profile, 102

Protection Surge Capacity Project, 57n.19

Pull factor, 3, 4, 22n.26

R

RAVU. *See* Refugee Access Verification Unit (RAVU)

RCUSA. *See* Refugee Council USA (RCUSA)

Real ID Act, 129, 129n.17

Refcoord. *See* Refugee Coordinator (Refcoord)

Refugee Access Verification Unit (RAVU)
development of, 51, 121
P-3 verification by, 49-50, 57-58n.30

Refugee Act of 1980
adjudication interviews and, 61-62
asylee adjustments and, 107-09
congressional consultation in, 107
passage of, 15, 23-24n.45
Presidential Determination and, 15-19
reconsideration of ceiling on refugee and asylee grants, 109-10
UNHCR and, 99
See also United States Refugee Program (USRP)

Refugee Admissions Committee
Presidential Determination process in, 34
proposed, 32-33, 120

Refugee camps, resettlement based on length of stay in, 10-11, 22n.23, 24n.46, 113, 114

Refugee Coordinator (Refcoord), 78

Refugee Council USA (RCUSA)
annual admission recommendations by, 30
formation of, 35-36n.5
group access recommended by, 45

Refugee Processing Center (RPC), 47, 69

Refugee status determination (RSD), 43, 67, 97

Refugees
admissions ceilings for, 16-17, 35n.3, 109-10
definitions of, 13, 109, 111-15, 117-18n.23
improved registration for, 101-03
legal definition of, 6-7
personal agency of, 3-4
personal histories of, 3
presidential discretionary admissions, 111-12, 113, 115
rescue of, 54-56, 121
worldwide numbers of, 2, 6, 21n.2

Regional security officer (RSO), 63

Registration of refugees, 101-03

Repatriation, 4-5

Request for reconsideration (RFR), 74-75, 89, 123

Resettlement
admissions process of, 67-68
allocation of resources for, 13-15
asylum *vs.*, 112-13
avoidance of human suffering and, 11-12, 22n.23
Baku Armenian, 38
based on length of camp stay, 10-11
Bosnian, 38
broader use of, 14-15, 119
camp populations and, 4
case-by-case decisions regarding, 8-9
cluster scheme, 19-20
corrupt practices in, 6
Cuban, 38
equity concerns in, 5
fraud concerns in, 5-6
of Hmong Lao, 38, 127
host country considerations in, 3-4
in-country designation and, 55-56, 121
increase in for FY 2004, 126
Iranian, 38
Liberian, 9-10, 127
of Lost Boys of Sudan, 38, 39
of Meskhetian Turks, 38, 127
migration choices and, 3
obstacles to, 4-5
of Ogoni, 39
OPE case preparation in, 69-71
Palestinian, 5
pull factor from, 3, 4, 22n.26
quota system of, 111-12
rescue-based view of, 9-13, 54-56
role of UNHCR in, 4-5
of Rwandan Hutus and Tutsis, 39
selection criteria in, 5
of Somali Bantu, 8, 19-20, 21n.2, 38
of Somali Benadir, 127
Soviet, 4, 12, 22n.29, 38
Vietnamese, 4, 10, 16, 38, 127
vs. assistance, 13-14
of "women at risk," 6, 43

Resettlement Management Working Group (UNHCR), 100

Resettlement registration form (RRF), 43, 67, 97, 100

RFR. *See* Request for reconsideration (RFR)

RPC. *See* Refugee Processing Center (RPC)

RRF. *See* Resettlement registration form (RRF)

RSD. *See* Refugee status determination (RSD)

RSO. *See* Regional security officer (RSO)

S

SAO. *See* Security advisory opinion (SAO)
Security advisory opinion (SAO), 89-90
  improvements to system of, 90, 123-24, 126
  and OPE screening, 72

T

Targeted response teams, 45-46
Temporary protected status (TPS), 114, 115, 118n.27
TPS. *See* Temporary protected status (TPS)
Transportation Security Agency, 59

U

UNHCR. *See* United Nations High Commissioner for
    Refugees (UNHCR)
UNHCR Handbook for Registration, 102
UNHCR Resettlement Handbook, 37, 98, 100
United Nations High Commissioner for Refugees
    (UNHCR), 3
  group referral capacity of, 100-101, 105n.22,
    124, 127
  improvement of refugee registration by,
    101-03, 124
  individual referrals by, 37, 42-43, 44, 55, 120
  P-2 referrals by, 41
  reforms to, 97-99
  repatriation and, 4-5
  role of, 97-105, 124
United States Committee for Refugees, 14
United States Embassies, P-1 referrals by, 37, 43, 55
United States Refugee Program (USRP)
  adjustment of status and, 93-94, 96n.36, 107-09
  admissions process of, 67-68
  admissions program ceilings in, 16-18
  allocation of resources in, 13-15
  complexity of, 7-8
  conflicting objectives of, 9-19
  and consistency of DHS interviews, 61-62
  cultural orientation and, 76
  DHS adjudication interviews in, 72-75
  distortions of, 104n.14
  family-based access in, 25-26, 27, 39-40, 46-54, 69
  funding for, 128
  group-based access in, 26, 38-39, 44-46, 67-68, 94n.7
  human right abusers and, 87-88, 95n.32
  individual referrals in, 25, 42-44, 55, 67, 99-100

interest group politics and, 11-13
  low admissions totals in, 2
  managerial approach to, 78-81
  medical screening in, 75-76
  OPE case preparation in, 69-71
  port-of-entry processing in, 76-78, 92-93
  priority system for admissions in. *See* Priority
    system, for access to USRP
  recommended statutory amendments to, 106-18,
    128-29
  refugee arrival at destination and, 76-78
  requests for reconsideration in, 74-75, 89
  role of Department of Homeland Security in,
    31-32, 59-66, 121-22
  role of Department of State in, 31
  role of PRM in, 28-31
  role of UNHCR in, 97-105
  security screening in, 71-72, 80, 89-90, 94n.5
  sponsor assurances in, 76, 94n.11
  travel and, 76-78
  See also Refugees; Resettlement
Urgent cases, 54-56, 121
USCIS. *See* Citizenship and Immigration Services,
    Bureau of (USCIS)
USRP. *See* United States Refugee Program (USRP)

V

Vietnamese Orderly Departure Program, 38
Visas 92, 48
Visas 93, 46, 47-48, 51, 57n.26, 121
  definition of, 39-40
  See also Family-based access
Volag. *See* Voluntary agency (Volag)
Voluntary agency (Volag), and interest group
    politics in USRP, 12-13. *See also*
    Nongovernmental organization (NGO)

W

Widows and Orphans Act of 2003, 21-22n.18
World Refugee Survey, 45
Worldwide Refugee Admissions Processing System
    (WRAPS), 47, 90-92, 124
  developments in, 127
  and OPE case preparation, 71
WRAPS. *See* Worldwide Refugee Admissions
    Processing System (WRAPS)